CASH-PAY
HEALTHCARE

How to Start, Grow & Perfect Your Business

Mark J. Tager, MD
Stewart Gandolf, MBA

PO Box 7303
Rancho Santa Fe, CA 92067

ISBN 978-0-9980315-0-7

Dedication

CASH-PAY HEALTHCARE
kæsh peɪ helTHker
adjective   noun

Everything your business does to obtain non-insurance based revenue.

Mark:

To the legion of physicians with knowledge in their heads, good intentions in their hearts, and healing energy in their hands. If you are striving to make a difference and to be different, then these words are for you. May your practices thrive!

Stewart:

To my wife Clara, two beautiful daughters Cristina and Natalie, and Cosmo, the wonder dog. Clara, thank you for being my friend and partner on this amazing journey through life. Cristina and Natalie, your creativity inspires me. And to Cosmo, well, I forgive you…

Acknowledgements

Putting together a book of this scope and depth is no easy task, especially since any of the clinically-related areas could be a book in themselves. We have leaned heavily on a cadre of physicians much more knowledgeable in the art and practice of healthcare than are we. I (Mark) am fortunate to consider them my MBFFs; my medical BFFs because I can ask them almost anything, almost anytime, and they are there to render guidance and assistance. Big thanks to Felice Gersh, MD; Andrew Heyman, MD; Marvin Singh, MD; Shilpa Saxena, MD; Adam Silberman, ND; Ira Goodman, MD; Farahan Taghizadeh, MD; Stephen Dayan, MD; Tahl Humes, MD; Mark Menoloscino, MD; and Rebecca Hunton, MD for putting us on the right path. Any clinical mistakes you find in the text are solely the fault of the authors, probably because we failed to heed their advice.

We've also received amazing support from well-respected industry leaders. Nutrition business guru Tom Aarts and Nate Freeman at Ortho Molecular helped us better understand the professional supplement market. We leaned heavily on Jay Keese of the DPC Coalition, and Michael Levin, VP of Sales and Marketing for Hint, to make certain we captured the landscape and nuances of Direct Primary Care. Michael Tetreault, Editor of *Concierge Medicine Today*, put the pieces in place for us regarding membership models as a whole. You'll find snippets of dozens of interviews we've conducted with other key opinion and industry leaders. Their words are their gift to the reader and our acknowledgment of their expertise.

Drafting a manuscript is just the first part of writing a book. You then must get it edited, designed, and printed. We are in debt to our three thoughtful and eagle eyed editors Karen Edwards, Carolyn Lange, and James Tager. James, Mark's son, has edited five of his ten books, and this time around asked, "When is enough, enough?" Simona Ramos and Kyle Hojem, from Healthcare Success, stepped in to create and clean up many of the illustrations and help with citations. We were blessed that Doug Crowe came into our sphere at just the right time. We were able to hand off a decent manuscript and have his talented team whip it into shape for delivery to the printer. We couldn't have done the book without the contributions of Gaella Aziz.

Stewart is deeply indebted to some of his mentors who shaped ideas for the book. These include Dr. Jim Merlino, whose leadership in patient experience provides daily inspiration. Dr. Jonathan Calure and Dr. Bruno Fang prove every day that doctors can be both great clinicians and excellent businesspeople. Stewart's real acknowledgment goes out to the entire team at Healthcare Success, not just for delivering superb service to their multitude of clients, but also for working extra hard while he disappeared to write a book.

TABLE OF CONTENTS

INTRODUCTION
___
Change for Good

Introduction

Change for Good

If you were drawn to the title of this book, chances are good that you want more from your healthcare practice. In fact, several mores: more freedom, more control, and yes, more cash-pay revenue.

If you follow our prescription, you stand a greater chance of getting "more;" however, as noted in the popular Rolling Stones song title, "You Can't Always Get What You Want," the application of diligence and effort is more likely to result in you coming away with what you *need*. And when you get your needs and—more importantly—your patients' needs met, you will, in fact, make more money.

We've designed this book to meet the needs of a wide, and growing audience of health-related practitioners and organizations. We'll focus most of our attention on primary and specialty medical care providers; but the ideas, logic, suggestions, and exercises are equally applicable for the complementary, nursing, dental, chiropractic, naturopathic, acupuncture, nutritional, psychological, or coaching professional. Our approach is applicable to all-sized organizations: from the micro-practice, to the multi-specialty clinic, to the hospital/healthcare system.

We also realize that, when it comes to cash-pay, our readers are at different levels of experience. Some practitioners want to start cash-pay, either in whole—by moving totally out of insurance—or, by adding some incremental cash-pay products and services to their mix. We'll not only be providing the revenue models to do so, but we'll also share the experience of practitioners who have taken the leap and have found enjoyment and success in either augmenting or transforming their practices. You'll find the pros and cons clearly outlined as you consider your best path, including whether to go it alone, or buy into a "packaged system" such as a franchise, licensing/service agreement, or other business affiliation. We'll guide you through the steps of creating a business plan that includes mitigating risk and maximizing the possibility of success.

There are practices that already have a cash-pay component, either in whole or in part, and for them, the goal is to *grow* their business. For these practices, the formula is straight forward: increase sales of existing offerings, selectively add ancillary products or services, change pricing/bundling models, decrease expenses, or do a combination of all these. We'll be presenting some assessments and checklists to help with the myriad of decisions you'll need to make. We'll introduce public relations and marketing basics, as well as the strategies and tactics that are essential in today's digital world. Growing your business means growing your presence. We'll discuss ways to get your business noticed, known, and remembered.

Throughout this book we will be pointing to resources that can help you succeed. These are companies that offer services and products. You may be wondering how and why we have selected them. First, a disclosure: other than several companies for whom Mark provides scientific talks, and Stewart's ownership of Healthcare Success and PatientFetch, we have absolutely no vested interest in the companies we reference. In the parlance of CME, we have no relevant disclosures. These are companies with whom we either have direct familiarity or they have been recommended by colleagues. In the course of researching this book, we reached out and interviewed more than 100 companies. You will find the web addresses of these curated vendors next to their names. When we mention other companies in a category, but do not have direct experience with them, there will be no inclusion of their websites. Then there are those companies that were just not on our radar. We apologize for overlooking them.

We've designed *Cash-Pay Healthcare* to be your go-to resource for everything you need to grow your business. To this end, we have put together a comprehensive toolkit (cashpayresources.com) that includes all the urls of the recommended companies, as well as additional resources from ChangeWell Inc. and Healthcare Success. In a few places in the text, we will be reminding you of the availability of this toolkit.

There are also successful cash-pay practices that are doing well. They have systems and procedures in place. Many can be found in the aesthetics, dentistry, and vision-correction fields. The best of these organizations have an insatiable thirst for fine tuning. They strive to *perfect* their efforts. Here is where incremental changes, spread throughout the entire business, can yield big pay-offs. What if:

- Your staff were ten, twenty, or thirty percent more comfortable with the notion of selling?

- You could double attendance for talks and seminars?
- Substantially grow your opt-in email list?
- Gain more social media followers?
- Rapidly populate your digital presence with great testimonials?
- Increase your phone conversion rates by a significant percentage?
- Capture more visitors who come to your website?
- Ensure more patients show up for their appointments?
- Gain better outcomes from your consults?
- Reduce training time for new hires?
- Enhance staff engagement?
- Make more "passive income?"

The list of potential improvements is long, but the thread is the same: a step-wise approach to constantly re-examining all facets of your business. For these organizations, you will find many pearls in the pages ahead.

Finally, the rise of high-deductible health plans (HDHPs) is forcing many insurance-based, medical specialty practices to adopt some of the strategies pioneered by their cash-pay colleagues. Back when insurance covered almost everything, patients followed their doctor's advice and moved forward with medically necessary procedures without much thought about the cost. Today, however, over 43% of US adults under 65 are enrolled in high deductible plans.[1] As a result many patients delay treatment because they cannot afford the out-of-pocket expenses. What's more, patients who *pay* more *expect* more from their doctors. Many of the principles outlined in this book (especially Chapter 7: How to Create the Ultimate Patient Experience) can help these practices adapt to the new and very different healthcare landscape.

The ABCs of Cash-Pay Healthcare

You are undoubtedly familiar with the basic ABC behavioral model. Attitudes affect behavior and behavior creates consequences. Because all change starts with a shift in attitude or perspective, let's look at some of the attitudinal prerequisites for starting, growing, and perfecting your cash-pay practice. These include a willingness to:

- **Overcome fears and embrace change.** Many conventional physicians are locked into golden—make that iron—handcuffs. While they may have a steady income, it is often not on par with their expectations nor consistent with their future needs. Many younger physicians struggle with debt. For those who toil as employees, the regimentation and physical exhaustion of a heavy patient load, and the burdens of bureaucracy rob energy and erode confidence. Yet healthcare practitioners have so many attributes going for them: intelligence, strong work ethic, clinical abilities, patient-centered skills, and an ethos to serve and heal. These attributes more than buffer the fears of change, and by proper planning, identifying good role models, actively learning some new skills, and taking some measured risk, it is possible to derive greater satisfaction from patient care.

- **Acknowledge the new competition.** When you enter the cash-pay world, you are directly competing for the hard-earned dollars of your patients. And unless your treatment is absolutely medically urgent, you are now in the retail world. Your competition not only includes other practitioners who do or don't provide your same products and services, it also includes a new outfit, a family vacation, an expensive dinner, or tickets to a concert. You must adopt an attitude that supports the exquisite, sensitive, attentive, detailed-oriented customer service proposition known in healthcare as the patient experience. This means that your vein, vision, body sculpting, integrative, facial rejuvenation, functional, acupuncture, chiropractic, or wellness clinic must provide an experience equal to the best that today's premier retailers deliver.

- **Move from being a director to a guide.** Many healthcare consumers are seeking practitioners who will treat them as partners rather than passive patients. Partners see their physician as their guide. Passive patients see their physician as their benevolent dictator telling them what they "should" and "must" do for their health. Layer on the element of cash-pay and the nature of the balance tips even further toward consumer choice. Reflecting on this shift, one of our colleagues said the following about new patient acquisition, "You now have to interview to be their physician." This dynamic is most relevant for those practices seeking to attract millennials (born 1981-1996), who now number 73 million in the US.[2] Growing up in the sharing economy, and schooled in working collaboratively, they see you as a member of their team, not the captain.

- **Give up some preconceived notions.** This means avoiding, like the plague, idea-killing thoughts such as, "We've never done this before;" "It won't work;" "We've always done it that way;" and "No one in our community will pay for this."

- **Revamp your attitude about your worth.** When it comes to setting prices for services, or providing in-office products, a sub-segment of medical practitioners struggles with the concept of what their services are worth. Both the practitioners and patients have been disintermediated by an insurance scheme that obfuscates the financial primacy of the transaction. Most physicians feel, rightly so, that medicine is a noble calling; but confound this with the belief that they are duty-bound to provide care for the never-ending masses who show up at their doorstep. The problem with this way of thinking is the following:

If you don't have enough resources to provide well for yourself and your family, you have very little to give to others. And if you don't have enough to give, you can't be successful.

How do you resolve this conundrum? Figure out what you are worth by keeping in mind that your years of experience, training, and judgement are more valuable than you think. When in doubt, compare your proposed hourly rate to the successful attorneys in your area. Charge a fair price to those who can afford it. In your spare time, you can always donate time and resources to those who are in greatest need.

- **Look at selling as a natural component of providing value to the patient.** Many in healthcare believe that selling is somehow manipulative, dirty, or not-dignified. It is the purview of used car salesmen. The reality is that we all "sell" whenever we recommend a pharmaceutical agent, an elective surgical procedure, or a lifestyle or self-care regimen. Selling is simply a way of influencing others. As long as it is born from a genuine, informed, and measured approach to providing value to the patient, and is consistent with the patient's wants and expectations, it is no less ethical than any other non-elective treatment we propose.

- **Abandon the notion that the conventional way is the only way.** A companion attitude to the negative view of selling is the wholesale rejection, by some physicians, of innovative products and services because they are not evidenced-based, supported by peer-reviewed, double-blinded studies. Hence, a segment of the medical profession will label these techniques alternative at best, and witchcraft or voodoo at worst. While conventional physicians can take comfort from association guidelines—and we are not saying to disregard them—most fail the real-world test of applicability. This has been substantiated by multiple assessments that show,[3,4,5] "Only a fraction of what physicians do is based on solid evidence from Grade-A randomized, controlled trials; the rest is based instead on weak or no evidence and on subjective judgment. When scientific consensus exists on which clinical practices work effectively, physicians only sporadically follow that evidence correctly…Half of what physicians do is wrong, or less than 20 percent of what physicians do has solid research to support it."

- **Get turned on by the ever-changing nature of healthcare.** The healthcare universe is expanding at a dizzying pace, the result of a multitude of forces colliding in synergistic or antagonistic ways. The worlds of personalized, predictive, and precision medicine are driving new understandings of health and disease. This is fueled by advances in many fields including neuroscience, genomics, the microbiome, and regenerative medicine. Practitioners are becoming enthralled by more whole-person healthcare models that go by names such as integrative, functional, anti-aging, holistic, or wellness. In addition to spending more time with patients, these practitioners have a toolkit that is more extensive than that of their conventional medicine colleagues. Patients now come to their doctors armed with Dr. Google, quantified self-data, mobile health apps, and a powerful social media voice. We know that aging baby boomers want to turn back the clock; millennials relate differently to their practitioners; and everyone wants to look good. An ever-expanding array of tech companies are focusing on the healthcare market with solutions for process improvement aimed at every aspect of your business. All of this means that that—if you want more satisfaction and greater revenue—you will constantly need to attend to the dynamics of this new world. We believe it is best to go forth into this world with an attitude of excitement, inquisitiveness, discernment, and engagement.

- **Strive to Make a Meaningful Difference in the World of Healthcare.** We've all seen the stats on the epidemic of chronic, lifestyle-based diseases affecting Americans. If we just examine weight, almost 3 in 4 men are considered to be overweight or obese; for women, it's about 2 in 3.[6] Every clinician must help contribute to stemming the rising tide of chronic disease, beginning with obesity.

The other, less publicized crisis is the demise of primary care in America. As the entry-point into healthcare, PCPs (primary care practitioners) are in the trenches on the war on chronic disease. The problem is that by 2020, the US will experience a deficit of up to 90,000 primary care doctors. Right now, nearly one in five Americans, or 60 million people, lack access to a PCP.[7] Admittedly, some of this burden has been lightened by the emergence of health extenders: physician assistants and nurse practitioners, many of whom take on enormous responsibilities when they serve the needs of rural populations. This access problem becomes compounded by the rising costs of health insurance that have forced millions of Americans to go without coverage.

There is an emerging model known as Direct Primary Care, which we'll describe in detail in Chapter 3: How & What Should I Charge for My Services? It seeks to solve the issues of access and cost through a membership model that does not involve insurance reimbursement. We see great promise in membership models, but like direct-pay, this is only a payment model. We'd like to see primary care expanded to include the best of integrative medicine, which solves the need for both whole person and precision healthcare.

The concierge model is a comfortable one for many clinicians who seek to retain insurance reimbursement, but also obtain membership revenue for non-covered services. Concierge practices offer improved access and an annual wellness, "executive-physical" examination that holds high promise for improved disease detection. While many of these practitioners may not be comfortable with integrative/functional medicine, they can drive more meaningful societal change by mastering the counseling and coaching skills to help patients make meaningful health behavior and lifestyle changes.

The Move Toward Better Behaviors

Modifying dysfunctional attitudes is a prelude for change, but we all know that the acid test lies in behavior. If you want to start, grow, or profit from a cash-pay model, you'll want to do the following:

- **Do your homework on the market.** Start and continue to gather market intelligence as follows:
    o   Scan your competitor or potential competitor's websites on a regular basis.
    o   Note their branding, positioning and pricing models.
    o   Look at their patient reviews (as well as your own, a process we'll discuss later).
    o   Mystery shop their practice, either by phone or in person.
    o   Compare their offers and positioning to your own; modify your approach as necessary to distinguish yourself in the market.
- **Create, periodically review, and modify a business plan.** The old adage goes that, "If you don't know where you are going, any road will take you there." The problem is the strong likelihood that you'll wind up someplace you don't want to be. Many practitioners freeze at the thought of crafting a business plan. It need not be a daunting task. It is merely a helpful crystallization of your market research and a thoughtful approach to how you will fund your efforts and, over time, distinguish and profit from your products and services. The best cash-pay practices routinely re-evaluate their business plan at least annually and modify it as needed. They create mini-marketing plans anytime they introduce a new product or service. We've devoted a good part of Chapter 6: How to Profit from Scientific Marketing, to creating such a plan.

- **Make major capital investments cautiously.** It is easy to get swept up in the excitement of a trade show or an impassioned sales pitch. This is particularly true in the aesthetics field where the world is littered with outdated, little-used, expensive devices, many which still have monthly payments. Always ask to speak to other customers who have purchased the product—practitioners who are not on the company payroll, nor being paid as a consultant, and have a reputation and market similar to your own. In our experience, most practitioners want to know the answer to these questions:
  - o Does it work? (Can you quantify the percentage of improvement?)
  - o Is it safe? (What side effects or complications have you had?)
  - o Are patients willing to pay for it? (Just once or on a repeat basis?)
  - o Are patients happy with the treatment? (Would they recommend it for friends and family?)
  - o Are you making money with it? (If so, how much are you charging?)
  - o Does the company stand behind their product?
- **Create a business team and solicit their input on a regular basis.** At the very least this should include a good attorney, insurance agent, and CPA, as well as other mentors or advisors in your field. Webmasters, SEO, and digital marketing companies are increasingly finding their way onto healthcare teams. Your accountant is integral in helping you establish and monitor the key metrics that determine the financial health of your business. Like it or not, you must attend to these numbers.
- **Get great training, and then get more.** There is no substitute for both formal and informal clinical and business training. In addition to programs conducted by your specialty associations, there are many organizations that offer certifications and fellowships, some of which provide CE or CME credits. Make time to participate and follow through on your involvement. You will find mention of these associations throughout the book.
- **Master one product/service/technique before going on to the next.** It takes time, diligence, and effort to learn how to perform a new procedure, as well as position and explain a new product or other offering to patients. We encourage you to pay careful attention to Chapter 4: What Products & Services Should I Add?
- **Commit to creating a learning organization.** For the most part, none of us does it alone. We all rely on others to help our patients get the results they want. The best practices are also those that invest the most in their people. They provide time, recognition, and remuneration for their staff to participate in ongoing education. This may take the form of conferences, online courses, certifications,

and educational staff meetings. In fact, if you have ever wondered how the key opinion leaders can speak at so many conferences, write books, conduct courses, and hold down a practice, each of them will credit a great staff for their success.

- **Become a better boss.** The next time you want a deep and moving insight into human behavior, look at a handful of negative patient reviews on the most common sites such as YELP, Google My Business, Facebook, Healthgrades, ZocDoc, WebMD, RateMDs, Vitals, or RealSelf. Ignore, for now, what they say about the providers (unless they are employees who report to you) and focus instead on the staff. You'll see adjectives such as "rude," "insulting," and "uncaring" or demeaning statements that the front office is a "joke." There is no way to put this gently. These types of reactions reflect a failure of leadership. It is the job of the leader to make people feel competent, valued, knowledgeable, and respected. The leadership role requires that you establish and promulgate values, set and monitor standards of behavior, and provide feedback and coaching on performance. While you must hire well and terminate early —a subject we'll tackle in greater detail later—the majority of cases of poor attitude, dysfunctional processes, and demeaning culture can be pointed squarely at the person(s) in charge. The good news is that this can be remedied with education and training. You'll find our thoughts on this matter toward the end of the book.

- **Take Advantage of the New Technologies.** There are so many opportunities to add efficiencies to your practice. Your selection of the right Electronic Health/ Medical Record (EHR/EMR) is a great place to start. Then you'll want to layer on the additional technological solutions to help you attract patients, communicate with them on a telehealth platform, and track and monitor their health through wearables and other mobile health initiatives. We'll have a lot more to say about this in the pages ahead.

- **Gain competence or more in the digital realm.** We've set aside two entire chapters for marketing in the digital age. We'll cover what you need to know about websites, SEO, digital advertising, digital marketing, and social media. It's a fast-paced world, and it's easy to feel that you might be getting left behind if you don't adopt and excel at the nuances of the current digital platforms. Your online presence is a particularly important determinant for millennials seeking services; most of them know all about you through your social media presence before they step into your office. It's important to have a good digital presence, but it is worthless in the absence of providing a great patient experience. There is a basic advertising maxim, which states that the fastest way to drive a bad business out of business is with great advertising/promotion. The cash-pay world is replete with very successful practitioners who have a low social media profile, but who provide a quality experience, a good value, and whose businesses are driven almost exclusively by great word of mouth.

- **Explore, as desired, non-clinical avenues for income.** Recognize that clinicians have many ways to generate revenue outside the traditional patient-practitioner relationship. Organizations such as SEAK (seak.com) provide training in how to become an expert medical witness, set up a consulting or disability file review business, earn money as a physician writer, etc. In this book, we will stay focused on the provision of direct clinical services.

What's in It for You?

The A's and B's result in the C's, the consequences of your attitudes and behaviors. You are already familiar with the consequences of your present path, and you are setting out to create a new set of consequences that provide greater satisfaction. Satisfaction comes in many forms. It might be:

- More meaningful and direct patient experiences
- Greater quality for the patient with more time and attention
- An increased set of practitioner skills with which to meet patient expectations
- Improved satisfaction for the members of the practice
- A better reputation in the community
- The potential of being part of a larger therapeutic community
- An opportunity for personal and professional growth
- The acquisition of transferable skills to help in both business and life, and of course,
- More money.

How this Book is Organized

For more years than we care to remember, we have been helping healthcare professionals—of all persuasions and specialties—grow their businesses. Mark has focused on personal development: how practitioners can go from good to great by becoming more influential in person, on camera and online. Along with his colleague Robert John Hughes at ChangeWell Training Academy (changewell.com), he offers live training, as well as online courses and coaching in presentation skills. Many healthcare companies take advantage of ChangeWell programs to grow their sales, marketing, or key opinion leaders' abilities. Mark also helps health-related companies clarify their physician-directed messaging.

Stewart has grown Healthcare Success (healthcaresuccess.com) into the country's premier medical marketing agency for doctors. They have helped hundreds of healthcare organizations, both large and small, attract more patients and retain those they have. Keeping abreast of the rapid move toward digital marketing, Healthcare Success helps guide healthcare systems, hospitals, and large clinics to make sense of, and gain success from, the ever-growing marketing options available today.

We've divided the book into two parts. In Part 1: OPTIONS & CHOICES, we'll discuss the range of possibilities open to practitioners today. We'll briefly touch on some of the dynamics of healthcare in Chapter 1: What is Driving the Cash-Pay Market? When you read this overview, we hope it sparks some introspection and generates some questions. We'll address three of the biggest ones in turn starting with Chapter 2: What Type of Practice is Right for Me? You'll be able to clarify your practice orientation and learn how to explain it to attract the types of patients you want to treat. In Chapter 3: How & What Should I Charge for My Services? you'll gain a deep appreciation for the pros and cons of cash-pay membership models (direct-pay, DPC, Concierge, and hybrid). We'll help you examine, and possibly change your relationship with healthcare insurance. You'll learn about some of the national companies that can help you transform your revenue model,

PERFECTING	Become nationally known Identify staff training efficiencies Promote & incent staff Consider additional locations Extract more from vendors Review business plan
GROWING	Carefully attend to key metrics Focus on staff training Add ancillary services & products Ramp up social media Raise practitioners' profiles Focus on patient testimonials Sell more existing services
STARTING	Create business plan Engage legal, accounting, insurance Develop website Obtain space, equipment, products Hire staff Get known in community Determine focus & financing
CONTEMPLATING	Attend conferences Seek a mentor Determine revenue model Decide on services Mitigate "cons" Prepare to practice

and whether affiliating with them makes sense. In Chapter 4: What Products & Services Should I Add? you'll find an alphabetized listing of the major options for adding products and services to your business. We've included some checklists you can use to determine which are right for you. At the conclusion of Part 1, we will introduce our Practice Change Readiness Model, shown on the previous page. Chapter 5: Where Do I Start? explores this framework to get you to focus on those changes that are possible, doable, and profitable given your interest and resources.

In Part 2: PRACTICE ENHANCEMENT, we'll cover the practical "how-tos" for building a successful business. Much of this will focus on marketing and patient engagement strategies. You'll learn skills such as how to attract the types of patients/clients you want to treat, how to become more Internet-savvy, how to spend marketing dollars wisely, how to ethically sell products and services, and how to avoid or plug leaks in your practice.

We recognize that your circumstances, as well as your needs and interests, are unique. We also know that cash-pay appeals to a broad spectrum of healthcare professionals. We will refer to our intended audience as physicians, doctors, and practitioners; their intended audience will be referred to as patients, clients, and every so often, customers. As you move forward, we encourage you to skip around and turn to those questions whose answers best meet your needs. We hope you find meaning and value in the pages ahead.

PART 1

Options & Choices

CHAPTER

WHAT IS DRIVING THE CASH-PAY MARKET?

Which Direction Is the Wind?

The wind powers every sailboat. Whether you are a novice or an experienced sailor, the first thing to do before leaving the dock is to check the wind. What direction is it coming from? How fast? Are there any shifts? Are storms ahead?

Depending upon the type of cash-pay adjustments you want to make to your practice, you are well advised to pay attention to the wind. Some of the forces may hold you back while others propel you forward quite smoothly. In this chapter, we'll provide a brief overview of these forces and encourage you to pay attention to those that are relevant for you. Here are our seven guidelines for more enjoyable sailing.

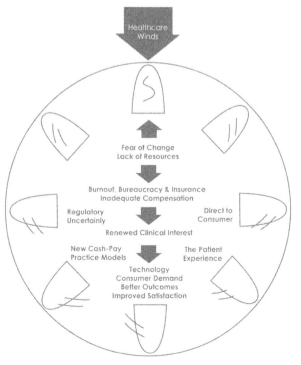

#1. Move Beyond Physician Burnout

Each year Medscape comes out with their survey on physician burnout. The latest for 2018,[8] tallied responses from more than 15,000 physicians representing 29 specialties. And like the years before it, the survey reveals that many physicians—in fact more than half—are not "happy campers." The Medscape stats show the spectrum of distress felt by clinicians:

- 42% reported they were burned out.
- 12% stated they were colloquially depressed ("feeling down"), and 3% admitted to clinical depression.
- The highest rates of burnout were in primary care, neurologists, emergency medicine physicians, and radiologists.
- 14% noted that they were both burned out and depressed.
- Interestingly, the percentage of physicians reporting burnout (42%) was equal between employed and self-employed physicians; the conjecture was that the pressures of running a business contribute to doctors' stress.
- Roughly a third noted that their depression affected relations with patients (less engaged, less friendly).

The stressors affecting physicians are all too familiar to clinicians and are summed up in this chart from the Medscape Survey:

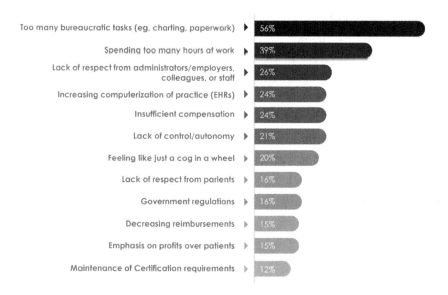

What Contributes to Physician Burnout

Too many bureaucratic tasks (eg, charting, paperwork) ▶	56%
Spending too many hours at work ▶	39%
Lack of respect from administrators/employers, colleagues, or staff ▶	26%
Increasing computerization of practice (EHRs) ▶	24%
Insufficient compensation ▶	24%
Lack of control/autonomy ▶	21%
Feeling like just a cog in a wheel ▶	20%
Lack of respect from parients ▶	16%
Government regulations ▶	16%
Decreasing reimbursements ▶	15%
Emphasis on profits over patients ▶	15%
Maintenance of Certification requirements ▶	12%

Modified from the Medscape National Physician Burnout & Depression Report 2018

Christine Sinsky, MD at the American Medical Association took a closer look at the first stressor: the ever-growing mountain of paperwork that physicians address daily. In her study,[9] she followed 57 US physicians in family medicine, internal medicine, cardiology, and orthopedics for a total of 430 hours. Additionally, 21 physicians completed after-hours diaries. She found that:

- Physicians spent 27% of their time in their offices seeing patients, and
- 49.2% of their time doing paperwork, which included using the electronic health record (EHR) system.
- In the exam room, they spent only 52.9% of the time talking to or examining the patients and 37.0% or their time was again devoted to paperwork.
- Physicians who completed the after-hours diaries indicated that they were spending one to two hours each night doing more paperwork.

The Far End of the Spectrum

While many physicians will soldier on, accepting the rigors of the profession and putting aside their personal well-being, there are others, for whom the toll is too much. Physician suicide garners little media attention; however, it is increasingly becoming a public health crisis. Pamela Wible, MD (idealmedicalcare.org) who runs a doctor suicide hotline has compiled a registry with more than 1000 doctor suicides, with men outnumbering women four to one.

Doctor suicide is a hidden and underreported public health crisis with more than one million Americans now losing their doctors to suicide annually—just in the United States. Wible points out that some drivers are specific to physicians: chronic sleep deprivation, patient deaths, and malpractice, but notes that physicians "have personal problems like everyone else—family and financial issues that are exacerbated by working for countless hours dealing with other's pain."

Wible takes an even more aggressive stance toward the system that employs "providers," noting that, "Words like 'burnout' and 'resilience' are often employed by medical institutions as psychological warfare to blame and shame doctors while deflecting attention from inhumane working conditions." She believes that graduate medical training perpetuates human rights violations, creating in young physicians, occupationally induced mental health problems, or at the very least exacerbating the problem in those with pre-existing disorders.

Where Do the Answers Lie?

If there is an answer to be found in the burnout epidemic (for all clinicians, not just physicians), it must be two-sided, addressing what psychologists term the PE fit: the interplay between the Person and the Environment.

The Medscape respondents made clear some of their desired environmental remedies. Fifty-six percent suggested fewer bureaucratic tasks, and 39% suggested fewer hours spent working. About one-third of physicians suggested more money and a more manageable work schedule. However, we all know that organizational change, even when not buffeted by resistance, only takes place with total organizational commitment and buy-in. Even then, it is often slow and painful.

There are positive system-wide programs that we can point to. Practicing Excellence (practicingexcellence.com), a company started by Stephen Beeson, MD is now touching the lives of more than 15,000 physicians in more than 70 partner healthcare systems. The Clinician Experience Project features a rich online suite of training and communication tools that, in addition to addressing clinician burnout, provides skills to accelerate improvements in patient care and more effective clinician leadership. There have been more than 25,000 shared member insights with clinicians helping their colleagues.

Organizations are increasingly offering training and education. The Institute of Coaching at MacLean Hospital, a Harvard Medical School affiliate, conducts outreach to healthcare institutions. They are also responsible for an annual Coaching in Leadership and Healthcare Conference at Harvard Medical School. (A good place to find a physician coach.)

There are many physicians who are making it their mission to help colleagues, offering programs and retreats. Dr. Wible offers private, group, and residency retreats of varying duration. Dike Drummond, MD (thehappymd.com) notes that he has done live burnout prevention training for more than 25,000 physicians in 140 organizations. Gail Gazelle, MD (gailgazelle.com) conducts coaching and retreats. Many physicians have turned to Starla Fitch, MD who brands herself as "The Connection Doctor" on her website (starlafitchmd. com). We've appreciated her transformative work for several years. The popularity of mindfulness training has resulted in many institutions offering programs for clinicians.

These types of interventions, however, may fail to thoroughly address one lingering, chronic irritant: the loss of control and autonomy that many employed physicians are experiencing. While the march of practice acquisition by larger healthcare systems has slowed, almost half of all physicians in the US are employees. A recent NYU School of Medicine study reported in the *Journal of the American Board of Family Medicine* shows that bigger isn't always better for the health of clinicians. The researchers found that physicians who work in small, independent primary care practices reported dramatically lower levels of burnout than the national average (13.5 percent versus 54.4 percent).[10] These findings indicate that the practitioner's independence and sense of autonomy in these small practices may provide some protection against symptoms of burnout.

Return to a Simpler Time?

The NYU study points to a small but steadily growing phenomenon in healthcare: the rise of the micropractice. Its popularity is rooted in a combination of simplicity in environment, coupled with cash-pay/membership reimbursement models. The micropractice includes the following features:

- A small panel of patients (400-800 versus 2,000-4,000)
- Minimal office staff, space, and equipment
- Physician may choose to work alone without staff
- Cash-pay, membership and hybrid (insurance plus cash-pay) payment models
- Many are Direct Primary Care, Concierge, or variations of Integrative/Functional Medicine
- Increasing reliance on telehealth
- May include home visits
- Affords patients improved access, less wait time, and more face time

Garrison Bliss, MD a Seattle based primary care physician and one of the founders of the Direct Primary Care movement, noted that being happy in the practice of medicine has "very little to do with how you get paid and is much more about whether your practice is on target for your personal mission."[11] Bliss believes physicians seeking to transform their economic model, must ask a more fundamental question, "What am I not doing, that if I were doing it, I wouldn't be burned out even if I worked all day and night?"

We recognize that many of the readers of this book may be reasonably happy with their giving-getting compromise. They like what they do and where they do it, but just want to make more money. If this is your situation, we'd encourage you to look at the chapters on reimbursement and adding products and services to your practice.

For those seeking to rekindle their passion for medicine, we offer a simple prescription, one that we'd encourage you to take under the advisement of a mentor, counselor, or coach:

- Take time to step back.
- Examine what's important in life.
- Identify your mission.

- Envision possibilities for the future.
- Anticipate and overcome barriers.
- Create a plan.
- Make a commitment and go forth.

To spark your thinking, we've included this insightful Venn diagram.

#2. Labor Less Under the Insurance Burden

Although Winston Churchill, in his 1939 radio address was discussing Russia, his remarks could well have been directed toward the American health insurance system: "It is a riddle, wrapped in a mystery, inside an enigma." David Belk, MD, points to the absurdity of the insurance system and how it has rendered physicians dumb, deaf, and blind when it comes to understanding patient reimbursement. In his blog,[12] he cites the reasons why physicians have no idea how much they are paid to see an individual patient.

- Different insurance companies will pay doctors a different amount for the same billing code.
- The same insurance company will also pay a doctor a different amount for the same billing code depending on the type of policy a patient has.
- There is almost no way to find out how much an insurance company might pay for an office visit in advance.
- It's not always easy to figure out how much insurance companies have paid us in the past for office visits.
- Different insurance companies will approve and disapprove of different services, so it's difficult to know in advance what we'll be paid for.

- The same insurance company might have several different methods of payment depending on the patient's type of policy.

Dr. Bliss likens this uncertainty to the classic Skinner box behavioral reward experiment with pecking pigeons. "Want to know how to make a pigeon peck its brains out?" he asks. "Provide it with a payment schedule that is totally unpredictable. Make it so it doesn't have any control when it gets its reward. It will peck 1,000 times to just get four pellets."

If you follow the money—the time and energy devoted to coding, pre-authorizations, denials, reconciliations, accounts receivable management and the like—you can see that a big chunk of your revenue goes toward the third-party payers. This may amount to 40% of your revenue.

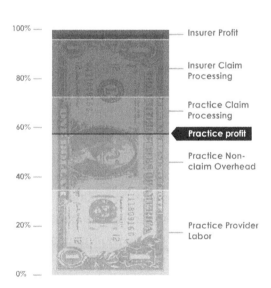

PRIMARY CARE PRACTICE INSURANCE-BASED REVENUE

Insurance consumes more than

40 CENTS
of each dollar

100% — Insurer Profit

80% — Insurer Claim Processing

Practice Claim Processing

60% — Practice profit

Practice Non-claim Overhead

40% —

20% — Practice Provider Labor

0% —

Adapted from Direct Primary Care Coalition

Medicare: In or Out?

Let's start with the bad news. Medicare has teeth. They can file felony charges, civil monetary penalties, and RACs (recovery audits) that sometimes compel enrolled physicians to comply with their coding and billing rules. If you are currently taking Medicare assignment and want to opt out, you'll have to do it carefully and follow all their guidelines. The best source for the specific forms to do so can be found on the American Association of Physicians and Surgeons website.[13] Before we summarize the major points here, **one big word of caution.**

> **CAUTION**: It is tempting for physicians who are working in a practice where they are accepting Medicare, to think that they can do their "day job" with assignment, and then not accept Medicare in their new location. This way they can hedge their bets, maintaining a good salary in their traditional practice, while getting their new cash pay venture up to speed. This is not legal under Medicare. In fact, they can reverse out all the payments made to you in your insurance practice, leaving you and your current practice with incredible liability. This holds true for physicians who think they can just stop taking Medicare assignment for new patients and then go on to offer cash-pay services for the new patients.

All fears aside, here are some basics for handling Medicare.

- **There is no law that says you have to participate in Medicare.** There are many physicians who decide not to enroll in Medicare. Since Medicare reserves the right to review medical records, psychiatrists, for example, have legitimate privacy concerns for their patients. Many pediatricians and pediatric specialists do not see Medicaid beneficiaries. There are physicians who cannot stay in business if they accept Medicare's regulated prices as payment-in-full. There are also providers who want to spend more time with patients and cannot realistically do so under the current compensation guidelines. If you are not planning to perform services for Medicare patients, enrollment in Medicare is not required. If you are not entitled to bill Medicare, your patients may seek reimbursement directly from Medicare after paying you a mutually agreed upon fee. Medicare may or may not reimburse the beneficiary.

- **Your relationship with Medicare differs depending upon whether you are a "participating" or "non-participating provider."** Non-participating providers haven't signed an agreement to accept assignment for all Medicare-covered services—but as a provider, you can still choose to accept assignment for individual patients. Participating physicians are those that have signed an agreement to accept Medicare.

- **To opt out of Medicare, you must do the following:**
  - o Participating providers are only allowed to opt out at the beginning of each calendar quarter. You must send in a valid affidavit postmarked 30 days prior to the first day of each new quarter (January, April, July, or October).
  - o Non-participating physicians and practitioners may opt out at any time. However, the opt-out effective date must be after the date the provider signs the affidavit.
  - o The opt-out contract lasts for a two-year period beginning the date you file and sign the affidavit. The opt-out automatically renews every two years. You may cancel your opt-out—and return to accepting Medicare—by notifying the Medicare carriers 30 days prior to the next two year opt out period.
  - o If you want to continue to treat Medicare beneficiaries on a cash-basis, you must enter into a private contract with them. This contract goes into effect when the opt-out period begins. You can then provide them covered services, for which they agree not to submit a claim to Medicare during the prescribed two-year opt-out period.
  - o Make certain you have office procedures in place to avoid billing Medicare.

#3. Stay Attuned to Changing Patient Demands

Patient behavior is often a mystery to physicians. Consider the patient who argues at length about their co-pay for primary care services, only to go down the hall in the same practitioner's office and pay hundreds, and sometimes thousands of dollars for Botox® and fillers. Or the patient who posts a negative review, but still wants to remain with the practice. Since we have inured patients to the true cost of medical care, and instilled in them the notion that healthcare is a right and should be paid almost totally by insurance, we've created the monster, one that physicians are all too familiar with.

Ironically, the movement toward patients having to bear greater costs is also driving them to pay more attention to value. As noted earlier, 43% of Americans were enrolled in high-deductible health plans (HDHPs) in 2017.[14] This shifts the physician-patient dynamic. Once patients finish complaining about the out-of-pocket fees, they increasingly direct their attention to value. The rationale is, "If I now have to pay cash for this medical service, am I getting value and am I being treated with respect?" Institutions are responding: Patient Engagement (PX) is now its own industry. You can find PX officers in all the major hospitals and healthcare institutions where they put on conferences and oversee the host of surveys that examine every health-related interaction.

Another trend—driven in large part by aging baby boomers—is a growing appreciation for wellness and integrative, anti-aging, functional and complementary approaches to health.

We'll define and discuss many of these emerging medical specialties in the next chapter. For those of us who follow the medical literature, it is interesting to note that a small, but vocal cadre of conventional physicians are always up in arms about "unproven therapies" and how physicians are turning into "witch doctors."[15] These physicians are swimming against a strong tide.

Healthcare is a business, and quality is defined as meeting and exceeding patient expectations. Clearly, the data provided by the National Center for Health Statistics,[16] show that consumers are putting their money where their beliefs lie. They are increasingly turning to multiple "non-conventional" modalities such as osteopathic manipulation, chiropractic, naturopathy, acupuncture, body-mind, massage, yoga, tai chi, and hypnosis.

This large segment of consumers recognize that western conventional medicine doesn't hold all the answers and that there are many paths to health and healing.[17] Fueled by the consumer dynamics as well as by growing physician acceptance, we are seeing the rise of a new type of multi-specialty clinic in which practitioners from different healing disciplines (see below) come together to provide a range of services for patients. These clinics display a vibrancy that comes from the multiple approaches to patient care. They also tend to cast a wider net in their community, attracting patients with diverse interests.

Expenditures on Complementary Medicine Approaches

- Adult, practitioner visits: $14.1 billion (46.7%)
- Adult, nonvitamin, nonmineral dietary supplements: $12.0 billion (39.7%)
- Adult, other approaches: $2.2 billion (7.3%)
- Children, nonvitamin, nonmineral dietary supplements: $0.8 billion (2.6%)
- Children, practitioner visits: $0.6 billion (2.0%)
- Children, other approaches: $0.5 billion (1.7%)

Source: National Center for Health Statistics, "Expenditures on Complementary Health Approaches: United States, 2012," June 22, 2016

In addition to MDs, DOs, nurses, and medical assistants, multi-disciplinary clinics may include:

- ND: Naturopathic Doctors
- DC: Doctors of Chiropractic
- FNP: Family Nurse Practitioners
- PA: Physician Assistants
- LAc: Licensed Acupuncturists
- LMT: Licensed Massage Therapists

- CNC: Certified Nutrition Consultants
- MFT: Marriage and Family Therapists
- CMT: Certified Massage Therapists

If you are interested in this type of practice model, we suggest you:

- **Check out some of the nationally regarded clinics.** You can learn a lot from the verbiage and positioning on their websites. Great examples from the integrative world include Anatara Medicine (anataramedicine.com) where Ahvie Herskowitz, MD practices with a cohort of complementary clinicians offering what he terms, "convergence medicine." The Center for Health and Well Being (chwbonline.com), founded by Janette Gray, MD is another example. Perhaps the most celebrated is Pacific Pearl (pacificpearllajolla.com), created by Mimi Guarneri, MD, President of the Academy of Integrative Health and Medicine (AIHM). Pain clinics are increasingly becoming interdisciplinary. We suggest you glance at the website for the Desert Clinic Pain Institute (desertclinics.com) to see the core specialists they have assembled.
- **Attend conferences.** The annual AIHM (aihm.org) conference brings together professionals from all the healing disciplines in early fall in San Diego. Many of the Osher Centers for Integrative Medicine hold annual multi-disciplinary conferences. Both IFM (ifm.org) and A4M (a4m.com) welcome practitioners from all healing traditions to attend their conferences.
- **Join a local network group.** The Functional Forum features local chapters that advance the cause of integrative and functional medicine. Created by visionary James Maskell, it's a great venue for meeting and mingling.
- **Take an "alternative" (alternative to you) practitioner for coffee.** Find those that are in close proximity to your practice. Consider gently asking your patients for recommendations. "Are you seeing anyone else for _____?"
- **Check the job boards.** Along with IFM (Institute for Functional Medicine), Lisa P. McDonald has established Integrated and Functional Connections (integratedconnects.com), a job-sharing site for integrative/functional medicine.

#4. Identify Opportunity in the Midst of the Direct to Consumer (DTC) Movement

We are all familiar with big pharma's direct-to-consumer drug advertising. These announcements are highly regulated, hence the long, complicated (for the patient) warnings of potential adverse events and complications. In 2016, the industry spent more than $5B[18] in an attempt to indirectly—through the consumer—influence physician prescribing patterns. In the case of pharma, the physician is still in charge of the relationship and the dispensing of medication. While the DTC moves of big pharma are most conspicuous, the DTC trend is rapidly increasing as other players—shown in the diagram below—circumvent the professional healthcare channel. These include a variety of laboratory testing services, often paired with products such as nutraceuticals, and/or telehealth counseling by a practitioner who might be a physician, nutritionist, pharmacist, or health coach.

THE DTC END-AROUND

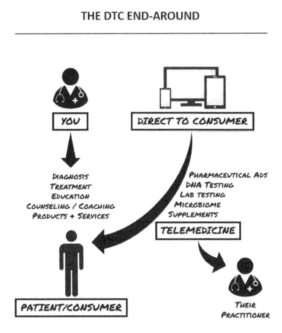

In the parlance of football, this is the classic end-around. However, if you know what play your opponent will run, you are in the unique position to counter their advance and perhaps gain possession and better field advantage. Here's your game plan:

Embrace Consumer Interest in DNA Testing

In 2017, the market for genetic testing "tipped." Driven by ANCESTRY.com and 23andMe, sales took a big uptick. By end of 2018, an estimated 12 million consumers became introduced to SNPs, the single nucleotide polymorphisms that reveal their genetic heritage. It also means that these companies hold a treasure of raw genetic data. While 23andMe provides a glimpse into carrier status for a limited number of conditions such as Late-Onset Alzheimer's Disease or Parkinson's Disease, many consumers want to dive deeper into their data to learn what to do to prevent illness and maintain health. While some clinicians might discount the validity and accuracy of home DNA testing[19] offered by an emerging group of companies, the train has left the station. If you want to serve your patients, it's time to get on board. The best way to do this is by helping patients make sense of their data.

Number of People Tested by Consumer Genetics Companies (in millions)

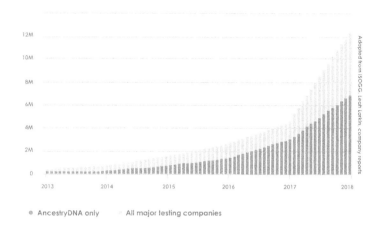

Pure Genomics (puregenomics.com) provides a physician-exclusive website application that translates the raw data into medically relevant results. The Pure platform also includes educational tools, protocols, E-script and core nutritional products. Pathway Genomics (pathway.com) offers DNA testing to both physicians and consumers. Pathway also features their suite of genetic tests on the Pathway Atrium™ patient management platform. Pathway supports insurance reimbursement with pre-authorization and other necessary forms, ICD-10/CPT codes, and interpretation guides. They also have a DTC "IQ" product that is readily available online and in large retail stores. Strategene also allows you to upload 23andMe data to get a more clinical genetic report. Color.com offers medical-grade testing for health conditions, like hereditary cancer including BRCA1 and BRCA2 identification. For patients with a family history of a known BRCA mutation, Color offers family testing for that mutation for $50. Supporting their DTC marketing, Color also has partnering physicians, whom the patient never meets, and who can sign off on the authorization.

At-Home Beauty: Threat or Opportunity?

Growing demand for new and innovative FDA-cleared beauty devices has led to the introduction of a variety of home-use beauty devices on the market. Valued at $5.5 billion in 2017, the global home-use beauty devices market is projected to reach a compound annual growth rate of 20.2% in 2023 according to Prescient & Strategic (P&S) Intelligence.[20] Sold directly to consumers without a prescription or a need to visit an aesthetic specialist, these home devices may represent, at first sight, potential new competition to your in-office procedures. However, you may be able to benefit from these tools and transform these "threats" into business opportunities. To begin with, no consumer device has the power and efficacy of the Class II lasers, IPLs and RF devices sold only to physicians. Many of the consumer aesthetic companies will offer their products to practitioners at a reasonable discount for resale. Practitioners can also elect to throw in or bundle a home device along with their more aggressive treatment to encourage self-care and maintenance. The most popular at-home devices are used for hair removal, acne treatment and rejuvenation of aging skin (wrinkles, pigmentation, etc.). Laser diodes are also used for hair restoration.

At-home devices will not replace the efficacy of in-office medical aesthetic devices. However, they can complement any aesthetic regimen to maintain results after or in between in-office treatments and add a revenue stream to your practice. You will want to stay abreast of the prices charged by the big retailers and online. It leaves a negative impression in the minds of your patients if they find that the same device is available cheaper from another outlet.

Pass Along Laboratory Savings

It's a simple law of economics. Volume drives prices down. Direct-to-consumer laboratory testing is experiencing dramatic growth fueled by consumers becoming more educated and proactive about their own health. According to a report by Kalorama Information, the market is expected to grow beyond $350 million by 2020 – up dramatically from the nearly negligible $15 million just a few years ago.[21]

Also known as Direct Access, these are state-by-state laws that allow consumers to directly access the blood, urine and other tests that are traditionally run through physicians. Consumers can order tests online through any one of several dozen DTC lab companies.[22] The menus may either be for individual tests or commonly prescribed bundles such as women's health, male health, etc. Many of the companies will provide practitioner accounts. Some of the companies have options for the consumer to research and select their test or wellness package with the company's network of nurse advocates, phlebotomists, or healthcare providers. The online companies also feature password protected patient portals. Compared to insurance-based pricing, the savings can be in the range of 50-80% off. Some companies will run specials. We are most familiar with Ulta Lab Tests (ultalabtests.com). They offer significant discounts, along with a streamlined process for testing at one of the many Quest locations. Their patient portal is marked by ease of use. The company serves several thousand clinicians. There are many others.

> An important note on laboratory testing. Both federal and state governments have some version of anti-kickback, Stark, or Stark-like laws on the books. About half of all states strictly limit the practitioner's ability to rebill or receive commissions from laboratory testing, even if the practitioner has opted out of Medicare and does not serve any Medicare patients. When in doubt, seek legal counsel.

Offer the Convenience of Telehealth to Your Patients

Telehealth services (not including telemonitoring) may include urgent and primary care, specialty diagnosis (e.g., dermatology), mental health, nutrition, coaching, health wellness, and more. Some of the companies that have developed their own platforms also employ their own physicians or other counselors who offer services directly to the consumer. These companies may "siphon off" selected categories of patients with their online telehealth service that include both a platform and a panel of physicians. Examples include Amwell, Teladoc, Babylon Health, and MD Live. These services are increasingly featuring mobile health. Physicians who work for them are usually paid based upon time spent and a percentage of revenue. Amwell.com, Doctorondemand.com, and Healthtap. com have robust mobile apps. Some of the services offered through telemedicine may or may not compete with those that you offer in your practice. For example, you may or may not want to do urgent care, or handle routine primary care questions, or you might. The best approach is to get comfortable with the telehealth technology and the different nature of the consult. Start integrating it into your practice. More on this later.

Become a Trusted Guide and Counselor to the Confused

Our final word of advice for handling the DTC end-run is based on three simple principles. The first is that consumer directed testing can—and often does—generate additional confusion on the patient's part. In addition to supporting the need for professional assistance, it can also ignite a desire for a deeper dive into health and healing. The second principle is a bit more nuanced. The consumer who has already got results in hand is an activated consumer and has demonstrated that they want more control of their health. They see clinicians as partners in the process. Third point: to grab these patients, your marketing can focus on both the confusion and your philosophy of being an advisor or guide. This is shown on the following page.

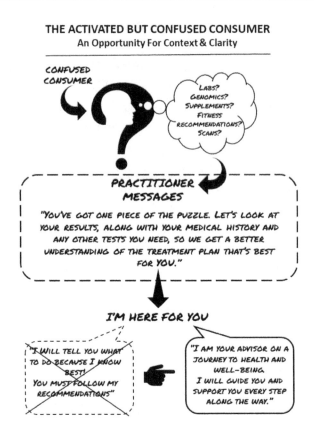

THE ACTIVATED BUT CONFUSED CONSUMER
An Opportunity For Context & Clarity

#5. Stay Attuned to the Changing Regulatory Environment

Healthcare is a highly regulated industry, and practitioners are often affected by the winds of policies and laws, both sensible and nonsensical. On the federal level, rulings by the Food & Drug Administration (FDA) may support or hinder emerging classes of therapeutics and the services you can legally offer. Many of these rules appear to favor big pharmaceutical companies. Between the passage of the Prescription Drug User Fee Act (PDUFA) in 1992 and 2016, the FDA received $7.67B in drug application fees from big pharma.[23] These user fees accounted for 68% of the Agency's review budget for prescription drugs, and 58% of the review budget for generic drugs. PDUFA expired in 2016; however, the fees were resigned into law in 2017. Below are examples of how some federal actions are impacting practitioners for good and, more often, not so good.

- **Epidiolex disrupting CBD market:**[24] The approval of Epidiolex to treat two severe types of childhood epilepsy in June of 2018 marked the first time the FDA has approved any product derived from cannabis, which the agency still classifies as a Schedule 1 narcotic. To date, the FDA has not attempted to halt the sales of CBD supplements, which are increasingly finding their way directly into the hands of consumers, and indirectly through practitioners. Now that there is precedent for a cannabis product to be classified as a drug, the industry fears that the FDA will utilize enforcement actions against companies marketing non-RX CBD supplements. The "pharmaceuticalization" of CBD will likely temper the billion-dollar market for CBD supplements.

- **FDA/JOD threatening adipose derived stem cell use:** When the FDA filed complaints in federal court seeking permanent injunctions against US Stem Cell of Sunrise, Florida and California Stem Cell Treatment Center for significant deviations in safety and manufacturing guidelines, they asserted the right to regulate autologous stem cell treatment. Depending upon the outcome of the case, the decision may affect hundreds of stem cell clinics that have opened around the country in recent years, offering new therapies for arthritis, neuropathy, degenerative disc disease and other chronic conditions.

- **FDA warnings to aesthetic companies for vaginal rejuvenation:**[25] The FDA notified seven aesthetic companies for deceptive marketing of unproven treatments. They asserted that these treatments may result in injuries as well as prevent access to appropriate recognized therapies for severe medical conditions. This action has put a damper on a rapidly growing aesthetic segment. For those physicians who have already adopted these technologies, we suggest you take a careful and thorough review of your informed consent forms.

- **FDA seeking to curtail 503A compounding companies:** The Agency is currently holding hearings on "Bulk Drug Substances That Can Be Used to Compound Drug Products in Accordance With Section 503A of the Federal Food, Drug, and Cosmetic Act; Establishment of a Public Docket."[26] These compounds include vitamins, herbs and other substances, that are made available to particular patients based on a prescription. This may have a dampening effect on treatments such as providing IV-nutrients.

- **Positive signs for telehealth:** A recently proposed rule released by the Center for Medicare and Medicaid Services (CMS)[27] includes several new proposals to pay physicians for telemedicine visits. This includes review of patient photos or videos using asynchronous or "store and forward" transmission. CMS also proposed three new monitoring codes as well as new billing for "prolonged preventative services."

- **Possible CMS payment changes:** Physicians who accept insurance will be affected by proposals to streamline payment. Tweaks to the system can benefit some types of practitioners and harm reimbursement for others. An example is the recent Trump Administration proposal[28] to collapse the major E/M codes (payments for different levels of Evaluation and Management) into one. Codes 2 through

5 would be combined into one payment. Some see benefit in the streamlining and may actually gain more revenue from the less complicated visits; others see threats to their income.

#6. Bring Digital Efficiency to Your Practice

You can get many of your work flow needs met by carefully selecting an Electronic Health Record (EHR), but you won't get *everything* you desire in one package. If you don't believe us, just poll your colleagues. To prepare for EHR adoption, or replacement, begin by listing your must-have criteria, then the nice-to-have, followed by the irrelevant. Your list might include some of these items as mission critical:

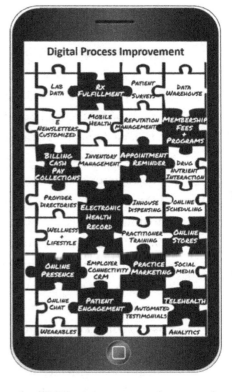

- Integration with the labs you use (API?)
- Patient reminders
    - o   Emails
    - o   Texts: any limitations on when they are sent?
- Practice Management: scheduling, confirmations, refill requests, etc.
- Payment management: insurance, cash, membership
- In-office dispensing: tracking and paying for supplements
- Pharmacy integration
- Patient portal
- Inventory management
- Provision for supplement sales
- Telehealth
- Others_____

Perform this exercise with the understanding that the EHR companies are constantly modifying, improving, and adding features. You most likely are going to settle for the one platform that meets many of your basic needs, and then add several separate digital solutions for your unique needs. We liken this to assembling a puzzle whose pieces reflect the landscape of digital process improvement. Displayed on your screen, this might look as shown on the illustration. There is no shortage of emerging companies competing to be one of your puzzle pieces. Throughout the next chapters, we will be mentioning many of them as they relate to separate management or marketing issues.

EHR (Electronic Health Record) Selection Guidelines

With more than 600 EHRs, finding the right system can be confusing. Also referred to as Electronic Medical Records (EMR), EHRs fall into two categories. There are the big enterprise systems that are multi-million-dollar system-wide installations. Cerner, McKesson Epic, Allscripts, and GE Healthcare fall into this category.[29] These EHRs must communicate across multiple specialties and departments, operate under HIPAA, and manage the onerous task of handling insurance, billings, and collections.

The second category caters to smaller practices varying in number from 1-25 practitioners. Some take insurance; some are cash only; some are hybrid models. Costs to the practice are in the range of $100-$500 per practitioner per month. In identifying the platform that works best for you, you are well advised to discuss the pros and cons with colleagues who have practices similar to yours. Among the EHRs to consider for mid-sized practices are AthenaHealth and ElationHealth Clinical First EHR. Both are robust and easy to learn. One of the interesting features of AthenaHealth is the speech to text Mobius Scribe™ designed to handle medical dictation.

The addition of patient portals provides important education and bi-directional communication. Patients can:

- Access treatment protocols and appointment summaries.
- Learn how to take medications and dietary supplements.
- Learn about their conditions through your educational library.
- Log daily health habits such as diet and exercise.
- Securely communicate with your office.

Depending upon what you do, you may want to consider these EHRs.

- **Integrative/Functional Medicine:** Power2Practice (power2practice.com) is built on a specialized EHR and practice management platform designed specifically for Integrative, Anti-Aging, and Functional Medicine practitioners. Through their innovative charting modules, including IV therapy, nutraceuticals, custom compounding, specialty labs, and customized note templates, Power2Practice helps practitioners simplify care and improve their business.

- **Micropractice and Direct Primary Care (DPC):** A number of the micropractice docs use Hello Health, Health Fusion, or Kareo. Several of the DPC physicians we interviewed had good things to say about the EHR from MDHQ.

- **Specialty Practice:** We have been impressed with Modernizing Medicine. They offer specialty-specific EHRs for multiple specialties including dermatology, ophthalmology, and orthopedics. NexGen is also oriented to meeting the needs of specialties.

- **Wellness & Complimentary Practitioners:** SimplePractice (simplepractice. com) is a feature-rich platform for practitioners in the health and wellness space including behavioral health, dieticians and nutritionists, chiropractors, substance abuse and speech-language pathologists. The extremely affordable platform allows for fully paperless intakes, scheduling, secure HIPAA-compliant messaging, and collection of payments, including e-filing of insurance claims. It is ideal for the smaller practice. Cash Practice Systems is an easy-to-use chiropractic EHR organized as simple pillars allowing for biomarker outcomes assessment, cash payments, and drip-email marketing.

#7. Make Inroads with Mobile Health

If you weren't overwhelmed enough with the 600 choices you have for an EHR, consider that there are now over 318,000 health apps available on the top app stores worldwide.[30] This is nearly double the number of apps available in 2015. In fact, more than 200 apps are being added each day. Overwhelmed yet?

Mobile health (mHealth) apps are divided into two categories: those that are patient facing and for the most part involve tracking of vitals, lifestyle and disease conditions, and those that are clinically useful for decision making. Here are some guidelines for becoming more mHealth savvy.

1. **Get in the habit of checking iMedicalApps.com regularly.** It provides great reviews of the latest clinical and FDA cleared applications arranged by specialty as well as mentions the best consumer apps. Integrative health makes the HealthNotes drug-nutrient checker available on their site.[31] You can also license the app from HealthNotes directly.
2. **Poll your patients and ask them which apps they are using.** What do they like/ dislike about them?
3. **Focus on your patients' needs.** If for example, you treat a lot of type 2 diabetics, there are many good apps available for them to monitor their health. For example, welldoc.com offers an FDA-cleared coaching app, BlueStar™ for type 2 diabetics.

Pediatricians may want to recommend that patients interested in tracking their newborn's development download thewonderweeks.com.

4. **Get familiar with a few of the basic consumer apps so you can make an intelligent recommendation.** (Recognize that some come with counseling; these services may either support or be in competition with your offerings.) Many of the apps fall into the category of lifestyle—fitness, diet, and stress—such as myfitnesspal.com, losit.com, lifesum.com, and fooducate.com. Many doctors will recommend using HealthMap's Inner Balance program.

5. **Charge for your service.** Increasingly, patients want to share their mountains of self-generated data with you, so consider establishing a policy or a service for which you are reimbursed for the time you take reviewing the mHealth data. In the membership model which we'll discuss in the next chapter, this can be an included feature, one that is often bundled with telehealth.

Now for the Big Questions

With a better understanding of the forces that may affect your practice, it's time to turn our attention to the two big questions: What type of practice is right for me? and What's the best way to get paid for my services? There are many options and choices available for you to find satisfaction in the practice of healthcare.

CHAPTER

WHAT TYPE OF PRACTICE IS RIGHT FOR ME?

Options & Choices

- In Overland Park, Kansas, board-certified OB-GYN Jim Mirabile, MD decides to no longer do obstetrics. He shifts his gynecology practice to emphasize Bioidentical Hormone Replacement Therapy (BHRT) for his patients. Mirabile adds both an aesthetic and a medical weight loss component to his practice. He now has three service centers each with ancillary, associated products. (mirabilemd.com)

- In Spokane, Washington, Amy Doneen, DNP, ARNP, a doctor of nursing teams up with Bradley Bale, MD to create the Bale-Doneen method®, based on a comprehensive discipline they call arteriology. The goal is to stamp out every bit of inflammation in the arteries through intensive diagnosis, conventional, lifestyle and nutritional treatment. They memorialize their work in a best-selling book and a successful training program for physicians. (baledoneen.com)

- Cardiologist Adel Eldin, MD, FACC, FACP in Florida, creates a successful direct primary care membership model for patients from 20 to 100 years of age. The tiered pricing, based upon age, also includes wellness for seniors. Dr. Eldin worked very closely with the legislature to help get the direct contracting model passed in Florida, saving thousands of dollars per year for each person enrolled, promoting disease prevention, wellness and also giving back to the community. (prontocare. co)

- Internal medicine physician Wiggy Saunders, MD joins an established practice, Robinhood Integrative Health, in Winston Salem, NC. Eloquent in nature and media-savvy, "Dr Wiggy" becomes the local TV doctor and focuses his expertise on thyroid disorders. Saunders adds a supplement store to his multi-provider practice that allows patients to reorder his recommended physician-grade nutraceuticals. (healthasitoughttobe.com)

- Naturopathic physician, Penny Kendall-Reed, ND realizes that one of the best ways to be known in a field as broad as naturopathy is to specialize. She dives deep into understanding neuroendocrine related diseases and lifestyle genetics. In addition to practicing natural therapies at the Urban Wellness Clinic in Toronto, she is on the lecture circuit speaking for a nutraceutical company and promoting her books. (pkrhealth.ca)

- For twelve years, Denver-based aesthetic physician Tahl Humes, DO has run a very successful practice under the brand name Vitahl. She now has three clinics: two in Denver, another in Chicago. Recognizing her patient's growing interest in wellness, she incorporates an IV lounge into her practice, branding it as Vitahlity Wellness (vitahl.com). The IV treatments, along with B12 injections, not only attract new patients, many of whom partake of aesthetic services, it adds a beneficial service to her existing patients, and serves to distinguish her brand.

- Dan Kalish, DC recognizes, at an early stage in his career, that a narrow chiropractic focus would not sustain his interest nor help him reach his financial goals. He moves heavily into functional medicine, masters the basics of science and treatment, and perfects his practice management techniques. He offers a year-long clinical course for practitioners, as well as provides business training to other healthcare practitioners. (kalishwellness.com)

- For Alan Reisinger, MD, a Baltimore based internist, the realization took a while. Working as president of a primary care medical group, and along with his partner, managing 4,000 patients in a traditional primary care practice started to take a toll on his energy and outlook. Reisinger signed up with MDVIP who helped him and his partner transition into a successful concierge practice. Reisinger now cares for some 450 patients and has the time and support to combine unrushed patient visits, lifestyle support and cutting-edge technology to provide effective, personalized preventive care. (mdvip.com)

- Tara Dall, MD, FNLA decides, for lifestyle and other reasons, to develop a total cash-pay practice whose major delivery is via video-based telehealth. A noted lipidologist, patients seek Dall out from around the globe to interpret their lab testing and to develop functional health plans. She charges both by initial consult, and in three-month or one-year increments for service. She passes along the lab savings to patients or provides forms for insurance reimbursement. Overhead is minimal; malpractice insurance rates are low. (advancemd.com) (taradall.com)

The list could easily go on to fill every page in this book, and more. There is a groundswell of innovation, experimentation, and restructuring of healthcare practice taking place each day in the United States and abroad. Many practices are thriving; some are still facing significant challenges, but almost universally, when asked to rate their satisfaction before and after adopting the changes, practitioners point to increased happiness, freedom, and quality of life.

As you ponder the type of practice that will bring you increased satisfaction and your patients better outcomes, you'll want to attend to two things. First, figure out what you want to do, the subject we'll cover in this chapter, and second, determine how you want to get paid for it, which we'll touch on next.

What Do You Want to Do?

No matter how you feel about labels, you will still need to identify what category of business you are in. When prospective patients search for a physician, they often Google a type of service (in addition to their problem). These categories represent your treatment orientation and the collection of services that are under this umbrella. You will find detailed descriptions of the products and services in these categories in Chapter 5: Where Do I Start? Here's a closer look at the most common categories along with resources that can provide further guidance.

Wellness: In 1977, when I (Mark) established the Institute of Preventive Medicine in Portland, OR, where I took cash only, saw patients for hourly visits, worked with a team of complimentary practitioners, and offered a robust collection of educational classes, "wellness" was the up and coming word. In fact, several years later when I served as Director of Health Promotion for Kaiser Permanente in the NorthWest region, my forward-looking boss, Marvin Goldberg, MD, told me upon joining that I only had one job. "When anyone in our region says the word wellness, the next words out of their mouth should be 'Oh, you mean Kaiser Permanente.'"

The term wellness has its roots in being the best you can be, and the viewpoint that absence of disease is not wellness. The issue with wellness is that the word has gone mainstream.

It is now an over-arching term encompassing any and every type of therapy that makes people feel better. It's also increasingly tied to lifestyle and sustainability.

Type the word "wellness" into a LinkedIn search and you will get more than 5.6 million hits. Considering that there are only about one million physicians in the US, and the overwhelming majority would not utilize this descriptor, there's a whole lot of "other" types of businesses offering wellness. If you are one of them, that's fine. Just realize that there is little specificity in this category. There are some excellent wellness software tools that you can incorporate into your practice.

- HealthSnap (healthsnap.com) is a lifestyle platform for the "proactive provider." It features assessments and reports in a variety of wellness areas including nutrition, fitness and musculoskeletal health.
- BodySite (bodysite.com) is another practitioner-oriented wellness platform that allows you to deliver lifestyle education for your patients.
- The Medical Wellness Association (medicalwellnessassociation.com) provides ongoing support and education for many of these practitioners.
- The National Wellness Institute (Nationalwellness.org) offers certification and may be an excellent venue for staff training in the basic principles and tools for health improvement.

Holistic/Wholistic: This was an emerging healthcare term in the 1980s. It most commonly refers to a body-mind-spirit orientation—a more encompassing view of the human being. A LinkedIn search for "holistic" generates more than 760,000 hits.

There are a great number of healthcare practitioners who define themselves as a Wellness or Holistic physician, practitioner, doctor, dentist, or healer. A great resource for practitioners of all types is *Holistic Primary Care*, a monthly publication available in print and online.

Integrative/Functional/Anti-Aging: These are more well-developed and more specialized disciplines, aimed more squarely at licensed healthcare practitioners. We have lumped them together because they have a number of shared beliefs. They differ, in large part, based upon where the practitioner received his or her training and which modalities were taught. While a host of smaller organizations have emerged with these descriptors, the field is being driven by several large, established, and growing associations.

- **AIHM** (aihm.org): Academy of Integrative Health and Medicine. Spearheaded by noted cardiologist Mimi Guarneri, MD, it is the most multi-modal association, representing health care providers and healers from multiple disciplines. AIHM offers conferences and a fellowship. The American Board of Medical Specialties now provides certification that allows successful candidates to present themselves as qualified medical specialists in the practice of Integrative Medicine. Integrative Practitioner (integrativepractitioner.com) is emerging as an excellent source for education, featuring an annual symposium, a quarterly journal, and other learning opportunities.

- **IFM** (ifm.org): The Institute for Functional Medicine was created by noted nutritional biochemist Jeffrey Bland, PhD in 1991. It has evolved significantly over the 25 plus years. IFM provides a coherent and structured framework for exploring functional medicine, as well as an organized set of tools for its conference attendees and fellowship trained physicians.

- **A4M** (A4M.com): The American Academy of Anti-Aging Medicine is the largest of the associations offering two congresses each year, as well as a robust fellowship program provided under the auspices of the Metabolic Medicine Institute. More than 7,500 physicians have been fellowship trained by A4M. Many doctors are curious as to the origin of the term "anti-aging." I (Mark) posed this question to Ron Klatz, MD one of the two emeritus founders.

> "The year was 1984 and I was attending a meeting of the American Aging Association held in Philadelphia. The group mainly consisted of older researchers, a mix of academics and public policy people. In a field of salt and pepper, what stood out was the bright purple button worn by each member, a button that said, 'Support Aging.' This didn't seem to make much sense to me. Aging seemed to be doing just fine on its own. It didn't need any support! What really required our support and encouragement were the techniques to *slow down* aging, to reverse some of its effects, to strive toward the ultimate goal of immortality. In my mind, the concept of Anti-Aging was born. It was years later in 1991, when I teamed up with Dr. Bob Goldman that this nascent idea sprouted wings, and the American Academy of Anti-Aging Medicine was born."

The Basic Tenets of Integrative/Functional/Anti-Aging Medicine

Each of the societies and associations noted above espouse deep appreciation for the best of US healthcare. There's no question about it, when it comes to acute care, the United States leads the world. In fact, if you suffer trauma, a heart attack or stroke, or come down with a treatable infection, there's no better place to be. However, if you are one of the 117 million Americans who have one or more chronic conditions—like heart disease, diabetes, cancer, or arthritis, conventional medical care may leave much to be desired.

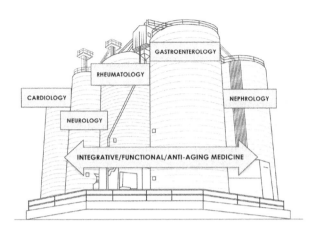

Why? Most medical care for chronic disease is delivered in a time-constrained system, one that affords patients scare minutes to dialogue with their practitioner, and even then, usually only about one "chief complaint". It is care that takes place primary in silos. A cardiologist takes care of the heart, a gastroenterologist the gut, a rheumatologist the joints, a dermatologist the skin, and so on. Each specialist has a vertically stacked body of knowledge, but rarely is there a practitioner who is looking across each of the silos to find an integrated approach to treating illness and disease.

And as we know all too well, the most common outcome of the conventional visit is a prescription. Last year, nearly 4 billion prescriptions were filled in retail US pharmacies. Many of them, of course, were born out of true medical necessity, but there is a growing trend to overmedicate our population. We see this in the inappropriate use of antibiotics and the burgeoning opioid epidemic. There are seven traits that form the backbone for this changing paradigm of healthcare.

1. **An anti-aging viewpoint that normal is not optimal.** These practitioners will focus not just on extending longevity, but adding quality of life to this extended lifespan.

2. **A search for the root cause of disease.** IFM offers a structured history taking approach that helps to identify the triggers that initiate illness. This is plotted on a timeline that provides clues as to where the clinician should focus.

3. **A personalized approach to diagnosis and treatment.** There is a plethora of emerging testing in areas of genetics, microbiome, inflammation, gut health, food sensitivities, environmental toxins and more. You will find these tests discussed in Chapter 4: What Products & Services Should I Add?

4. **An appreciation for the importance of lifestyle and environment.** Most conventional physicians do not have the extended time and training to help patients with their fitness, nutrition and stress issues.

5. **An emphasis on teaching and empowering patients.** The role of the doctor returns to the roots of the word meaning a teacher. The practitioner serves as a guide, often using motivational interviewing techniques to surface the patient's ambivalence and involve them in deciding on a course of action.

6. **An integrated—or comprehensive—viewpoint**—one that is open to input from other healthcare disciplines, and draws from other healing traditions.

7. **Enough time for the patient to tell their story,** to discuss the diagnosis and get agreement on the treatment plan. This is in stark contrast to the conventional medicine visit in which the practitioner typically interrupts the patient's narrative within the first 23 seconds.[32]

Take Note: Andrew Heyman, MD and Jim LaValle, RPh, CCN have developed a unique system to organize clinical decision-making and patient education for integrative/functional practitioners. The Metabolic Code® (metaboliccode.com) employs a robust algorithm engine that takes the patient history, biometrics, and commonly used laboratory tests and organizes the results into a series of five easily understood triads. An example of a triad is the Gut-Immune-Brain grouping. The Metabolic Code report can be printed out and used as a basis for educating patients. It can also be customized to communicate your supplement recommendations.

Lifestyle & Preventive Medicine: Many practitioners find their "tribe" in the American College of Lifestyle Medicine (ACLM). ACLM offers their own board certification for both physicians and other licensed healthcare specialties, e.g. PhDs, Masters level health disciplines, PAs, Doctors of Chiropractic, Occupational Therapy or Podiatry. They also hold conferences and provide extensive educational opportunities. The members tend to be appreciative of population health; many hold MPH degrees. ACLM defines lifestyle medicine as follows:

> *Lifestyle Medicine involves the use of evidence-based lifestyle therapeutic approaches, such as a predominantly whole food, plant-based diet, regular physical activity, adequate sleep, stress management, avoidance of risky substance use, and other non-drug modalities, to prevent, treat, and, oftentimes, reverse the lifestyle-related, chronic disease that's all too prevalent.*

Doctors who operate under a lifestyle medicine banner will often incorporate health risk appraisal, cooking classes, meal planning, fitness and nutrition assessment, and disease reversal programs into their offerings. Many practices employ health coaches and utilize support groups. Some incorporate telehealth.

The American College of Preventive Medicine on the other hand, is a medical specialty recognized by the American Board of Medical Specialties. It focuses on the health of individuals, communities and defined populations with emphasis on occupational medicine, public health and general preventive medicine.

Precision Medicine: According to the Precision Medicine Initiative, a long-term research endeavor, involving the National Institutes of Health (NIH) and multiple other research centers, precision medicine is "an emerging approach for disease treatment and prevention that takes into account individual variability in genes, environment, and lifestyle for each person." We want to emphasize the "emerging" part of this branch of medicine. With the cost of genetic testing plummeting, and knowledge of the "omics" and the microbiome rapidly escalating, this area of medicine continues to expand exponentially.

Much of the initial impetus came from Craig Venter's Human Longevity Inc. (HLI) (humanlongevity.com) whose subsidiary called Health Nucleus,[33] co-founded with Peter Diamandis, MD combines DNA analyses with a whole-body MRI scan, metabolomics screening, two weeks of constant heart monitoring, pedigree analysis, microbiome sequencing, and a plethora of standard laboratory tests. The screening has turned up cancer in 2% of the study participants.

LINKEDIN SEARCH BY TITLE (USA, 10/18)		
Descriptor	Physician	Doctor
Integrative Medicine	10,900	1,900
Functional Medicine	35,100	64,100
Anti-aging Medicine	3,700	6,900
Holistic Medicine	10,300	31,900
Concierge Medicine	2,900	2,300
"Direct Primary Care"	1,100	580
Wellness	135,000	252,800
Lifestyle	24,700	50,700
Precision Medicine	610	700

Aesthetic/Cosmetic Medicine: Aesthetics has always been pure cash-pay, so there is no discussion about insurance (except on rare occasions), hence the influx of practitioners focusing on facial beauty and body shaping.

Basically, the field is divided into "core" and "non-core" practitioners. There are approximately 20,000 core residency trained dermatologists; plastic, facial ENT, oral maxillofacial and oculoplastic surgeons in the USA. Increasingly physicians of all disciplines from emergency medicine to primary care are getting involved in many of the non-surgical treatments. While core physicians are not happy about this influx, the reality is that physicians with state medical licenses are allowed to administer all types of treatments. State laws limit other practitioners in terms of device use, injectables, and supervision. If you are a physician delegating services, or another licensed non-physician providing them, always check with your state medical board to find out what is legally permitted.

One of the drivers of the boom in aesthetics is the medspa.[34] In 2017 there were 4,200 medical spas operating in the US, part of a $4B industry with the average spa generating $945k in revenue. According to Alex Thiersch, JD, founder and director of the American Med Spa Association (AmSpa), approximately 60 percent of all medical directors at medical spas are non-core.[35]

The technologies, described later, have been refined. With adequate training, most practitioners can deliver good results with injectables, most notably if they stay away from any of the trickier areas of the face. Devices produce predictable and safe results in competent hands. Non-core practitioners interested in focusing on aesthetics can avail themselves of the resources listed below.

SELECTED AESTHETIC RESOURCES FOR THE NON-CORE PRACTITIONER (Alphabetical)		
WHAT TO PERUSE	WHAT TO CONSIDER ATTENDING	WHERE TO TRAIN
Modern Aesthetics	The Aesthetic Show	American Academy of Anti-Aging Medicine
Prime Journal	Aesthetic Everything Beauty Expo	American Board of Aesthetic Medicine
The Aesthetic Guide	SCALE Conference	Empire Medical Training
Medesthetics Magazine	American Academy of Cosmetic Surgery	American Institute of Aesthetic Medicine
Aesthetics Medicine Magazine	The Medical Spa Show (AmSpa)	National Laser Institute
Beauty Wire Magazine	International Esthetics, Cosmetics, & Spa Conference	American Association of Aesthetic Medicine and Surgery
Dermascope Magazine	5 Continent Congress (ex USA)	
Skin Inc	IMCAS (ex USA)	
	Cosmetic Surgery Forum	
	South Beach Symposium	

Weight Management: Given that 160 million Americans are either overweight or obese, every practitioner needs to attend to this issue. Adding a weight management offering, as in the case of Dr. Mirabile, detailed previously is easy, and can add cash-pay revenue to your practice. There are also physicians who focus exclusively on weight management and define themselves as a weight management physician. Among the questions: put together your own program, or work with one of the national companies that either provide franchises or licensed systems to structure the offerings and help market the program? HealthyHabits Medical Business Consultants (healthyhabitsmc.com) offer a variety of solutions for practitioner and patients. The Center for Medical Weight Loss provides extensive training and a robust online provider site. Many weight loss practitioners attend the annual meeting of The Obesity Society.

Regenerative Medicine: Most practitioners of regenerative medicine in the United States limit their procedures to outpatient orthopedic procedures. Platelet rich plasma (PRP) or fibrin, bone-derived mesenchymal stem cells, or the stromal vascular fraction of adipose, are extracted, and refined usually via centrifuge (depending upon the type of cell, with enzymatic action) and then injected into the joint, ideally under ultrasound guidance. Amniotic cells and umbilical cord tissue products may also be injected. Many practitioners will combine the cellular products, sometimes adding other tissue healing compounds. PRP is also used in aesthetics, applied to the face in conjunction with minor invasive procedures, and sometimes used in the genital area, where the growth factors can enhance tissue regeneration.

The FDA is increasingly active against the use of intravenous, intra-cardiac, or intrathecal administration, unless performed under IND. Physicians who are interested in participating in the latest research utilizing these more advanced techniques would do well to consider an affiliation with Bahamas-based Okyanos (okyanos.com), operated by reputable US physicians. The center operates under Bahamian law, following rigid, approved protocols for safety and quality. Referring physicians from the US monitor their patients along with a Contract Research Organization. Two organizations that focus on the emerging science include the World Stem Cell Summit and the International Society of Stem Cell Research.

Pain Management: often goes hand in hand with regenerative medicine. Major therapies include a variety of injections: epidural, caudal, trigger point, facets as well as spinal injections, and ligament/muscle/trigger points. Increasingly, pain management clinics are becoming much more multi-modal incorporating chiropractic, acupuncture, physical therapy, massage therapy, behavioral health and naturopathic treatment. A glance at the website of the Desert Clinic Pain Institute (desertclinics.com) shows this diversity of treatment approach.

Sports Medicine: Most sports medicine practices are offered by orthopedic physicians; however, practitioners who are personally passionate about human performance can attract sports-oriented patients. There is room for clinicians, especially Integrative and Functional physicians to create partnerships with local health clubs and corporations. The American College of Sports Medicine (ACSM.org) offers both clinical and non-clinical certifications. ACSM enjoys a partnership with Wellcoaches to deliver behavior change programs. A major focus of sports medicine is exercise testing and the exercise prescription. These tests are often incorporated as an included benefit in many cash-pay membership medical practices.

Women's/Men's Health

Practitioners who promote themselves as Women's or Men's Health experts usually have solid grounding in understanding, balancing, and replacing hormones. In women, this often centers around menopause; in men, low testosterone levels. There is increasing emphasis on pellet implants (see Chapter 5: Where Do I Start?). Men's health also deals with ED, premature ejaculation, and prostate health. Cardiovascular health, hair removal, and aesthetic services naturally fit under a gender umbrella. Companies such as BodyLogicMD and Hormone Treatment Centers of America have created education, training and marketing systems for physicians.

Other Foci: We've touched on some of the major types of practice; however, there are many others. Some are broad-based and well established such as cosmetic dentistry, LASIK, vein clinics, or executive health; others such as mold, Lyme disease, memory or neurocognitive clinics are more narrow, or just emerging. No matter what umbrella you choose to place your services under, you will need to be aware of the following issue.

The Problem with Knowing Who You Are or Want to Be

There's an all too common disconnect that we have seen repeated time and again as well-intentioned clinicians, well versed in their paradigm, go out and try to represent themselves in person and online. They suffer from "the curse of knowledge." If you spend some time glancing at websites, as we do, you will find the following examples:

- **Technospeak:** The use of big medical terms that you are familiar with, but patients don't quite get. When in doubt, define the terms you are using. Explain functional, integrative, or precision to a middle-schooler.

- **Feature Focus:** This is all about you falling in love with your tools and techniques, many of which are not understood by patients. Worse yet is when you present them as a laundry list of things you do. (See the physician example below, as well as the remedy.) Features are worthless unless they are attached to benefits for the patient.

- **All About Me:** If the first thing that hits the patient is a long list of your accomplishments, you will be missing the opportunity to let them know the most important aspect of attracting patients. What do patients want?

In addition to demonstrating that you are a kind, caring, compassionate clinician who really listens, prospective patients want to know that you hold the solution to their problem.

So, what might this look like? Here are some examples:

Functional Medicine: This is an opportunity to thoroughly explore and get to the root of your patient's problem, but you must begin by noting the emotional toll disease takes on the individual. Many of your prospects have most likely exhausted many of the conventional routes and are frustrated and concerned. Others have the vague sense that they are losing their edge, or they are not as vital and vigorous as they want to be.

Sports Medicine: Not only can you help with the nagging injuries, but you have the tools to help these patients reach higher levels of performance. You'll help them go faster, longer, and harder.

Women's Health: You understand their frustration with being told, "It's normal," or "It's a part of aging," or "Your symptoms are all in your head." You will listen to and work with them as a valuable partner. You may also note that your treatments may be more "natural" and in tune with the hormones that the body produces.

Aesthetics: This is a bit of an exception, in that patients really want to know the clinician's experience—so you can take this opportunity to tout your credentials. Before and after pictures are quite important, as well as positive reviews. Practitioners just starting out might want to let patients know that you have both an eye for beauty and if you practice integrative or functional medicine, a whole-person philosophy that emphasizes beauty from the outside in, and inside out.

Always emphasize that you will be your patient's guide and partner in working through whatever issue they might have.

Does What You Say Match What They Want?

Mark's colleague at ChangeWell Training Academy, Robert John Hughes, often guides practitioners through a clarification exercise in which he has them compare the language on their website with the patient's Yelp reviews. Here's a typical example:

Same Doctor - Different Perspectives

Dr's Website	Online Patient Review
Doctor _____ uses traditional naturopathic approaches, which include, herbs, vitamins, minerals, amino acids, homeopathy, foods and counseling. ___ also uses energy healing techniques such as craniosacral therapy, visceral manipulation, NET Neuro Emotional Technique, brain gym, EFT	_____ is very easy to work with and is exceptional. I had been feeling continuously tired and fatigued and nothing I tried seemed to help. _____ suggested a few things for me to try and to change some areas of my diet and life. Within a short time I felt much better. Finally I found someone that could help. Other doctors just chalked it up to being over-worked.
Method, Process, Techniques	Problems, Solutions, Results

It's pretty easy to see the disconnect. The doctor is focusing on method, process and techniques; the patient focuses on problems, solutions and results. Another way of examining this disconnect is to put your promotional verbiage through one of the popular word cloud programs such as Wordle (wordle.net) WordArt (wordart.com) or TagCrowd: (tagcrowd.com). Here's what this looks like when compared to the patient's wordcloud.

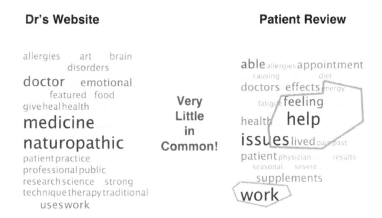

Create a Better Invitation

The best way to let prospective patients know about your work is to focus more on them, than on you. In the example above, if we were to take into consideration the patient's viewpoint and needs, here is what this clinician's statement might look like.

*Many of my new patients complain that they **feel** continuously **tired and fatigued**. Nothing they've tried seems to **work**. Even worse, sometimes they're told "you're just overworked" or "it's part of **getting old**."*

I don't believe that. Hi, I'm Dr Julia Smith. I practice integrative medicine. That means we treat your body as an entire, integrated system. When you come in, we'll *do a very thorough analysis of your body and all its systems. Then, based on the results, we'll suggest a few things for you to try. If you're like most of my patients, within a short time you'll be **feeling much better**. I look forward to **helping you**.*

Click here to schedule your first visit with us.

Before we move on to the next chapter, there's one more exercise that will help you focus your efforts. It is described in the box below.

How to Better Describe What You Do

No matter your flavor of healthcare, you will want to be able to describe your services using terms that appeal to your prospects, patients, or clients. We've found that staff often have valuable inputs. A great team-building exercise is to raise these questions and discuss the answers:

- What adjectives do you think our patients use to describe the services we provide?
- What adjectives would you (staff) use?
- Write the patient descriptors on the left side of the page, staff on right, and compare. Identify the ideal set of descriptors
- When looking at our online presence, advertisements, and internal promotion, are these the descriptors that come to mind? If not, what must we do about this?
- How should we organize our office to better reflect these terms?

You Are Multipotent

To borrow an analogy from the stem cell world, most healthcare practitioners are multipotent (given the right signals from the environment, capable of transforming into a different cell type). With years of training, a strong work ethic, and ample experience meeting and exceeding the needs of their patients/clients, there are multiple options for reworking these assets into a shape that provides enhanced satisfaction. Transforming and augmenting your practice does require that spark of energy that helps you rekindle what you love about caring for others. Fortunately, there are many organizations and individuals who can help you in this process. Once you get a clearer notion of what you really enjoy doing in your healthcare practice, you'll need to figure out how to get paid for it. We'll start following the money in the next chapter.

CHAPTER

HOW & WHAT SHOULD I CHARGE?

Following the Money

Generating revenue in healthcare is simple; however, it's often not that easy. You can make money from:

1. Your services
2. The services of others
3. Product sales
4. ~~Referrals/commissions~~. Not a good idea. There are both federal (Stark) and state laws that prohibit physicians from receiving rebates, commissions, kick-backs, or fee splitting.[36] Most states also have laws prohibiting markup of laboratory services. You are advised to seek legal counsel in your state.

Money may come to you in the form of:

1. Insurance reimbursement
2. Direct-pay (sometime called private-pay)
3. Membership
   a. Direct Primary Care
   b. Concierge
4. Combinations of the above (Hybrid)
5. Passive and Residual Income

In this chapter, we'll examine these numbered items in greater detail. We'll also discuss two emerging technologies, group visits and telehealth, and discuss how they can generate additional revenue, while keeping costs down.

In-Office Laboratory Testing and Dispensing

At the end of this chapter, we will provide some guidelines for pricing your services, and the services of those practitioners who extend your care. We cover product sales in the next chapter. There are two other potential revenue centers for your business that are worth considering: (1) Physician office lab testing, and (2) In-office medication dispensing. Both offer convenience, and usually lower costs for the patient, as well as improve compliance. With physician office lab testing, other benefits include immediate diagnosis leading to faster treatment decisions and medication adjustments.[37] For most primary care practices, the "big three" chronic conditions will be diabetes, hypertension and hyperlipidemia. Hence, practices who wish to adopt in-office testing could check blood glucose levels, A1C levels, lipids and PT/INR (for anti-coagulation status).

The second growing trend is the adoption of in-house pharmacies. The numbers make sense. For a conventional doctor who sees 25 patients and dispenses about 40 prescriptions a day, adding $10 on each of these would result in a daily profit of $400, and would not take up any more of the doctor's time. In-office dispensing is regulated by each State, so if you are considering doing so, check with your local healthcare attorney. The larger clinics may want to use the service of a company that offers fully equipped mini-pharmacy systems, with storage and tracking. In this case, a significant percentage of revenue obtained from the patient goes toward their service. More commonly, in the Direct Primary Care model described below, physicians will stock the most commonly prescribed generic medications, and charge the patient the wholesale price, often adding a 10% fee for the handling.

INSURANCE REIMBURSEMENT

Health and Human Services has been heavily promoting value-based care that centers more on specific outcomes. This has given rise to accountable care organizations (ACOs), bundled payments, and patient-centered medical homes. Reflecting the dominance of insurance-based medicine, the 2018 Medscape survey shows that physician participation in ACOs is approaching 40%, in contrast to the 9% of physicians who are in cash-only or concierge practices.

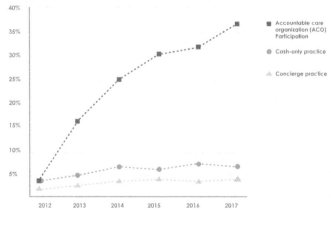

Modified from the Medscape Physician Compensation Survey, 2017

For most practitioners, especially primary care, billing is based upon the:

- time spent with the patient
- severity of symptoms
- extent of history-taking and examination
- degree of complexity of medical decision making
- counseling and coordination of care provided

The most commonly-used CPT codes and Medicare reimbursement rates for 2018, and approximate visit times are shown on the chart below.

CPT Code	2018	Approximate Time [38]
KE99211	*$30.90	5 min
99212	$61.67	10 min
99213	$101.39	15 min
99214	$149.32	25 min
99215	$200.52	40 min
*non-MD or qualified healthcare professional		

We won't be discussing much about the world of insurance reimbursement, other than to make the recommendation that, if you choose to take insurance, you are well advised to engage the services of a firm that has expertise in billing and coding, and/or you train your office staff well. Karen Zupko and Associates is a great source for training. Facilitating medical coding and billing is a feature built into many of the insurance-centric EMRs.

One of the questions that practitioners ask their billers and coders is whether the practice can receive insurance reimbursement for some of the wellness or integrative functional assessments or counseling provided to patients. Insurance pays for medically necessary services that are properly coded and documented and delivered by licensed practitioners. It pays for treatment of conditions such as hypertension, hypercholesterolemia, migraines, and diabetes, but not for helping a 175 lb., six-foot male athlete, go from 13% to 10% body fat.

That being said, there are CPT codes for conditions such as fatigue, mood disorders, alcohol withdrawal, or dehydration for which IV nutrient therapy would be indicated. It may also be possible, for example, to bill for an eye exam for headaches. There are some reimbursement codes for education and counseling. We reached out to a number of companies that provide coding and most were reluctant to share details of their procedures;

in part due to the complexity and the "it depends" nature of the process, and in some measure the desire to maintain their intellectual property.

DIRECT-PAY

You develop a menu of services and products, and price these out on an `a la carte basis. It is quite common for the physicians, or the most sought-after practitioners in the practice to bill their time out at higher rates. We have commonly seen physician rates of $300-$600 an hour, depending upon the market. In general, fees for well-trained extenders are usually about half that of the physician. Most direct-pay practices do not accept insurance. They will; however, give the patient a superbill to send to their insurance for any eligible reimbursement, or recommend a third-party biller who can handle the transaction. You will want to state your payment policy clearly and in writing, and have patients acknowledge your terms. An example of a cash-only payment policy looks like this:

Our Payment Policy
- Payment is required at the conclusion of your visit.
- We will provide you a copy of your bill and you may directly submit it to your PPO insurance plan as "out of network."
- We regret that our office is unavailable to answer questions or provide additional documentation that your individual insurance plan may request.*
- Your reimbursement will depend upon your individual insurance plan. Please contact your insurance company for information on your coverage for "out of network" providers.
- We are not providers for any HMO insurance or Medicare. Medicare patients are also required to pay upfront and per government regulations may NOT be eligible for reimbursements.
- We accept all major credit cards.**

*Some practices direct patients to a third-party billing company to help them submit their bill to their insurance company.
** If offered, mention patient financing here.

Your communication can also include a cancellation policy, as follows. This can be enforced by having the patient's credit card information on file and billing them accordingly, provided they have been informed of, and agreed to these terms.

Cancellation Policy

As we have set aside this time specifically for you, and we do not overbook appointments, if you need to cancel or reschedule your appointment, please call our office 48 hours prior to your appointment in order to avoid a cancellation fee. Cancellation fees are as follows: _____

☐ **Take Home:** *Cash-pay practitioners are increasingly offering patient financing. CareCredit (carecredit.com) provides a health and wellness line of credit accepted by over 175,000 health providers.*

In the same way that a restaurant determines the pricing of each dish on their menu, so too must you identify the prices you will charge for your services. Setting price points will depend upon:

- **What the market will bear.** Here is where you'll want to do research on practices offering similar cash-pay services. If you price yourself too low, you may give the impression that your services aren't that good; too high, and you will price yourself out of the market, or only draw the few who are willing to pay your fees. You can always offer some introductory bundles, or limited time offers that appeal to the value shopper. Cash-pay services often tend to work well in more sophisticated markets where educated patients know what they want.
- **What your costs are.** You'll need to factor in the total cost of goods and services. For products, this means product cost plus shipping and taxes, cost to maintain inventory, bundled pricing and free product. Service costs should be fully loaded including rent, insurance, utilities, taxes, supplies, equipment, legal and accounting. Work closely with your CPA to get these numbers.
- **Minimizing risk.** If you want to provide both an affordable patient option, and minimize the risk of a new venture, consider creating a minimally viable, "thinner" product in the beginning to test the waters.
- **The margins you want to achieve.** In the ideal world, you would maintain your overhead at 25-30%, somewhat higher if your mix includes extenders at 50% markup, or large supplement sales volume (also at 50%).

☐ **Take Home:** *Your homework includes setting the prices of your services and products. Use the list below as a starting point and add those that are relevant to your practice.*

DIRECT- PAY SERVICES FEE SCHEDULE

Visit Time

- Initial visit (1-2 hours) _____
- Annual exams (90 min) _____
- Follow up (30/60 min) _____
- Phone/Telemedicine consultations (15/30/45/60 min) _____

Typical Services (Examples)

- B12 injection_____
- IV drip_____
- Pap_____
- Skin biopsy_____
- Steroid joint injection_____
- In office lab tests:
    o Finger stick glucose_____
    o Pregnancy test_____
    o Rapid strep test_____
    o Urine dipstick_____
    o Venipuncture_____
- Medical records requests
- Neurotoxins per unit _____
- Body composition testing _____
- VO2 Max testing _____
- Other_____

Direct-pay models are not just limited to primary, integrative, and functional medicine practitioners, this model is expanding across the healthcare spectrum.

- Tony Mork, MD, a minimally invasive spine surgeon with offices in Newport Beach, CA and Miami, only accepts cash for procedures. He offers a concierge-like/destination medicine approach to spine care. Prospective patients, from around the world, upload their MRI in advance. Mork then conducts a 30-minute telehealth consultation and creates a treatment plan for the patient. Appropriate candidates are scheduled for surgery. Patients are directed to Mork's YouTube channel for further education pre- and post-procedure. In addition to routine follow-up care, he provides his cell phone number for patients to call or text him 24X7 no matter when their procedure was performed.

- Patrick Bitter, MD, a noted San Francisco bay area dermatologist did what many dermatologists do: accept insurance payments for medical dermatology, and cash only for aesthetic procedures. Bitter recently dropped insurance, and patients who want his medical dermatology expertise pay cash.

- G. Keith Smith, MD founded the Surgery Center of Oklahoma in the mid-1990s, only to part ways with insurance companies when he decided to become transparent with the Center's cash pricing. The Center lists the prices for more than 200 outpatient procedures on their website.[39] Smith has gone on to co-found the Free Market Medical Association (fmma.org) that brings together other like-minded cash-pay clinicians. Transparency in pricing has a great allure for companies that are self-insured for employee healthcare.

For these, and other specialty practices, direct-pay seems to be a good model for the long term. However, one of the challenges with direct-pay in primary care, and a reason why many physicians who start out this way eventually move to a membership model, is that some patients will have a nagging feeling that they are being "nickeled and dimed," or perhaps feel slightly pressured to buy additional products or services.

Should You Want to Skew High-End

Depending upon your market, your reputation, the desirability of your services, and the strength of your brand, you may want to bundle and package a suite of services tailored to patients who will pay $5,000-$25,000 to work with you. There are a number of very successful "destination health" doctors who can command these fees. Examples include Mark Menoloscino, MD whose patients make the trek to the Meno Clinic in Jackson Hole, WY for his detailed functional assessment, or noted Integrative/Anti-Aging physician Mark Houston, MD in Nashville, TN. Houston runs a two-day intensive cardiovascular consult program that is concierge in flavor. Patients come into Nashville where they undergo extensive testing day one, then meet with Houston for 1.5 to 2 hours the second day. They are then followed up for a year by phone and with repeat visits. Patients pay an annual fee and insurance is billed for medically indicated testing. The Health Nucleus program in San Diego commands high patient fees and draws both national and international patients. Canyon Ranch Medicine combines diagnostics and personalized medicine under the umbrella of a comprehensive resort spa experience. The Pritikin Longevity Center (pritikin. com) also offers medically-based lifestyle programs in a luxury health resort setting.

Destination aesthetics is well established in the world of plastic surgery where patients fly in for procedures, have surgery, and stay at a local upscale hotel for recuperation. Practitioners aiming at this end of the market are advised to mingle with high net worth prospects at golf and country clubs, C-suite business organizations, community and civic events, and consider sponsoring and advertising with organizations that support the arts.

After spending time with Florence Comite, MD, Director or the Comite Center for Precision Medicine (comitemd.com), it is easy to see why her recently-opened, state-of-the-art 13,000 sq. foot precision-medicine center, in the heart of midtown Manhattan, is a magnet for higher end cash-pay patients. Chances are, you will not be creating this large a footprint, but you can benefit not only from Comite's clinical acumen and 20-year history as a precision medicine pioneer, but also her business system, both of which she teaches in preceptorship and training programs. We've grouped the business side features into four "Fs:"

Focus, Friend, Front-Load, and Follow-Through

Focus: The Comite precision medicine model builds around the n-of-1 concept: Each person is unique and deserving of data-driven, personalized and tailored interventions for optimal longevity. The emphasis is on integrating and interpreting as much data as possible, from hormones, metabolomics, genomics, the microbiome, and other advanced diagnostics, and marrying this to the client's lifestyle, within the context of the personal and family history, to create a personalized treatment plan.

Note Well: The more complex your offerings, the more important it is to present your program in a simple visual scheme as Comite represents below. (We might quibble that most patients would not understand the word "metabolomics," but it does have the ring of "metabolism" in it, and that is an engaging term for consumers.)

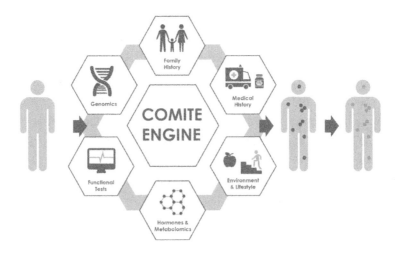

☐ **Take home:** *Clarify your model and your messaging. Use simple diagrams that allow comprehension at a glance.*

Friend: This would seem to be an odd word to juxtapose with precision; however, the mandate at the Comite Center is to forge a bond of likability and trust with the client. This means that the Center staff—including Dr. Comite—are often generous in conducting free, exploratory phone consultations with prospective clients, many of whom are referrals from existing clients. According to Comite, "I try to understand both the patient's pain point, and their concerns. Some want to know what they can do to stop the decline in their health. Others may say that they are not on their 'A game.' Many are dealing with specific issues, or they are scared because a close friend or family member has been diagnosed with a particular condition. Being a doctor on the phone conducting the intake can be invaluable to really understanding the person. A bonus, too, is leveraging your effort in the future. Yes: Time is money; but investing in each of your client's health will bring the best return."

☐ **Take Home:** *The person who is the best listener (and has time to do so), possesses the most passion, and has a reasonable understanding of the products and services, should be the chief communicator with prospects. If you are a physician, never think this is somehow beneath you or a waste of time to field prospect calls. A successful cash-pay healthcare practice is based on creating strong relationship equity with potential patients.*

Front-Load: Comite's six to eight-week client enrollment process is heavily front-loaded—a great deal of data is gathered before the first visit. This makes the office visit more efficient. Clients fill out a proprietary precision health questionnaire on a secure client portal. This is followed by advanced laboratory testing with a mobile phlebotomist who draws blood at the patient's home, office, or hotel. Alternatively, clients are directed to a specific laboratory in possession of Comite's proprietary biomarker kit. Patients are asked to release their medical records (sharing data from wearables and health apps is also encouraged – a rarity among physicians). Once all this information is in hand, Dr. Comite and her clinical team conduct a telemedicine consult (referenced by Comite to her clients as a "TeleMed"). In anticipation of the first office visit, clients are also scheduled for bone studies, a bone density including a body composition at a neighboring facility. The first office visit includes additional assessments including vascular and cardiorespiratory fitness. This work results in a customized treatment plan that include, among other things, lifestyle modifications (sleep, nutrition, exercise, stress reduction), supplements and medications, if indicated, and recommendations for advanced diagnostics.

☐ **Take Home:** *Once you develop a relationship with the prospect and they agree to become a client, determine what you can front-load in your offering so that you can maximize your and their time in the office. Consider using a mobile phlebotomist; it says that you value your client's time and that you are providing a higher level of client service.*

Follow-Through: As we've reinforced throughout this book, Comite positions herself as her client's quarterback and partner through a journey to optimal health; it is a process that unfolds over time. Earning a client's buy-in isn't difficult, because the rewards of the n-of-1 approach are soon evident. Her clients report looking and feeling better. Over time, parameters of aging and disease biomarkers reverse at the cellular level; and conditions such as diabetes and heart disease disappear.

Comite lets clients know that they can always reach the Center via email, phone, text or video chat. Most important is the discussion she has with clients about the real value of advanced testing, the biomarkers, and the serial data it generates. Namely, any and every laboratory test is a snapshot in time. It is a piece of a puzzle, and the real value—as Comite shares—is not in the data points but in the patterns. Repeat assessments and analyses reveal, in the data, the reversal of aging: herein lies the n-of-1 magic.

☐ **Take Home:** *Establish a structured follow-up schedule and discuss with your patients the importance of serial check-ups. One more take-home tip: Always do what you say you are going to do for a patient; stay compassionate and open to their evolving lives.*

MEMBERSHIP MODELS

On the most basic level, membership medicine involves a contract between the practitioner and the patient. The patient agrees to pay a monthly, quarterly, or annual fee for a set of services determined by the practitioner. At the minimum, these services include enhanced access, e.g., same day and longer appointments and often 24X7 access via phone, email and text; reduced-price or included screenings; and referral care. Home visits and telehealth may also be included. However, the bundling of included services and products can be quite extensive, depending upon the interests of the practitioner and the desire of the patients. This drives up the monthly or annual cost; alternatively, extra services can be priced separately. For practitioners who accept insurance, known as a hybrid model, the membership fee is for non-covered services (access, education, nutritional counseling, etc.). The practitioner bills insurance only for those services that are covered by insurance.

24X7 Phone Abuse?

Many physicians considering membership medicine are reticent to include 24X7 phone access as part of their bundled services for fear of potential abuse, e.g., too many calls, calls at night or weekends. Neither the surveys, nor the informal discussions with membership practitioner support this notion. According to surveys conducted by Michael Tetreault, Editor of the *DPC Journal* and *Concierge Medicine Today*, when asked about phone access, membership practitioners noted the following distribution of calls:

- 82% normal business hours 8 am-5 pm
- 8% weekdays after hours 5 pm-7 am
- 8% weekends; of these about half (~4%) came in from 8 am-5 pm
- 2% of calls came on weekends from 5 pm-7 am.

The advantages of a membership model are quite obvious. It allows the practitioner to provide greater access, and hopefully better care to a smaller panel of patients. Many malpractice insurers will lower the rates they charge physicians. A membership model provides the practitioner a better quality of life and smooths out cash flow. Consumers are increasingly accepting of membership models, from gym and spa participation, to streaming online services, and even subscriptions to non-profit causes.

Much has been made of the distinction between the two major membership models: Direct Primary Care (DPC) and Concierge practice. They are more alike than dissimilar, and most of our recommendations hold for both models. In each, the panel size is limited. Traditional DPC practices usually care for 600-800 patients, down from the 2,000-2,500 in a conventional practice. Concierge practices usually round off at about 400 patients.

In the DPC model, the practitioner does not accept insurance, and the monthly fee pays for both enhanced access and routine non-urgent and urgent healthcare issues. Because DPC practices follow a quasi-insurance model, they are state regulated. Currently 17 states have passed DPC laws and there is legislation currently moving in Congress to expand this.

Many concierge practices will accept insurance for medically necessary services covered by insurance; the membership fee covers the access fee, and most commonly an annual comprehensive wellness exam.

While there are adjustments for age, the typical fee for an adult under the age of 65 to join a DPC practice is ~$70/month, and this fee is often paid monthly. It is usually adjusted upward in more affluent markets. Concierge fees are usually higher, in the range of $110-$200/month or more and are often paid annually or quarterly.

DPC: A Fierce Sense of Freedom

Small, but mighty. Growing and passionate. These are adjectives we would use to describe the approximately 900 DPC practices in the United States, most of which are one or two physician micropractices with low overhead.

There's a pioneering spirit you can feel in the self-employed DPC practitioners. These docs are passionate in their vision of greater control and it's reflected in the relative simplicity of the model. Harkening back to a simpler time, they are adamant that this is medicine as it "ought to be." It's primary care, pure and simple. For those who have previously been employed physicians, there is a seething, residual anger at corporate medicine. Some of these entrepreneurial-minded physicians take umbrage at the larger, multi-physician corporate primary care models that feature improved access. These may be membership-based (Nextera Health), hybrid (OneHealth), Medicare insurance focused (Iora Health) or primarily workplace-oriented (Paladina Health). Physicians in these structures participate as employees. For those physicians who want the security of a job and a paycheck, and eschew dealing with business, these organizations can offer a better work experience compared to employment in a conventional practice.

Leaning more toward an insurance capitated model, DPC relies on there being a bell curved distribution of patients, many of whom are non- or low utilizers for the practice to make money. On the other hand, membership models for more functional/integrative practices, tend to attract more high-touch, high-need, high-utilizers which usually require a different revenue model.

KEEPING THE DPC VISION ALIVE AND WELL

We hope the powerful vision of the primary care physician as entrepreneur remains a driving force in healthcare. We applaud the recent decision of NYU to make medical tuition free. With the shackles of debt removed, young physicians may increasingly turn to primary care, and hopefully to DPC models that provide both autonomy and increased patient/provider satisfaction. It will remain the work of today's DPC physicians to help counter the mindset, among today's housestaff, that the best career path is employment in a large healthcare system. This is best done by actively promoting the vision and the benefits of this more personalized, proactive and entrepreneurial model of care.

Fortunately, there are some excellent resources for physicians who want to explore, advocate, initiate, and gain success in DPC. These include:

- **DPC Frontier** (dpcfrontier.org): an academic DPC authority founded by Phil Askew, DO, JD, MBA featuring a state-by-state summary of state laws and practices.
- **Direct Primary Care Coalition** (dpcare.org): Dedicated to addressing the political barriers to DPC, the Coalition has a lobbying component designed to advance the movement as well as provide solid resources.
- **DPC Alliance** (DPCalliance.org): A membership organization that provides mentoring, materials, education, support, and discounts on goods and services for DPC practitioners.
- **The American Association of Family Physicians** (aafp.org/Practice-Management/Payment/DPC.HTML): AAFP is the national advocacy organization for family practitioners. They have embraced the DPC concept. AAFP puts on seminars and also has an excellent startup toolkit for primary care docs.
- **American College of Private Physicians** (acpp.md): provides advocacy for physicians whose practice designs include a direct financial relationship between patient and physician.
- **Access Healthcare Direct** (accesshealthcaredirect.com): the brainchild of Brian Forrest, MD, AHD offers a DPC boot camp as well as practice transformation services, GPO discounts, prevention and wellness tools, and a patient portal.
- **DPC Journal** (directprimarycare.com): Essential reading for practitioners who want to understand the latest trends and acquire the necessary tools to start and grow their DPC practice. Editor-in-Chief Michael Tetreault is also in charge of the sister publication for concierge physicians, ***Concierge Medicine Today.***

Clarity of Offer Is Essential

Because membership medicine, in this case DPC, is a contracted service, it is critical that you clearly outline the services that are included in your offering. You need to tell patients what they are going to get and what it's going to cost them. We are in strong agreement with Garrison Bliss, MD, a DPC physician in the Seattle, Washington area who believes practitioners should use "plain speak" in describing their services. This is how he represents his membership practice.

- BlissMD will provide primary care services to all member patients. I will act as your full-time medical advisor and the most available physician you are likely to ever meet.

- BlissMD will provide routine medical care, urgent care, chronic disease management and care coordination with specialists, hospitals, ERs, etc. We will provide high quality well-vetted referrals to the best medical services we can find and help you navigate this crazy medical world intelligently.
- We will provide a limited list of injectable medications either at no charge or at our cost.
- We will provide a substantial array of splints, walker boots, crutches and other items at no charge.
- We will handle minor surgical issues (like draining superficial abscesses, removing splinters and repairing uncomplicated lacerations) in our office - and refer out surgical problems beyond our scope of practice.
- We will provide a limited list of joint and tendon injections (Elbow bursa, elbow epicondyles, hip bursa, knee joint and shoulder joint primarily) at no cost.
- We will provide free flu vaccine annually for all of you who are interested and free Tetanus/Diphtheria/Pertussis vaccine every 10 years to members. Since we are not set up to bill your insurance for other vaccines, we will send prescriptions to your local pharmacy to receive these injections.
- Blood draws and IVs will be free. We are affiliated with Quest Labs for laboratory work. We can draw your blood in our office (at no charge). Quest will process the labs and bill your insurance.
- Bliss then goes on to list his current prices.

You may choose to offer these basic primary care services, or note that you also provide others such as school and sports physicals, sleep hygiene, weight management, functional medicine assessments, or more. The choice of services, the pricing, and what is included in the membership fees is up to you.

Most practitioners build in a good deal of flexibility in their offerings. They bundle different services for different aged-patients. They must also charge the patient appropriately. Hint (hint.com) provides a workflow automation platform that supports the unique requirements of direct care. The platform allows for enrollment, packages and plans, activation and payments, as well as displays financial records on an easy to use dashboard. Many of the DPC physicians will pair Hint up with their EMR, as well as offer Spruce Health (sprucehealth.com) to handle the more advanced patient communication options including text, secure messaging, telehealth, email, and website live chat.

Concierge Medicine

Some physicians have a bit of a knee-jerk reaction to the term "Concierge" as it tends, in their minds, to connote an equal measure of exclusivity and snobbery. The horse is out of the barn. Concierge medicine is in the lexicon, and for many practitioners it is the easiest way to describe their practice in a few words and have it understood by the consumer. Those who study population health also frown on the ever-increasing movement toward concierge care, in large part because it exaccrbates the shortage of primary care physicians.

There are some practices—marked by extremely high annual fees in the tens of thousands of dollars—that are aimed squarely at the high-end of the market. Like the Ritz Carlton, Seabourn Cruise Lines, or Bentley automobiles, the branding and imaging of these practices is consistent with the higher price points. For the most exclusive clients, some concierge physicians may even travel with their patients. There are a number of concierge physicians, most of whom are in major metropolitan areas, who can command high prices, most often by limiting their panel to no more than 50 high net worth individuals or families.

For the more typical practice, in addition to the enhanced access and convenience, the centerpiece of the concierge offering revolves around a "wellness visit." This annual visit includes a complete history and physical exam, labs, selected imaging tests, nutrition and lifestyle counseling. The popularity of this combination—access/convenience plus testing—has allowed many of the traditional healthcare institutions to add the concierge moniker onto their one-and-done executive health physical programs. Patients can now select a concierge physician within the confines of the hospital system.

How Do I Become a Concierge Physician?

It is easy to understand the allure of concierge medicine. For physicians who have a big panel, say 2,000 or more patients, in which they are dependent upon insurance reimbursement, the possibility that they could reduce the panel to 300-500 patients, receive $1,000-$2,000 or more per patient in membership fees, partake of insurance for medically indicated problems, and possibly sell products such as nutraceuticals in office sounds almost too good to be true. It's a great bottom line: work less, enjoy the experience of providing care, and make more money.

Concierge Medicine: Do It Alone or Go with a Partner?

The answer to this question revolves around two things that most physicians are terrible at: practice administration and marketing. The lack of these skills, coupled with risk aversion, are what drive most physicians to work as employees. Most physicians are used to patients just showing up for care because they are in network. The staff in a conventional practice are neither inclined, nor trained to sell the physician's services to the patient. In the ideal world, most practitioners just want to take care of patients and let someone else attract the patients and run the practice.

How difficult is it to become a successful concierge doctor? First of all, it depends upon both your starting point and where you want to end up.

- **If you are an employed physician**, and you want to migrate your patients into a concierge model, you must be cautious. You do not own these patient records, your employer does. You may very well have some level of non-compete or non-solicitation in your employment agreement. (This varies by state, and again, seek legal help). You may need to build your potential patient base outside the practice by being active in the community, getting together mailing lists, connecting with potential referral sources, etc. well in advance of opening your doors. It is usually much more difficult to build a concierge practice de novo.

- **If you are in private practice and have a good-sized panel,** you can take advantage of three types of conversions:
    o **Full conversion.** You move totally into retainer-based care. In this case, if your patients like, trust and value your services, with an excellent conversion strategy, up to 20% of your panel may agree to pay a membership fee for enhanced access, more time and wellness services. You may elect to continue taking insurance for covered services.
    o **Hybrid conversion.** In this scenario, you keep 100% of your patients; however, you layer on an annual fee for the non-covered access, time, and wellness services. Anywhere from 5-10% of your patients may avail themselves of these concierge services. This is a good solution for physicians who want to test the concept. Many physicians who are successful with the hybrid conversion eventually move to the full program. One advantage of the hybrid conversion is that it is applicable to both solo and group practices.
    o **Specialty conversion.** This is one of the fastest growth areas in concierge care. It tends to favor the internal medicine specialists who see patients with chronic conditions. Hence, it is ideal for neurologists, pulmonologists, endocrinologists, rheumatologists, obstetrics and gynecology, and non-invasive cardiologists. Sports medicine, and even physical therapy practices can successfully convert to a full or hybrid model.

- **If you are confident in your abilities to establish and oversee legal, practice management, and marketing, you might be able to go it alone....** but much like the trials and tribulations of putting on a large, do-it-yourself wedding, most physicians can benefit from professional help. Each state has unique regulations regarding membership models and government programs. Private insurers can become finicky when it comes to conversion. Do you have the right staff for the job? Are you confident in your pricing model? Do you have a strong program to attract new patients? An even bigger question is whether you and your practice are a good candidate for concierge conversion, and if so, how are you going to get your existing patients to commit?

Here's where the national and local concierge companies come in. You still own your business, but they help you get through the stages of change: from contemplation, through analysis and conversion to ongoing management, marketing and growth. There are a handful of well-run companies that have successfully guided physicians through these stages. These include MDVIP, SelectMD, Cypress, Specialdocs, SignatureMD, Diamond Physicians, and Paragon Private Health. To acquaint you with variations in the concierge model, we'll be discussing the pros and cons of several with which we have the greatest familiarity.

MDVIP is a network of more than 950 doctors around the country. They are the big boy on the block. With so many practitioners, a patient base of over 300,000 members, a standardized annual wellness program, and uniform record keeping, MDVIP has been able to conduct several large-scale aggregate studies on its patient base. As compared to patients in traditional primary care practices, they have shown that Medicare patients who joined MDVIP-affiliated practices were hospitalized 79 percent less.[40] MDVIP patients with private insurance were hospitalized 72 percent less. MDVIP gets high satisfaction ratings from their patients. These data validate the MDVIP model, namely that a small panel size, attentive physicians who have time, a focus on prevention, and expertise to deliver comprehensive care, will provide better outcomes and greater patient satisfaction as opposed to conventional primary care.

MDVIP is a full-service partner. They help analyze your practice to see if you are a good candidate, and provide a definitive number of patient conversions that they will either meet or exceed. They assist with the conversion, as well as handle the legal, accounting, medical record keeping, and marketing support to help grow the business. They pass along their negotiated discounts with vendors. There are ongoing educational opportunities that the physicians can partake of. Given the size of their network, they can also offer support for consumers who travel domestically. This is accomplished by contacting their MDVIP physician who can arrange a local referral.

The annual fee for MDVIP-affiliated practices is $1,800. Patients typically pay the fee quarterly, semi-annually or annually. MDVIP is your partner in the membership component—not the insurance reimbursement portion—of the practice, and for their services they retain one-third of the fees that the patient pays directly to them, and the balance is passed along to the physician. The overwhelming majority of the physicians (95%) are in-network and take all commercial and Medicare insurance. With their 18-year history including a stint owned by Procter & Gamble that helped scale the business, they have the experience and support to help physicians successfully transition into and grow a concierge business.

Diamond Physicians is on the other side of the size spectrum. Created by James Pinckney, MD, Diamond has just a handful of practices in the State of Texas, however they are poised for growth. Diamond Physicians features a flexible model, with three ways to join. The first is as an employee. The second is through a joint venture partnership in which the physician brings the capital, Diamond runs the practice, and they share the net profit. The third model is franchise based. The physician pays an upfront fee, and an ongoing royalty on the gross sales. While Diamond will do a hybrid conversion, they move physicians over to a full conversion once the practice has become established. Similar to the other concierge companies, they have negotiated deeply discounted prices on lab services, generic medications and other services. Diamond takes great advantage of technology, using Drlink (thedrlink.com) a HIPAA-secure telehealth platform Pinckney has created with Anthony Lyssy, DO. It is user friendly in that it is "DPC within an app," and is easily assimilated into any EMR.

Paragon Private Health takes pride in that they are the only concierge medicine company honored on the 2018 Inc. 500 fastest growing private companies in the United States. Their payment model is similar to that of MDVIP, but there are a few differences in their offering.

The first stems around the use of PracticeDiagnostics™, Paragon's proprietary real-time HIPAA-compliant big-data analysis platform. It provides a report on the practice and the likelihood of successful conversion. PracticeDiagnostics is a deep dive into your patient panel, which provide the following insights:

- active patient numbers
- socio-economic distribution
- age composition
- likely patient enrollment
- comparison of full versus hybrid program

- projected revenue
- patient satisfaction insights

Using this sophisticated tool, Paragon is able to quickly rule out the practices that won't qualify under their model. According to CEO Hiren Doshi, 90% of the screened practices don't qualify for full conversion and 70% fail to meet their criteria for hybrid conversion. Interesting, Doshi notes that some patients who are rejected by MDVIP fit their model and vice versa.

Another difference relates to the degree of standardization. Outside of performing the standardized annual wellness program, MDVIP physicians are free to practice as they choose. However, most tend to stay close to a conventional model of care. Paragon's approach is more boutique in nature. In the conversion process, they focus on determining the services that the practitioner is excited about delivering, and then develop the model and pricing based upon what is covered under membership and what is not.

Specialdocs (specialdocs.com) also provides the classic practice transformation services including conversion, regulatory, patient communication, billing, and practice growth. Physicians remain independent and autonomous. The company works hard to brand the individual practice. Their program is differentiated in several ways. Physicians make a four-year commitment to their services. At the end of this time, there are no non-compete clauses; physicians re-up with Specialdocs because they choose to. Specialdocs' percent of the membership fees also scales downward beginning from approximately 20% over the four-year period. They also offer personalized succession planning.

Physicians should also look into **Cypress**. Rather than taking 1/3 of the membership fees, they work on a lower percentage.

The bottom line to implementing a successful concierge conversion—regardless of the partner you choose—is the ability to match or exceed your current income, provide improved patient care, and improve your work-life balance.

☐ **Take Home:** *Remember, you are partners with the concierge company and you should not be lulled into the false sense of security that they will do all the marketing of services, and you just sit back and collect patients. Market forces are constantly reshaping healthcare, and no matter which organization you affiliate with, you would be wise to continually grow your presence in your community and online. Stay abreast of trends in products and services to augment your income.*

The Hybrid Model as a Buffer Against Acquisition

I (Mark) first came across Paul Christakis, MD, a solo pediatric practitioner in Boca Raton, Florida, in a Sermo chat in which a group of cynical physicians were bemoaning the poor state of reimbursement and asking whether anyone was charging for phone visits. Offering a glimmer of hope, and a model for other practitioners, Dr. Christakis provided these comments.

"My practice (solo peds) is what I consider a hybrid practice for 10 years now. Our $325 per family annual fee covers lab callbacks, phone calls, email access, patient give outs, like books on infant care, safety, puberty, discipline etc. I have managed as a result to stay afloat without having to see 40 kids a day and the patients seem to like it. Still getting an average of a newborn a week, 30 years into practice. If you have a traditional practice, then it would be right and smart to charge a phone/email fee or consider anticipated time when coding the EM visit, for the circumstances everyone has discussed in the above responses."

Christakis later discussed with me, his initial hesitation, and how he replaced it with a bit of courage. Early on, he let the insurance companies know of his plans, and received two calls from them. When they realized that the member fee was for non-covered services, they were fine with that and he has never heard back from them. As you read his welcome to my practice notice to patients that is prominently placed on his website, we urge you to pay attention to the sentiment that accompanies the words and heed our take home point. (The three dot ellipses are ours, used for space reasons.)

What makes our practice a little different?

Christakis Pediatrics is a somewhat unusual pediatric practice in certain respects. We, like many of our colleagues, attempt to provide excellent and compassionate care to all of our patients. We do this by maintaining high standards in the areas of clinical expertise and patient satisfaction. I have had a strong desire to be a pediatrician since my own childhood. I began in 1988, by "hanging up a shingle," joining my older brother John, an internist. Fortunately, after 25+ years, I continue to thoroughly enjoy my work every single day. … My pediatric career has been everything I expected and more. On the other hand, we have also experienced the reality of trying to practice pediatrics as a traditional and solo doctor in today's medical business world.… My hope, going forward, is to continue to buck the trend of merging with a large group practice, or selling the practice to a hospital chain, but instead to continue working as I have been. By this I mean:

- A small, personal office setting, in which patients get to know each of us.… Our patients have taught us over the years that knowing what to expect when they come in to our office, and specifically who they will see is a highly valued characteristic of our office.
- Reasonable scheduling of well visits. We schedule adequate time to cover the many issues that I am expected to cover as a member of the American Academy of Pediatrics. We also try to carve out enough time in the day for the inevitable sick visits. I personally place great value in running on time, although it is not always possible. I very much appreciate the patience and understanding of our kind parents when I find myself apologizing for being late.
- Live phone response. I dislike voice menu phone answering systems so much, that I have vowed to never go that route for my own office!
- Excellent coverage after hours and on weekends. I rotate coverage with a number of long-term colleagues. This entails direct-to-doctor phone access after hours, and walk-in office hours at their east Boca office on weekend mornings, when I am not on call.
- 24/7 access to me if your child is in the hospital, during which time I personally collaborate with the hospital pediatrician.
- Email communication directly with me for non-urgent clinical questions, and with the staff for appointments, form requests and other administrative or billing issues.
- Availability for home visits.

In Jan. 2008 I reluctantly implemented an annual charge of $325 per family. There was simply no other way to maintain the kind of practice we are. This has allowed me to continue to practice pediatrics in the manner I envisioned when I first opened our doors in 1988. As a result of the understanding of our patients, we have been able to avoid closing, moving, selling, or merging with another practice. I feel very grateful and honored to have the trust and respect of our patients' parents, who, despite difficult economic times, have stayed with us. Our intention has never been to exclude patients. I am living a life-long dream to be a pediatrician, alongside my internist brother, in Boca Raton, where I have lived since 1974, and so I thank all of my families for that!

☐ **Take Home:** *Make certain your authenticity and sense of caring show through in your communications. Yes, patients want convenience and cost, but equally important, they want to know, like and trust you.*

The Key to An Insurance Hybrid

Question: *If you take insurance and want to add a membership component, how do you do it so as to not get cross-wise with either Medicare or commercial insurers?*

Answer: *You offer a suite of services that are "non-covered services." You take insurance for what insurance pays for and membership for what it does not. The services and products you choose to offer are based upon your interests, resources, and what the market wants and will pay for.*

The goal of membership is to create a value proposition that insurance doesn't cover. You will want to express this value proposition succinctly and clearly. On one hand, it can be all about access and referral. Shilpa P. Saxena, MD builds a more compelling case with her approach calling her model "functional integrative medicine with a collaborative care team that will know your case and care that you get better."

Examples of Non-Covered Services:

- Enhanced access. email, phone consults, 24X7
- Services associated with a health coach, or nutritionist related to education and counseling
- Education you deliver via video in the form of a video library on different disease topics, self-care and prevention
- Providing patients with books, posters, and other educational materials
- Classes and workshops in your practice, or in the community (e.g., cooking classes)
- Visits for personal training, going grocery shopping with patients, or going to their homes and doing a pantry test
- Telehealth coaching and counseling
- Review of non-disease related mHealth data
- Dry needling by physical therapists in states in which the technique is allowed.
- In office-tests. Examples: Endothelial testing with EndoPAT, Evoked potential brain wave testing with WAVI, VO2 max testing. However, note that if these tests become covered by Medicare for a disease indication, and your individual patient

has that indication, the testing can no longer be included in your membership services for that patient.

☐ **Take Home:** *Make certain to list all your non-covered services in your Patient Agreement. Also make certain that you have detailed privacy clauses, and/or specific HIPAA clauses.*

Cash-Pay: Not Just for Physicians

Most of our narrative has focused on physicians; however, cash-pay models are being adopted by many types of practitioners, some of whom provide primary care, others more specialty-focused services. We are increasingly seeing FNPs, PAs, RNs and other licensed professionals offer direct care and membership models, often in underserved areas. For example:

- KC Devine, FNP launched a membership DPC, Well Life ABQ in Albuquerque, NM.
- Kelly Engelmann, FNP-BC created Enhanced Wellness Living in Jackson, MS to offer nutrition, detox, exercise and mind-body-spirit programs for her clients.
- In Cottonwood, AZ, Julie Trainor, ARNP offers IV nutrients and PEMF (Pulsed Electro Magnetic Field) therapy to her patients.
- Atlanta based psychologist Rebecca Johnson Osei, PsyD has introduced the concierge concept into psychology with enhanced access including telepsych, in office or at-home visit options. Weekend and evening sessions are available at an additional cost. She couples this delivery with monthly membership pricing for a set number of coaching hours. Other services such as road trips and travel or hospital companion services are also priced separately.
- Physical therapist, Jarod Carter, PT converted his practice to cash-pay, authored a successful book on the subject, and has embarked on training other physical therapists to do the same (drjarodcarter.com).

The principles and processes for cash-pay and membership success cut across all disciplines in healthcare.

PASSIVE INCOME

Who among us hasn't dreamt of putting our healthcare knowledge to work while we sleep, thereby generating an ongoing source of passive income and getting out of the rut of just selling our time. The most readily available method for this is to develop an online product or service directed either to consumers or other professionals. Doctors such as Joseph Mercola, Josh Axe, and Julian Whitaker have built strong nutritional products sales businesses. Brad Bale, MD and Amy Doneen DNP, ARNP collect a monthly fee from practitioners who participate in their monthly online journal club. So, it's possible. But it takes work, planning, partners, and a really well thought out business plan to succeed. Here are a few starting points.

- **You will need to enhance your presence.** You will be leveraging your personal reputation, knowledge and brand to customers for your privately branded product or educational content. We'll cover this in part in Chapter 5: Where Do I Start, and in depth in Chapter 10: How to Get Noticed, Known & Remembered.
- **You will need to be known for something, to start.** Maybe you are the mold or thyroid doc, the detox expert, or the practitioner who holds the answer to good sex, healthy babies, or beautiful bodies. You need to fill a specific need. For example, Leslie Stone, MD, a family practitioner in Ashland, OR, who has delivered more than 5,000 children, created growbabyhealth.com alongside Emily Rydbom, Clinical Nutritionist to offer their expertise to a national audience. The business includes a series of online trimester-phased pregnancy modules coupled with their own preGenesis prenatal supplements. They offer the GrowBaby app for Moms as a monthly subscription service for $3.99/month. Additionally, GrowBaby Pro is an app for practitioners offering a way to implement prenatal nutrition in their practice. The practitioner app features a tiered monthly subscription package based on how many clients are added. You can follow their latest multi-scope collaborative effort online and on social media where they reach a community of 135,000+ people.
- **You need a compelling story.** This is the genesis of Liveli (Liveli.com), a nootropic developed by Stanford trained physicians Tess Mauricio, MD and her husband James Lee, MD. A benign brain tumor sparked James' interest in fortifying his brain with optimal nutrients, kicked off years of research, and resulted in a consumer-focused product line.
- **You want to start with a product or service that is in sync with your brand.** Jill Carnahan, MD (Dr. Jill) is a well-known functional medicine doctor with a large following. Known as an environmental medicine expert, developing an environmentally friendly skincare line was totally in line with her mission and her brand.
- **You'll need to take advantage of PR and social media (more to say on this later).**

- **You'll want to work with a company that can help you develop well-performing sales funnels.** There are a number of marketing/sales platforms that automate list and email management, as well as help you develop outbound campaigns. We have had some success with Infusionsoft but have found it to be a steep learning curve. Especially designed to sell online courses, Kajabi is a much easier system to use. The recently introduced Kartra platform seems to have great balance, and is quite robust. Consultants can help you get started on the design of these sales efforts. Other marketing automation programs include Hubspot, Sharpspring, Pardot, Eloqua and Marketo. Much of the strategy of product sales revolves around the concept of the sales funnel. This entails a series of well-orchestrated steps that usually follow the following formula.

The Sales Funnel

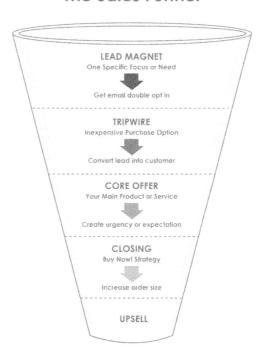

- o **Lead magnet.** This is to get the viewer interested. It focuses on one point of interest or need. It might be a "how to" blog or story, or the ability to download an E-book that solves a singular problem, e.g. "Get our Free E-Book: How to Close More Customers Online."
- o **Call to action.** This is all about getting them to click on the lead magnet so you can get their email. With rules, regulations and laws tightening around spam, the gold standard is the double opt-in. Following the first

click, the prospect receives an email in which they have to confirm (double opt-in) their interest in your offer.

o **Tripwire.** This is usually an offer for an inexpensive product for which they provide their credit card. Why the small sale? The purpose of this step is simple, it's all about behavior. A person who has bought from you is now a customer, not a prospect, and it is infinitely easier to get them to purchase the next product, which is your core offer.

o **Core offer.** This is your big ticket, money making offer.

o **Bonus offers and upsells.** These are all the extras that help close the sale by making it too good to pass up, or up the sales price with add-ons. Sometimes, deadlines are used to create a sense of urgency.

☐ **Take Home:** *The sales funnel formula is ubiquitous and tied to any number of products, many of which are promoted with overhyped language, and incredible buy-now pressure. Frankly, it can be a real turn-off. It's important to separate the value of the process from the verbiage and tone of offer. Healthcare practitioners can create funnels that are more professional in tone and demeanor.*

GROUP VISITS

According to functional medicine physician Shilpa P. Saxena, MD the group visit alleviates two conditions that practitioners suffer from: time scarcity and decision fatigue. It can also increase patient satisfaction and practice revenue.[41]

Each day practitioners of every type discuss common causes of illness, preventive strategies, self-care, and treatment instructions. They do it multiple times a day in three to five minute increments. Studies have shown that:[42]

- 40 to 80 percent of medical information is forgotten immediately.
- The greater the amount of information presented, the less that's correctly recalled.
- When patients do remember the information, almost half of that is incorrect.

Is there a way to better impart information and provide support for behavior change? Part of the solution lies in a process known as the group visit. Edward Noffsinger, PhD, the pioneer developer of group visits, constructed the first model, the Drop-In Group Medical Appointment (DIGMA), in the early 1990s after himself suffering from a serious illness. Noffsinger, who has spent more than a quarter-century at Kaiser Permanente, realized that group visits could offer patients more time, access, and support, both from their doctor and from a network of other patients.

The use of group visits has been steadily growing. according to the American Academy of Family Physicians (AAFP), an estimated 10 percent of family doctors offered shared medical appointments in 2015.[43] In addition to patient satisfaction, AAFP notes that positive benefits on dietary compliance and intermediate markers for diabetes and coronary artery disease. Organizations like Cleveland Clinic, Harvard, Yale, and the Veterans Administration, are all employing group medical appointments. CMS Medicare has no prohibitions on patients being seen in the group setting, so this works in insurance, cash-pay, membership, and hybrid practices. Here are the details:

The Implementation Model
- Enlist the office staff to help promote and fill the class. You can start out doing one every two-three months, then increase frequency. Let patients know about the class in your online and email outreach.
- 10-16 patients gathered lecture style.
- 90-minute session with approximately 30-minute lecture education and 60 minutes of discussion and Q&A.
- Separate from the educational talk, if this is an establish patient, pull the participant aside and have a different licensed healthcare practitioner conduct, and document, and if appropriate, bill for an EM visit.

The Integrative Model
- Rather than group the patients by specific condition, e.g., a hypertension, or diabetes group visit, consider grouping by root cause, a key tenet of functional medicine.
  - o For example, Saxena will group patients with different sequelae of poor gut health (the root cause). She will pull in patients with autoimmune conditions such as rheumatoid arthritis, asthma and other atopic disease, irritable bowel, and GI-related symptoms. She will deliver a lecture on increased intestinal permeability and how it may influence not just the gut, but other organ systems.
- Consider utilizing Saxena's Group Visit Toolkit, which contains all the administrative, marketing and educational material to conduct sessions on cardiovascular disease, stress hormones, weight management, the blood/sugar connection, immune health and GI foundations. The Toolkit is available at Lifestylematrix.com. The Lifestyle Matrix Resource Center also has an implementation team who can work with staff to create a personalized game plan on becoming successful with this practice model.

- Cash-pay group visits also allow prospects to meet you and learn about your approach to healthcare.

The Financial Model
- Insurance: Collect an individual copay for each participant. Bill the appropriate level 1, 2, or 3 code for the EM.

Take Note: For insurance, you are billing only for the office visit and EM with a licensed provider and not the education.
- Cash Pay: Charge for either the class alone (e.g., $50-$75 per participant), or bundle the class fee with a cash-paid EM.
- Membership: Bundle the class and include it with the patient's membership fee. It is a great value-add.
- Recommend and make available supplements and other products for purchase.

The group visit is your antidote for decision fatigue. It provides great education and support for patients, and the math really works in terms of practice revenue enhancement.

TELEMEDICINE

According to a recent marketing report,[44] the global telehealth market was valued at $6 billion in 2016 and is projected to expand at a compound annual growth rate (CAGR) of 13 percent from 2017 to 2025. It is being fueled by the rise of chronic disease, a demand for self-care, and growing interest in medical imaging and mobile solutions. We see five major benefits to telemedicine.

Improved Access – Telehealth not only improves access by patients, it allows practitioners to expand their reach. Attesting to this, the VA hospitals offer close to 50 telehealth specialties. During fiscal year 2016, more than 700,000 veterans completed approximately 2 million telehealth appointments.[45]

Cost Efficiencies – Telemedicine has been shown to reduce the cost of healthcare as well as increase efficiency.

Improved Quality – Studies have consistently shown that the quality of healthcare services delivered via telemedicine is equal to that delivered with traditional in-person consultations.

Patient Demand – Consumers want telemedicine, and multiple studies have documented patient satisfaction with this technology.

Better Practitioner Life Balance – Telehealth dramatically expands your options, and allows you to charge patients for a visit in which overhead is negligible. The options with telehealth are many. You may choose to do full-time or part-time telehealth, either as a self-employed, cash-pay practitioner offering diagnosis and treatment. You can go to work for one of the telehealth companies such as American Well or InTouch Health that employ physicians. As we see below, there are increasing opportunities to become a virtualist.

Telehealth Curious?

If you have ever wondered whether telemedicine is either here to stay, or its own unique sub-specialty, look no further than this recent advertisement from a major health insurance plan in the Pacific Northwest.

Wanted: Family Medicine/Internal Medicine Virtualist Physician. We are currently seeking a Board-Certified Family Medicine or Internal Medicine physician to join our growing medical group as a Primary Care Virtual Physician. The Virtualist physician will provide telephonic and virtual care for our members and will facilitate desktop medicine cross coverage for on-site clinic physicians.

As we've seen above, some practitioners use the telemedicine visit to check in with patients in advance of a longer appointment, or to review images and labs making special use of screen sharing to explain information. Telemedicine works extremely well in rural settings, allowing for much easier patient follow up and health maintenance. And, should you choose to take a vacation, you can still be connected and conduct a telehealth visit with a patient.

There are three types of telehealth services. (Texting, email, and phone are not considered telehealth.) These include:

- Live, synchronous transmission. You are interacting in real time via video
- Store and forward. The image (usually still, but sometimes video) is captured, uplinked and stored for retrieval.
- Remote patient monitoring. Bluetooth devices transfer data from devices such as home blood pressure, weight, or glucose monitors.

If your telehealth visit involves the practice of medicine, notably diagnosis and treatment, you will want to check with your state licensing board as rules vary as to whether you must first see the patient in person, and whether you can treat patients across state lines. Telemedicine is still the practice of medicine, and you may need to be licensed in the various states for which you treat patients. The state laws also differ in terms of extenders and prescription writing. Currently nine states have specific licenses for state health. The telehealth policies for all 50 states can be found at Connected Health Policy (cchpca. org). The American Telemedicine Association is a non-profit industry-focused lobbying organization that can help you keep abreast of the ever-changing regulatory landscape. A few more to-dos: You will also want to get legal review on your consent forms. Check with your malpractice carrier to make certain you are covered for telemedicine. Finally, consider adding a cyber liability policy to your D&O insurance.

Many of the physicians we spoke with had great things to say about the features and benefits of Spruce (sprucehealth.com). They appreciated the robustness of the system. Spruce's HIPAA-compliant model includes support for cell phones, desk phones, extra lines, phone trees, SMS texting, secure messaging, secure voicemail with transcription, fax, and telemedicine. The cloud-based platform allows healthcare teams to interact internally, and also with patients or other external parties. All communication is treated as part of a unified, chronological medical record. We have also been impressed with the educational content provided by eVisit (evisit.com), and recommend downloading their materials to better acquaint you with the field.

Have It Your Way

Physicians are incorporating a rich assortment of services and access opportunities in their cash-pay models, including a focus on telemedicine. This is the case for Matthew Haden, MD, a primary care DPC physician with two locations in and around McLean, VA (pureprimarycare.com). Haden does traditional primary care with some unique offerings: genetics and personalized medicine, pharmacogenetics, food allergy testing, and other functional medicine tests. Along with a colleague, he also specializes in fertility awareness. Haden offers both member and non-member prices (direct-pay) for both office visits and telemedicine consults.

In order to start a practice and keep overhead low, Haden initially offered only house calls and telemedicine. Recently he has opened brick and mortar facilities, and this at the request of patients. Haden uses Spruce (spruce.com) for telemedicine, noting that most patients prefer the secure texting feature. Most recently he has switched his EHR to MDHQ, chosen because he feels it was built around a very functional patient portal.

FIVE MORE TAKE-HOME TIPS FOR CASH-PAY SUCCESS

1. **Determine whether you have the entrepreneurial spirit.** This is one of those gut-check issues. Only you can determine the extent to which owing and running a cash-pay practice is consistent with your vision and worth the effort. If you

want the freedom and the up-side, you will have to have the courage to handle the responsibility and be ever vigilant of the downside. If you don't have the courage, or wish to play it safe, consider employment opportunities that may provide you a better quality of life. If you decide to join or stay in the ranks of the employed, know that the physician universe is split almost equally physicians who have an ownership stake in the practice and employed physicians.[46]

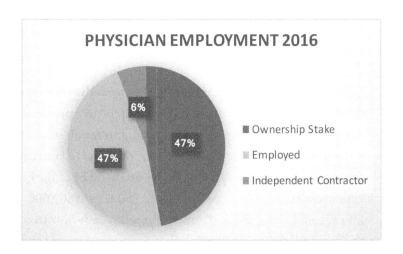

2. **Make certain patients are going to "love you."** We know this sounds sophomoric, but patients will pay cash out of their pocket for docs where there is reciprocity of caring. You must demonstrate you care about patients with each and every encounter. Michael Tetreault noted this quite elegantly in speaking at the Concierge Forum in Atlanta, in October of 2018.

> *"There is a mystique, a temperament and a curious fascination about doctors who spend an inordinate amount of time with their patients. It's so simple, it's weird. There is just nothing like that in healthcare today. And like it or not, a patient wants and deserves your time and attention. That's why they pay the subscription, keep calling you and keep texting you. They want and expect that their doctor will be 'present' and 'mentally' dialed-in. Concierge doctors, known to provide innovative, patient-centered care environments, are in a unique position to take advantage of the growing number of personalized data resources matched to patient profiles and preferences to improve patient care. A patient wants their doctor to explore new technologies and dig into new medical research. They are entrusting you with their life. Today, we're hearing routinely that a patient will leave a private, direct style medical practice in a matter of weeks if they feel they*

are not a priority. That's not fair, but it's true … While the human spirit is willing to forgive your colleagues for long wait times, errors, staffing, etc., patients will remember and share what their last doctor's office visit was like."

3. **Build your pricing model by working backwards.** If you are just considering taking the leap into cash-pay healthcare, there is an orderly set of steps you can take. What is less orderly, and less logical, and fraught with some confusion, is the emotional state, fears, and hindrances keeping you from making the jump. The best process to identify the components of a cash pay business is to work backwards.

    Determine how much you want to make annually. This will guide many of your decisions. Let's say you want to take home $250,000 pre-tax a year, roughly $20k per month and have time for yourself and your family. If you are migrating from an insurance based private practice, your overhead (all in: rent, staff, professional services, insurance, equipment purchases) might be in the range of 50%-60% so your gross receipts will need to exceed $500,000-$600,000. This does not take into account the stress and strain of uneven cash flow from collections. With this in mind, there are several ways to get to your desired annual compensation.

    a. The micropractice in which you no longer take insurance, and patients pay cash for your services. You can drop your overhead to 20%-25%...in the range of $8-$10,000 per month. In this scenario, you could hit your target with a gross revenue of $400,000. If you keep your expenses low enough, you might clear even more than the $250,000.

    b. You could get to the gross revenue of $400,000 with a membership panel of 300 patients paying $1,333 ($110/month). In some markets, this might be a price point more along the lines of a concierge practice (which tend to be priced higher than Direct Primary Care). Or you could have 476 patients paying $70/month (an average price for a 40-64-year-old).

    c. If you bill your services by the hour, let's say $350 hour (the billing rate of a junior attorney in a mid-sized law firm), and you want to see patients 30 hours a week for 48 weeks a year, assuming full booking, you would generate $500,000 plus you'd enjoy a good lifestyle.

    d. However, as they say on those late-night infomercials, Wait…it gets better! If you were to add product sales, e.g., nutraceuticals, cosmeceuticals, home devices, and were modestly successful selling $3-4,000/month with a net profit of $1,500-$2,000 per month, you would pick up an additional $18,000-$24,000 net on top of your service costs.

e.   You'll want to work with your accountant to calculate your actual expenses, which will vary depending upon the services that you offer and whether they are included in membership or charged as extras. Also, make sure to have adequate cash reserves to allow for the practice to scale. You are not going to have a full practice day one, and it will usually take you longer than you anticipate to get a full panel.

4.   **Start and stay lean**. We learn more from our failures than from our successes in life. These episodes make a great and more lasting imprint on our brains. Getting started, you would do well to heed the advice of Ajainder Shergill, DO, MBA who penned a great article for LinkedIn entitled "Six Lessons I learned from My Failed Direct Primary Care Practice." In the article, he discusses the difficulty of making the jump from being a hospitalist, to opening a DPC practice, a business which two years later he shuttered. This type of conversion is challenging for physicians without a patient base. Shergill points to the need to advertise and build a patient base well in advance of opening a brick and mortar clinic, and how he should have reached out to businesses in his area. He shares his marketing naivety.

A big component of his downfall; however, was investing too much in fixed assets. He leased a large clinic space and bought expensive waiting room equipment and all kinds of medical supplies. His epiphany can best be summed up in one remark, "I never needed more than one exam room the entire time I ran my practice." Our advice, from, this story: "Stay lean, my friends."[47]

☐   **Take Home.** *It is not enough to start and stay lean, you will also need to monitor and track not just income, but expenses and other key metrics that determine the health of your practice. More on this later.*

5.   **Choose your products and people carefully.** In the next chapter, we'll provide a roadmap for adding products and services to your practice. At some point, you may well consider adding personnel to help you extend your reach, and to profit from their services, engaging them either as employees or independent contractors. You'll find hiring (and firing) guidelines in Chapter 5: Where Do I Start?

Many types of practitioners (if not, most) are better at counseling and educating patients than physicians. They have time, training, patience, and can often relate better. Traditionally, most Physicians Assistants and Nurse Practitioners have a clinical focus in either primary care or a surgical specialty, where they "extend" the scope of services provided by the physician. In this setting, as licensed providers, their services are billed under traditional insurance. Many also have interest and advanced training in motivational interviewing, patient education, and counseling. They can be great assets to your practice.

There is an ever-growing cadre of wellness, health, and nutrition coaches that you could bring into a cash-pay practice to counsel patients in health behavior change. Many are young, passionate, articulate, trainable and, best of all, affordable. If you have a new patient coordinator with interest in expanding their skills, you might consider training this person to be a health coach. The field is replete with many different degrees and programs. Many are in the field of nutrition and represent some of the following certificates:

- Registered Dietician (RD)
- Certified Clinical Nutritionist (CCN)
- Certified Nutritional Consultant (CNC)
- Certified Nutritionist (CN)
- Certified Nutrition Specialists (CNS)
- Board Certified in Holistic Nutrition (BCHN).

Depending upon whether they are licensed providers in your state, their services may also be insurance reimbursable. The following Integrative, Wellness and Sports Medicine programs tend to graduate well-schooled coaches who may fit readily into cash-pay practices:

- The National Society of Health Coaches
- American Council on Exercise (ACE)
- Dr. Sears Wellness Institute
- Duke Integrative Medicine
- Functional Medicine Coaching Academy
- Wellcoaches, and
- Institute for Integrative Nutrition.

Go Virtual with a Lifestyle Extender

All clinicians share the belief that lifestyle education and counseling is a key element in helping patients improve their health. They also know that they can't count on insurance for reimbursement in this area. Even practitioners who believe strongly in the need for lifestyle education are reluctant to bear the expense of bringing a full-time counselor or coach into their practice.

Enter Virtual Health Partners (VHP) (virtualhealthpartners.com). With a team of several hundred registered dietitians at hand and a host of educational opportunities for the patient, VHP provides low-cost, turnkey solutions for adding online lifestyle counseling/coaching to your business. Practitioners can customize VHP subscriptions to support both their health philosophy, and the scope of their offering. For example, a practitioner can work with the online dieticians to offer vegan, paleo, halal, pescatarian, or vegetarian education. According to CEO Jillian Cohen, "If, for example, the doctor believes no patient should drink milk, our nutritional counselors will follow the physician's guidelines." She goes on to note the scalability and comprehensiveness of the HIPAA-compliant platform. According to Cohen, "The consumer must be invited into the program. They can then take advantage of the features the practitioner has selected. These may include live one-on-one or group counseling for nutrition and fitness, support groups, access to recipes, cooking demonstrations, texting support, and more. There is a small set-up fee for the practitioner in addition to the monthly subscription for each patient." VHP fits seamlessly into cash-pay where the services can be marked up, or tailored to fit within a variety of membership tiers. The platform can also work in conventional medical practice. The doctor—who does not participate in the financial transaction—makes a strong recommendation to the patient to enroll in VHP. For physicians looking to transition into cash-pay, seeding your practice with VHP-counseled patients can help generate an engaged patient base who already knows that you have their best interests at heart, and are more likely to follow you to your new business model.

Hopefully by this point, you've got a good handle on the nature of and reimbursement model for your practice, now let's turn to the all-you-can eat smorgasbord of products and services available to you.

Chapter

What Products & Services Should I Add?

This is the largest, and for many ongoing practices, perhaps the most helpful chapter in *Cash-Pay Healthcare*: understanding which products and services to add to grow your business. For some practitioners, the service and the revenue may be ancillary, contributing to their revenue mix. For others, it may be the basis of their practice and comprise the majority of their income. Many of the products and services can be incorporated under the umbrella of a larger concept such as Anti-Aging, Women's Health, Functional, Integrative, or Wellness. Others can find their way into specialty practices.

Understanding the Economics

There are a variety of ways in which you can profit from ancillary products and services. These include:

- **Purchase and mark-up of products.** In general, professionals can purchase products at 40-50% off a manufacturer's suggested retail price. The practice must carry inventory and sometimes, the discount is proportional to the quantity ordered; with greater commitment, the practice may negotiate an additional 5% or more off. Practitioners must stay vigilant to make certain the product is not available at a lower price online, as this can generate patient ill will. Companies that pride themselves on serving the professional market are incentivized to control their sales channels and to watch for grey-market or counterfeit products.

- **Third party vendors for products.** These are companies that provide you with a branded online store to facilitate convenient patient ordering. This typically entails a suite of nutritional products from various manufacturers; the vendor pays for and manages product inventory, order entry, and shipping to the patient, as well as customer service inquiries. You receive reimbursement monthly, and an administrative portal allows you to track and manage your data. An online store allows you to profit from reorders while reducing or avoiding inventory lode and the potential risk of accumulating outdated supplements. While practices usually enjoy a 50% margin when they stock and sell products, gross margins when using an online dispensary are typically 35%. The companies allow for some customization of the practitioner's online store and depending upon the level of customization, the store can work to extend both the physician's brand and his or her education and outreach efforts. The recent merger of FullScript (fullscript.com) and Natural Partners (naturalpartners.com) has expanded the formulary available from these companies. An example of the admin page of a FullScript Smart Pharmacy online store is shown below.

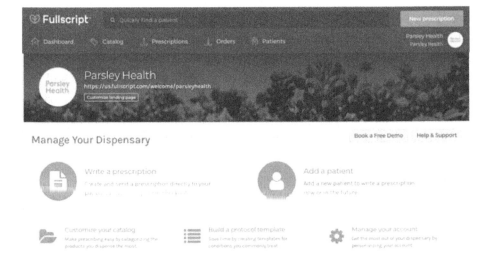

Power2Practice (power2practice.com), a leading EHR tailored to the integrative health clinician, incorporates the FullScript Smart Dispensary into their platform. Below, you will find a reasonable scenario showing how a small increase in reorder rate, experienced through the virtual dispensary on the Power2Practice platform, more than compensates for the lower gross margin.

	In Office	Virtual Dispensary
Physician margin	50%	35%
Retail Sales (+20%)	$5,000	$6,000
Physician Margin on Supplement Sales	$2,500	$2,100
Physician Margin on Reorders over the year (2 vs. 6)	$5,000	$12,600
Monthly Costs (Staff + Inventory)	$640	$0
Total Monthly Gain	$6,860	$14,700

Other companies that offer online dispensaries are Emerson Ecologics (Wellevate) and Kaerwell. Kaerwell also features a directory of both CME and non-CME educational events, many of which are sponsored by the professional brands, as well as links to conferences, educational webinars, and white papers. Kaerwell also offers direct-to-consumer fulfillment on private label nutraceuticals.

The larger supplement companies also have provisions for online patient reorders solely for their products versus the online dispensaries that carry multiple brands. Physicians may receive between 35% and 50% on the sale which is carefully handled so as to not be considered a "commission" or "rebate" which is prohibited in some states. The practitioner can elect to provide patients with a discount. Most recently, Exponential Faces has developed an online store that handles a variety of cosmeceutical skincare brands. HintMD (hintmd.com) has introduced manufacturer-direct-to-patient cosmeceutical fulfillment as part of their aesthetic membership model.

- **Group Purchasing Organizations.** These are businesses that have negotiated special pricing based on leveraging the group's purchasing power to get discounts from vendors. Medigroup is the largest of these which services physician offices, surgery centers, and specialty clinics. They work with the medical products distributors as well as extend perks to employees on things like cell phone plans or travel. MedResults Network (medresultsnetwork.com) is a buying group specific to the aesthetics industry which allows members to obtain discounts between 5 and 10% on a suite of several dozen products and services. One of the advantages of the Y Lift™ (See **Y** on page 135) is the ability of members to obtain deep discounts primarily on Allergan products.

- **Mobile Services.** These are companies that come to your practice and provide equipment and a technician under your supervision, or who can provide the service independently.

One example involves assessing cardiovascular disease. Abdominal Aortic Aneurysm screening is covered under Medicare. Carotid ultrasound with Carotid Intima-Media Thickness (CIMT), is as well, when there is greater than 50% plaque in the artery or localized thickening of 1.3 mm. According to Joseph Ence, CEO of Vasolabs (vasolabs.com), this a chicken and egg situation. "If, as a clinician, you believe there is an indication to screen, and the report shows 'plaque or stenosis' insurance will generally reimburse." The device can easily be brought into a practice along with a registered ultrasound technician to conduct multiple patient scans. Ankle-brachial index testing (ABI) for vascular occlusion can also be covered by insurance. It's important, however, to structure the relationship appropriately and in compliance with insurance requirements, including Medicare requirements. You may mark up the service if the technical component or the professional component of the services is supervised or performed in the "office of the billing physician or other supplier" by a physician owner, employee, or independent contractor of the billing physician or other supplier. The ordering physician must regularly furnish care at the location.

For those physicians who have opted out of insurance, or included screening in your membership package, you can add this service in the same way you do any other. Remember the onus is on you to fill the schedule, so you may want to ensure that your policies account for cancellations.

Renting aesthetic devices is a great option when you want to test-drive the latest aesthetic technology but you don't have the patient base to justify a purchase, nor do you have staff well trained on the device. With rentals, you avoid having to deal with maintenance and obsolescence. Monarch Laser Services (monarchlasers. com) is the leading purveyor of aesthetic laser device rentals in California. In addition to providing superbly trained technicians, the company has an extensive practitioner education program. An Internet search of "laser rentals" in your area should turn up several vendors. Kevin Meyers, CEO of Monarch, cautions that you want to avoid long term contracts, and opt for those companies that have a full spectrum of equipment choices as well as a call center and techs who can support you.

☐ **Take Home:** *Remember: no matter which products and services you elect to bring into your practice, a large part of your success will depend upon the quality of the patient experience you provide. Success will also directly relate to how well your staff communicate the benefits of the products and services to your clientele.*

Product & Service Additions from A to Z

To organize the major options, we've arranged them alphabetically. Each of these categories could easily be a book in themselves, so we will touch on some of the major adoption criteria for you to consider. In the body of the text we will mention either some companies whose offerings we are familiar with, or those recommended by colleagues. Our apologies to those treatment modalities or products we have overlooked. Feel free to skip around and read those sections for which you have interest.

AESTHETIC PROCEDURES (NON-SURGICAL)

There are few categories that are as well-aligned with cash-pay and consumer demand as aesthetics. If you are a specialty-trained aesthetic practitioner, this is the heart of your business. For other non-core practitioners, aesthetics can also be the sole focus of your practice; however, we are increasingly seeing hybrid models that combine nutrition, anti-aging, and functional medicine with aesthetics. The growth of the medspa industry has also shown the benefits of forging a strong connection to wellness and lifestyle. The American Med Spa Association estimates that there are 4,200 medspas in the US, generating $4 billion, with the average business bringing in almost one million dollars a year in revenue.[48] The top three medspa services are injectables, aesthetician services, and laser hair removal.

The major components of an aesthetics program are covered below. Other specialty areas are discussed later in alphabetical order.

Devices for Skin Rejuvenation
The main targets include the face, neck, the décolleté, and hands in an older population. The goal is to improve tone, texture, coloring, fine lines and wrinkles, as well as to tighten the skin. Some devices can also address active acne and a variety of scars. For skin rejuvenation, the most common modalities are lasers and Intense Pulsed Light (IPL), although microneedling (See **M**) is becoming quite popular. Radiofrequency (RF) or ultrasound brings heat deeper into the dermis and allows for skin tightening. Increasingly, companies are introducing combination devices such as RF and microneedling. Factors to consider when adding aesthetic devices include:

- **Cost:** There is great variation in aesthetic devices depending upon the type of energy, where the devices are manufactured, and the level of service and support offered by the company. The "hottest" new technologies are also premium priced until competitive products come on the market. Most device salespeople will provide you with a Return on Investment (ROI) calculation. Carefully consider whether this scenario is realistic given your location, type of practice, and patient mix. Always make your buying decisions on the lowest ROI projections, or cut the salesperson's rosy forecasts at least by half.

- **Fractional versus non-fractional:** Fractional devices treat small columns of skin and leave non-treated skin in between. This allows for much faster wound healing and usually a greater safety margin. The more powerful devices can be turned up or down to bring more or less heat into the skin. Given Mark's involvement with Reliant Technologies, developer of the Fraxel® laser, we have an inherent bias for the safety and tuneability of fractional technology.

- **Multi-platform versus stand-alone device:** There is greater versatility in having a platform device, especially since you can usually configure it with different energies and/or wavelengths, and add additional hand pieces as your familiarity and needs grow. Platform devices tend to be costlier than single-focus devices, and they lock you into a major commitment to that particular manufacturer.

- **Disposables versus non-disposable:** Some device disposables, such as solutions, filters, and tubing, are absolutely necessary for patient safety. Other disposables and usage charges are purely high-margin incremental revenue for the manufacturer. This is not all bad. Disposables establish a partnership between manufacturer and practitioner and with it, the incentive for the vendors to help you succeed. Disposable income is what fuels a vendor's marketing, and you just want to be sure that some of these marketing dollars go toward helping you get patients. Disposable costs are incremental rather than fixed costs, so your business/marketing plan must take into account not just the percent of disposable cost (cost of disposable/ treatment price), but what happens when increasing competition drives down what you can charge, and how this will affect your margins. As a rule of thumb, a ~15% disposable/treatment percentage ($15 on each $100 charged to the patient) is reasonable. Note that you will also have to manage inventory so you have enough disposables on hand. Make certain you know the time lag to get new disposables shipped and delivered, as well as the minimum order quantities. Also, ask about volume discounts. Often, to close sales on new device purchases—especially at the end of the month or the end of the quarter—companies are able to provide you with a very good starter kit of disposables, so negotiate accordingly.

- **Downtime and pain:** Simply put, all aesthetic devices utilize energy to wound the skin and allow the body's natural healing processes to create new, healthier skin. The downtime is proportional to the degree of thermal, cryo, or mechanical wounding. Make certain you understand the clinical course of treatment and the need for compounded topical anesthesia. These are blends of higher-percentage lidocaine with additions of tetracaine and sometimes benzocaine. All staff should be aware of toxicity and adverse events, as well as State regulations that limit products from a multi-use container.

- **Service contracts:** Service contracts beyond the first year of warranty can add an additional 5-8% on to the price of your device. You will need to include this expense in the cost of operation. While there are some third-party vendors who can repair machines, as well as companies who have bundled support into the price, if you anticipate active use of your device, go with the manufacturer's program.

- **Marketing support:** You have the greatest leverage at the time of purchase. You may be able to negotiate for co-op advertising dollars, financial support for an open house at your practice, placement on a find-a-practitioner menu, creation of a landing page or mini-site, or other considerations. Get promises in writing.

- **Safety:** Class II devices will require safety training, signposts, and appropriate eyewear. State laws differ as to who can use each device. Make certain you are familiar with these guidelines, and always err on the side of safety.

- **Insurance changes:** Check with your insurer to make certain that you are covered for aesthetic procedures.

One of the most exciting, and emerging areas in aesthetic rejuvenation has been the opportunity to deliver biologically active ingredients such as peptides and various cytokines directly into the skin via light or mechanical disruptions. We can now easily break up the tight junctions of the epithelial cells and create microchannels anywhere from 100 microns and up for "drug" delivery. The challenge will be broadening our understanding of which actives in combination with which devices, yield the best results. Amnio Aesthetics (amnioaesthetics.com) is a company at the forefront of this research. Their products are derived from the human amniotic membrane obtained from the placenta and are used in combination with multiple aesthetic devices.

Injectables

These include neurotoxins and fillers. Who is allowed to inject them is regulated by State law, so make certain you stay current on any regulatory changes. The efficacy, low startup costs (say, versus a device), and consumer demand are driving the market. According to the American Society of Plastic Surgery (ASPS), there were 7.23 million neurotoxin injections in 2017. As with any procedure, safety is paramount, and there is no substitute for totally understanding the anatomy of the face, and for the injector to know his or her limitations. Artistry levels vary, especially with fillers. It takes extensive training to master the amount and placement of dermal fillers. No matter what type of injectable you use, you will need to clarify patient expectations as to duration of effect, especially if your experience differs from the manufacturer's estimates.

As with every procedure, take time with the informed consent. If a patient feels you are rushing through it, they may also feel that you might rush their treatment. Be aware that while serious complications are rare (if you know your anatomy), adverse events are common. One of the reasons for the popularity of the hyaluronic acid (HA) fillers is the ability to correct placement errors by dissolving the HA with the enzyme hyaluronidase.

Compared to other countries, the US has a limited number of FDA-approved products in both the toxin and filler categories. The three commonly-used aesthetic neurotoxins include Botox Cosmetic®, Xeomin®, and Dysport®, with slight differences noted among them. Fillers are grouped into categories depending upon their ingredient and physical properties. The most commonly used products feature different configurations of hyaluronic acid (e.g. Juvederm® and Restylane®). Other ingredients include calcium hydroxylapatite (Radiesse®), polylactic acid (Sculptra®), polymethyl-methacrylate (Bellafil®), and polyacrylamide (Aquamid®). In addition to added practice revenue (a short visit and a good-margin product), other advantages of an injectable practice include:

- **Immediate patient gratification:** Once any swelling or bruising resolves, if your technique is solid, you have a happy patient.
- **Recurring revenue stream:** A major benefit—assuming competence and a good patient experience—is that the patient will come back several times a year for their neurotoxin and once or twice a year for fillers. This allows you to cross-sell other products and services.
- **Attract millennials into the practice:** Selfies are ruling the world. A Samsung executive estimates that the average millennial will take 25,000 selfies in their lifetime.[49] So the pressure is on to look good, and this means no wrinkles, nice skin and full lips. The ASPS estimates that, among patients 20-29 years of age, neurotoxin use is up 28%, and fillers up 32% since 2010.
- **Bundling of products/services:** Margins can vary on injectables, but most practices double the cost of the product to the patient; some mark them up several times. There is ample room for discounting to attract new patients and/or if patients avail themselves of other services.
- **Ample training & staffing opportunities**: In addition to training by the manufacturer, and courses at the major aesthetic meetings, there are independent companies that provide instruction, such as Empire Medical Training, The National Laser Institute, American Academy of Facial Aesthetics, Aesthetic Medical Educators Training, and the American Academy of Procedure Medicine. Many practices contract with an experienced injector (usually nurse practitioners, nurses, and physician assistants) who comes to the practice on selected days and times. Some injectors have their own patient following. There are a number of

devices devoted to safe injections: Accuvein® (accuvein.com) sells a modestly-priced device that provides real-time non-invasive imaging of veins. Life/form® provides soft vinyl skin that mimics the injection sensation. Recently Galderma introduced LucyLive™ at selected trade shows. LucyLive is a three-dimensional program that allows layered visualization of the anatomy of the face and the hands. Cadaver courses are excellent for those practitioners who want to gain an in-depth knowledge of anatomy and ensure patient safety during procedures. EuroMedicom offers a clinical facial anatomy dissection and live injection course each quarter, held in Europe.

Body Contouring

This is a rapidly growing field of aesthetics. According to IMARC Group's latest report,[50] the global body contouring market reached a value of US\$ 5.7 billion in 2017. While liposuction is intended for significant fat volume reduction, non-invasive body shaping technologies target stubborn fat, e.g., love handles, muffin tops, and bra fat that are not well addressed by diet and lifestyle. There are two ways to permanently remove small amounts of fat (lipolysis). This can be done by the application of either cold or heat. Freezing, or cryotherapy (CoolSculpting®) is done using specially fitted applicators. Lipolysis may be accomplished by heat directed into the subdermal fat layer using lasers (SculpSure®), radiofrequency (truSculpt®), or high intensity focused ultrasound (Liposonix®). The heat or the cold must be applied long enough to kill off the fat cells. We have not been impressed that so-called "cold lasers" produce permanent fat reduction. Recently, device applicators have been developed for use under the chin for many of the body contouring platforms. Emsculpt® from BTL is a device that stimulates muscle contractions and can selectively tone areas such as the abdomen and buttocks. There is also an injectable, Kybella®, that is FDA-approved for submental fat.

Vaginal Rejuvenation

While there are a dozen non-invasive and invasive procedures that can address aesthetic vaginal rejuvenation, the major new approach is vaginal tightening. It involves bringing heat into the dermis—either with radiofrequency or lasers that target water (the CO_2 laser)—to cause collagen remodeling and tissue tightening. This tissue tightening may also help with urinary incontinence. Usually several treatments are required. Note that that some of the device manufacturers have a platform that allows you to switch out the hand piece so it can be used for other applications. In addition to answering the basic device questions above, you'll want to determine if you and your staff are comfortable and prepared for holding an intimate discussion with your female patients. Among the most commonly used devices are Thermi's ThermiVa®, Cynosure's MonaLisa Touch®, and Sciton's diVa®. As previously mentioned, manufacturers are currently dealing with the FDA's warning regarding safety.

ARTERIOLOGY

Arteriology is a recently introduced term that describes a diagnostic and therapeutic approach to snuff out inflammation in the arterial walls, reduce their stiffness, and improve blood flow. These efforts are directed toward decreasing the death rate for cardiovascular disease (heart attack and strokes) that kills 2,150 Americans a day. Most practitioners interested in aggressively improving arterial health will provide a suite of diagnostic services including, but not limited to body composition, blood lipids, inflammatory biomarkers, blood-pressure monitoring, in-office testing for arterial stiffness including pulse pressure and pulse wave velocity, and arterial calcium scans. More conventional testing such as stress tests, echocardiograms, and cardiac catheterization should certainly be done under the care and supervision of a trained cardiologist. Arteriology services are skewed to attract a mid-aged and older population.

Two popular, easy-to-use in-office devices that assess endothelial health are EndoPAT from Itamar Medical and Vendys® II from Endothelix, Inc. Both of these devices involve arm-cuff based reactive hyperemia. Each is a 15-minute test. Measurements are conducted at the fingertip, with EndoPAT sensing pressure or Peripheral Arterial Tone (PAT), while Vendys detects temperature changes.

Increasingly, practitioners are emphasizing the importance of nitric oxide (NO) for endothelial health. HumanN (humann.com) offers a salivary strip test to test for NO. The results help drive dispensing of their Neo40® and SuperBeets® NO formulations. As of the writing of this book, a clinical trial is underway in which patients are using the Lightstim® LED bed for lowering blood pressure. It is hypothesized that the mechanism of action may involve nitric oxide. LightStim (lightstim.com) also manufactures handheld LED units for skin rejuvenation and pain reduction.

Arteriology-focused practitioners will usually have comprehensive fitness, nutrition, and stress management programs and rely heavily on nutraceuticals to reduce inflammation, serum lipids, and minimize pharmaceutical medicine use. A great review of both advanced testing and nutritional protocols can be found in Mark Houston, MD's review article in *Therapeutic Advances in Cardiovascular Disease.*[51]

Brad Bale, MD and Amy Doneen, DNP, co-authors of *Beat the Heart Attack Gene,* also emphasize the importance of poor periodontal health as a risk factor for CVD[52] and point to the effectiveness of the OraVital (oralvital.com) system to identify and control biofilm and oral infections. Arteriology-focused medical practitioners should consider forging strong referral connections with local dentists who have this orientation. A listing of dentists can be found on the OraVital website.

BODY COMPOSITION TESTING

Dexascan

The Dexascan is the gold standard for body composition testing. The Dual-energy X-ray Absorptiometry accurately measures bone density, lean muscle mass, and subcutaneous and visceral fat. As the measurement requires the patient to lie down, the device takes up significant space. Dexascans usually cost $30-$50,000 to purchase. Patient out-of-pocket costs range from $85-$375 per scan.

Impedance

Compared to a Dexascan, impedance machines take up a much smaller footprint, and can be acquired at much lower cost. It takes several minutes to get the results. These machines are based on Bioelectrical Impedance Analysis (BIA). BIA assesses the electrical impedance, or opposition to the flow of an electric current through body tissues. The current passes rapidly through water and meets resistance when it hits fat. The devices deliver a printout of total body water, lean muscle mass, and fat (including percent body fat). Although less accurate than the Dexascan, they provide a great counseling tool, especially when used for sequential measurements. Practitioners can decide to bundle the test with other services, or charge separately for it. The most commonly used devices are made by Inbody (inbodyusa.com) and Seca (seca.com) and feature stationary-hold hand grips. Fit3d involves measurements with the patient on a rotating turntable.

BRAIN HEALTH

Compared to diagnostics for some other bodily systems, there are fewer diagnostics, and fewer specific treatments available for brain health. However, clinicians point to CNS Vital Signs (cnsvs.com) as the "gold standard" in neurocognitive testing. CNS Vital Signs is a software platform that features a variety of patient tests which take about 25 to 30 minutes to complete. The assessment is automatically scored and integrated into a final report. Supported by multiple clinical studies, the assessment is well accepted by most payers for reimbursement.

The field of neurocognition is indebted to the pioneering work of Daniel Amen, MD, whose Amen Clinics (amenclinics.com) have scanned more than 150,000 brains and shown visible improvement with lifestyle and supplement treatment. On the diagnostic side, SPECT brain imaging (Single-photon emission computed tomography), a nuclear medicine test using gamma rays, can accurately reveal brain activity and blood flow patterns. PET and CT scans can also show structural changes, notably for Alzheimer's and traumatic brain injury. These scans are provided by local hospitals or specialized clinics such as Cerescan (cerescan.com). They may be insurance-reimbursable for specific disease indications (usually with precertification). EEGs also provide valuable data on the brain's electrical activity.

The FDA has been reluctant to clear EEG-related tests for stand-alone diagnostics; however, EEGs can provide a novel source of evidence to complement clinical evaluations. WAVi (wavimed.com) has created an affordable evoked potential EEG to test brain performance and provide benchmarks to clinicians looking to reverse mental declines associated with aging, trauma, and a variety of neurodegenerative diseases. Other companies that offer online testing for cognitive function (without the EEG component) include SMART Brain Aging and ImPACT who provides software for pre-and post- concussion testing.

Neurofeedback devices, such as Neuroptimal are commonly employed by practitioners for brain training. Many practitioners will also recommend that patients utilize home devices such as the Muse Brain Sensing Headband (muse.com). The company has a full-service program for professionals to promote the program in-office. Wellbrain (wellbrain.io) offers both products and a training program that enables practitioners to better understand and teach mindfulness. Transcranial magnetic stimulation, as offered by the German-based neuroCare Group, features in-office devices that address ADHD, depression, chronic pain, and stroke rehabilitation. Devices include near infrared spectroscopy, transcranial and magnetic stimulation, and neurofeedback. Cranial Electrotherapy Stimulation devices such as Thync and Alpha-Stim can help with mood and provide anxiety relief. The Fisher Wallace Stimulator is FDA-cleared for depression, anxiety and insomnia. Brainmaster Technologies (brainmaster.com) offers a hardware/software package that provides reliable, comprehensive neurofeedback training for patients.

From a functional standpoint, many of the brain related treatments are oriented around reducing neural inflammation through a lifestyle, diet, and supplement-related approach. Increasingly, as the science develops, practitioners are incorporating nootropics into their practice. Nootropics are substances such as drugs or supplements that improve cognitive function, especially the higher executive functions such as memory, creativity or motivation. Percepta™ (perceptabrain.com) is a plant-based nootropic that combines cat's claw and MemorTea™. The manufacturer, Cognitive Clarity Inc. is the brainchild of neuroscientists Rudolph Tanzi, MD and Alan Snow, PhD and is supported by nineteen peer-reviewed publications.

Some practitioners will also include urinary neurotransmitter levels in their assessments. (See **L** Laboratory Tests below.)

CANNABINOIDS

Welcome to the Wild, Wild West. It is difficult to avoid the ever-growing legion of consumers, quasi-health, and health professionals who are touting the miraculous benefits of cannabinoids.

The marijuana plant contains dozens of cannabinoid molecules with THC and CBD possessing different pharmacologic properties. Marijuana, medical marijuana, and cannabis (medical marijuana)—in their many forms (edible, drinkable, volatile)—refer to the plant. The FDA neither approves, nor regulates their use, rather there are both federal and individual State laws that govern their legality. Medical marijuana has been approved in 30 states and the District of Columbia.

THC is the major cannabinoid responsible for producing intoxicating effects. It has been used to treat chronic pain, anorexia, and Alzheimer's.[53]

Cannabidiol (CBD) is a non-psychoactive compound that can be extracted from medical marijuana, but more commonly is derived from industrial hemp. In order to not run afoul of the FDA, many physicians will note that they provide hemp-derived phytocannabinoids. One of the driving forces behind the surging popularity of CBD has been that it is non-euphoric. The laws and regulations surrounding "hemp" are very different from marijuana. Hemp is not as strictly regulated. Hemp-based CBD is available in all 50 states and is even sold online. CBD oil has been used to treat anxiety, epilepsy, depression, Parkinson's disease, spasms, and pain.

Cannabinoids basically include three chemical classes of compounds. The first are the naturally occurring molecules found in the cannabis plant. The second are synthesized molecules, several of which have FDA approval as drugs (Marinol, Syndros, and Cesamet). In June of 2018, the FDA approved Epidiolex®, an oral CBD solution for the treatment of seizures associated with two rare and severe forms of epilepsy. The third category are those substances that the body produces, the endocannabinoid system (ECS). This endogenous system consists of lipid-based neurotransmitters and cannabinoid receptors. It is found throughout the central and peripheral nervous system where it is involved in appetite, pain-sensation, mood, and memory.

David Bearman, MD, a California-based cannabinoid expert recommends that physicians interested in incorporating these treatments make certain to attend conferences specially designed to provide the necessary education. He recommends the International Cannabinoid Research Society, as well as Patients out of Time (patientsoutoftime.org), noting that the latter organization offers 12.5 hours of category 1 CME. He has found value in an annual conference, Marijuana for Medical Professionals. Bearman's own organization, the American Academy of Cannabinoid Research, also offers certification.

COSMECEUTICALS

The term "cosmeceutical" was introduced by Albert Kligman, MD in 1984 to refer to substances that exerted both cosmetic and therapeutic benefits. Cosmeceuticals are not regulated by the FDA, as opposed to prescription and OTC topical drugs. Manufacturers are thus not permitted to claim that their product cures, treats, mitigates or prevents disease; nor can they make structure or function claims. The Federal Trade Commission (FTC) oversees the manufacturers, making sure the promoted product benefits can be substantiated.

In 2017, wholesale revenue of physician-dispensed cosmeceuticals reached $1.2 billion globally ($2.4 billion to patients). The market is expected to grow at 8.6% a year through 2022.[54]

Skincare products account for the largest share of the cosmeceuticals market. They are specifically designed to maintain, protect and condition the skin and to help address specific cosmetic concerns. Cosmeceutical products usually include cleansers, toners, exfoliants, peels, serums and moisturizers mostly found in retail size for your patient home-care use and professional size for your in-office use. The most common skin concerns that cosmeceuticals target are wrinkles, fine lines, hyperpigmentation, acne, redness, scars, skin texture, and skin tone. Some of the most popular active ingredients in cosmeceuticals are retinol, peptides, growth factors, antioxidants including vitamin C, brightening agents, exfoliating agents including alpha hydroxy acid, botanicals, and moisturizing agents such as hyaluronic acid. Topicals are often used in combination with other skincare treatments. Many cosmeceutical skin care products are compatible with in-office procedures such as lasers, microdermabrasion or injectables.

Similar to stocking nutraceuticals in your practice, you will want to acquaint yourself with some go-to products. We've broken out some of the active categories as well as included representative companies.

- **Sun Protection:** Three companies dominate the professional market with their silky, mineral based formulas, available in multiple strengths, both tinted and untinted. These are EltaMD, Tizo and Colorscience.
- **Serums:** These are increasingly popular with patients. Our favorites include NeoStrata's Tri-Serum Lifting Serum, and serums by iS Skin and Teoxane. A time-tested serum for skin brightening is Skinceutical's CE Ferulic.
- **Moisturizers:** With hundreds for the professional to choose from, we lean toward those from Epionce, SENTÉ, and Nia24, each of which features unique bioactives.
- **Lightening and Brightening Agents:** Skin lightening involves reducing pigmentation. It addresses discoloration and uneven skin tone. Brightness involves increasing radiance and the glow of the skin. It is more about restoring vibrancy. Traditional lightening agents will include hydroquinone, kojic acid, arbutine, vitamin C, and retinol. Increasingly, these ingredients can be specially compounded to meet individual patient needs. Brightening products will feature vitamin C, retinol, alpha and beta hydroxy acids. An excellent brightening topical is SkinMedica's Lytera.
- **Growth Factors/Skin Rejuvenation:** In addition to the category leading SkinMedica products, other excellent choices include products produced by Neocutis, DefenAge, Aivita, and AnteAgeMD.
- **Peels:** Obagi and PCA are popular, tested medical grade skin peels.
- **Retinol:** Skinbetter Science produces an excellent retinol product.
- **Multiproduct Lines**: Many companies produce full-service lines. You may be able to obtain additional discounts by buying across their spectrum of offerings. Check out complete product lines from ZO Skin, SkinCeuticals, Obagi and BioPelle.

NOTE WELL: There are also local and national contract manufacturing laboratories that can produce your own private-label cosmeceuticals. You lose out on any cache the brand has—and have to replace it with your own. Private labeling can ease your worries about the products being found at lower prices online. Companies are readily available from a Google search.

DETOXIFICATION

We live in an increasingly toxic world that creates a major burden on our bodies. Toxins enter the body through the air that we breathe, the chemicals on our skin, and the food and water we ingest. The liver is the primary organ responsible for removing these toxins. If the liver is not working at full speed, every other system in the body is at risk from the fat-soluble toxins that are stored in the body and are poorly excreted. Detoxification is usually performed by addressing two enzymatic steps known as Phase I and Phase II detoxification.

Detoxification is a popular and accepted concept among the lay public, as well as a mainstay of treatment for integrative/functional physicians. Detox is frequently used along with an elimination diet. The most commonly removed food ingredients include dairy, gluten, wheat, soy, eggs, tree nuts, and shellfish. After a period of several weeks, individual foods are reintroduced and the patient is observed for reactions. The major nutrition companies provide detox kits for nutritional support during the process. Often in the form of powders, these products include vitamins, antioxidants, minerals, and amino acids necessary to support the phases of liver detoxification. Some of the more dedicated practitioners will employ fir saunas for detoxification.

ENERGY MEDICINE

I (Mark) sometime lapse into classic-physician skepticism when I am confronted by Energy Medicine advocates. Then I remember we are beings fueled by energy produced by the mitochondria in our bodies. I personally have always found it poetic that our heart contains the most mitochondria: a heart cell contains 5,000 mitochondria, a liver cell 1,000, and a brain cell 400. We detect the vibration of these various organs through the routine tests— the EKG, MRI, PET and ultrasound scans that we routinely use for conventional medical diagnoses. Some complementary medicine experts recognize these differences in vibrational energy being reflected in the chakras and the meridians that course through the body.

From the work done by the HeartMath Institute (heartmath.org),[55] we also know that "vibrations" are contagious. When we come into contact with other individuals who are in a relaxed, loving state, we too tend to relax, as we are subject to their vibrational aura. We know that the magnetic field produced by the heart is more than 100 times greater in strength than the field produced by the brain. Using sophisticated magnetometers, we can detect the heart's energy up to three feet away from the body. Many people feel transformed in the presence of a guru, a master, or true teacher of one of the ancient healing disciplines, such as yoga, tai chi, meditation, or mindfulness.

We see two types of energy medicine practiced today. The first is related to the concept of biofield therapy, the idea that energy fields surround the human body and can be influenced to affect healing. The most commonly known therapies are acupuncture and homeopathy, but also reiki, healing touch, craniosacral, and qi gong.

The second deals with utilizing vibrational energy to both detect and treat energy abnormalities in the body. One such system has been created by Ondamed (ondamed. net), manufacturers of a biofeedback device that can also guide therapeutic decisions. The device has been used by physicians and patients around the globe since the mid 90's. According to founder Silvia Binder, ND, PhD, the focused electromagnetic fields can help with inflammation, infectious processes, and other physical imbalances by improving microcirculation, lymphatic flow, and immune response.

FELLOWSHIP TRAINING

Receiving proper training is critical for great patient outcomes. Many of the recommendations in this chapter may be outside your core training, yet you want to feel both competent and confident in incorporating new products and services. Many societies offer clinical certificates or provide more formal fellowship training programs. This is notably the case with Integrative/Functional, Regenerative and Aesthetic Medicine. Of note is the recently created American Board of Integrative Medicine (ABOIM) certification. Acceptable programs can be found on their website. https://www.abpsus.org/integrative-medicine.

GENETIC TESTING

The emergence of direct-to-consumer genetic testing (the identification of SNPs in populations, discussed in Chapter 1: What is Driving the Cash-Pay Market?) has shined light on genetics. It also drives the need for healthcare professionals to help consumers make sense of their data—for one thing, to realize that genes are not their destiny. Our lifestyle choices turn on or off the genes that contribute to illness or wellness. The companies that provide translators take the raw genetic data from 23andMe to determine which are the clinical relevant SNPs and use this data to counsel the patient. The three most-commonly used translators, mentioned earlier are from Pathway Genomics, PureGenomics, and

StrateGene. OneOme's RightMed® provides a comprehensive pharmacogenomics test (also called a medication response test) that analyzes a person's DNA to predict how well he or she is likely to respond to a medication. DNAlife, a European-based company, relatively new to the US, offers both nutrigenomics and pharmacogenomics. Genome Medical (genomedical.com) is a specialty medicine practice in genomics that offers testing, and telehealth genetic counseling to support physician referrals in 48 states. The company provides three lines of services: hereditary cancer, reproductive health, and genetic health screening. This allows physicians to easily add highly-skilled virtual counselors to their collaborative care teams. It is also important to note that the price for full genome testing, as is now done by Human Longevity Inc., is coming down and will most likely be more widely adopted.

GUT HEALTH

Functional medicine practitioners will often begin their presentations by quoting Hippocrates: "All disease begins in the gut." Our expanding knowledge of the gut microbiome, the hormonal and neural pathways that connect the gut to the brain, and food sensitivities, has dramatically elevated the status of this organ system. The major laboratory tests for gut health are described below. Treatment for the most part, revolves around:

- Removing sensitizing agents, foods and toxins
- Adding necessary digestive enzymes
- Restoring the integrity of the intestinal lining with bovine colostrum and minerals
- Eating more dietary fiber for short-chain fatty acids; augmenting with butyrate
- Reintroducing probiotics

Having spoken extensively for Sovereign Laboratories (sovereignlaboratories.com), on behalf of their Bovine Colostrum-LD® product, Mark appreciates the ability of this mammalian biologic to help heal the increased intestinal permeability caused by common GI assaults such as NSAIDs, gluten, antibiotics and the standard Western diet. Studies have shown that bovine colostrum can decrease zonulin excretion (a marker of a "leaky gut").[56] With more than 100 bioactives,[57] including immunoglobulins, anti-infectives, and growth factors, this whole- food supplement provides the necessary elements for tissue repair. The unique lipososomal delivery of Sovereign Laboratories' products protects the colostrum as it passes through the gut and facilitates absorption. Mark has also created a 40-minute online video certification course on bovine colostrum available from the company.

HYDRODERMABRASION

Microdermabrasion continues to be a popular treatment. The American Society of Plastic Surgeons (ASPS) estimates that their core members performed 740,000 procedures in 2017; this figure doesn't take into account procedures done by non-core practitioners. Hydrodermabrasion, the process of exfoliation augmented with fluids, provides a more comfortable experience. Patients leave the painless procedure with a nice glow to their skin from the cleansing and infusion process. Procedures can be done on the face, neck and décolleté in one sitting usually within 15 to 20 minutes. Most practices sell a package of treatments offered over several months. The popularity of the procedure, along with its modest cost make it an ideal "top of the funnel" treatment to gather new patients and have them come in repeatedly. The two major devices are the Hydrafacial®, and Dermalinfusion by Envy Medical. There are minor costs for the disposables including serums.

HAIR REMOVAL

Hair removal continues to maintain its popularity, most notably for the low-cost, low-skill level for treatment, increased safety, better training, and universal demand, but just as much from better, faster, safer devices. Hair removal may be an adjunct treatment or even a teaser to bring people into your practice. Multiple visits (3-6) are needed for desired results, depending upon gender, hair location, and hair color (only dark hair can be removed) which lends itself to service and product bundling. Two types of energies are used: lasers and IPL, with both being efficacious. Recently Venus Concept introduced a revenue sharing program for their Venus Velocity™ diode laser hair removal system. They place the aesthetic system with qualified customers and charge a flat fee based on monthly usage. One final note: as with all laser and light procedures, make certain the technician understands the importance of using appropriate settings on darker-skinned individuals to prevent burning or scarring.

HAIR RESTORATION

Hair restoration is enjoying a renaissance. Women of all ages suffer from changes in or loss of hair. This provides many bundling opportunities. For example, treating hormonal-related hair loss in middle-aged and older women might best be accomplished with a combination of BHRT (Bioidentical Hormone Replacement Therapy), nutritional support, and PRP (Platelet-Rich Plasma). Hair restoration can also serve as the doorway to get more men into a practice, as a receding hairline is of great concern to millennials and GenX men. You'll want to determine your degree of commitment based upon patient interest, and whether to make this a major, or a more nuanced part of your offerings. The treatment spectrum consists of the following:

1. **Nutritional support:** These are specially formulated professional supplements that have shown clinical efficacy. Nutrafol® (nutrafol.com) has specific formulations for both men and women. With 21 nutritional ingredients, it provides clinically tested, standardized botanical bioactives with targeted action against the underlying causes of hair loss, including inflammation, DHT, oxidative damage, and stress. In a recently published double-blind, placebo-controlled clinical trial, Nutrafol has been shown to increase hair counts and improve clinical appearance of hair loss.[58] Depending on the severity and need of the patient, it can be used as a stand-alone for preventive or restorative purposes. Viviscal is another well-regarded professional brand.

2. **Light based therapy:** You may elect to offer in-office LED treatment, but given the length of time the treatment takes, as well as the necessary frequency, many practitioners are better advised to offer home devices to your patients. These wearable devices take the form of caps (Capillus®) or bike-type helmets (Theradome®). They feature an array of LEDs, with the price point tied to the number and type of LEDs offered. The companies feature professional versions that allow for practitioner markup.

3. **Growth factors/PRP:** PRP therapy (platelet-rich plasma, see **P**) for hair loss is a three-step medical treatment in which a patient's blood is drawn, processed, and then injected into the scalp. Although there hasn't been much scientific research done on PRP for hair loss, PRP therapy has been in use since the 1980s. There is great anecdotal support for PRP among leading dermatologists.[59,60]

4. **Surgical punches:** These allow for excision of follicular units of several hairs, whose artistic use prevents the corn row approach of older techniques. NeoGraft® and SmartGraft® dominate the category.

5. **Robotic hair replacement:** Given the cost, space, and training necessary, only physicians who intend to make hair restoration the focal point of their practice should consider a robotic approach. The Artas ® System is offered by Restoration Robotics.

HORMONE REPLACEMENT THERAPY (HRT)

HRT is a significant category for integrative cash-pay practitioners who place the majority of emphasis on the sex hormones, thyroid, and adrenals, as well as hormones involved in insulin resistance. Before beginning any treatment program on a patient, it is critical to obtain and be able to intelligently interpret hormone levels, available through most laboratories. There is no substitute for obtaining ongoing continuing medical education to become competent in this area of medicine. It takes more than one weekend course to master hormone treatment.

The HRT treatment philosophy is tied, in large measure, to the need for a longer patient visit. This increased consultation time is especially critical for the pre- and menopausal patient who often comes away from the conventional 10-minute primary care visit feeling that her symptoms have been downplayed; she hasn't been heard; or that the treatment alternatives which often include anti-anxiety medications, are unsatisfactory.

While the term "natural" has multiple meanings, increasingly patients will seek out more natural alternatives, leading them to practitioners who offer "Bioidentical" hormone replacement therapy (BHRT) involving compounded medications delivered orally as capsules, sublingually, vaginally, rectally, IM or more preferably, transdermally. The insertion of hormone pellets is also becoming more commonplace, driven in equal measures by patient convenience and practitioner preference. The larger compounding pharmacies such as Wells Pharmacy Network provide sterile implantable pellets produced in their FDA registered 503B facilities.

Pellecome LLC (pellecome.com) has created the Re3™Advanced Pellet Delivery System for both women and men. In addition to providing the pellets, they have developed a kit that helps make insertions easier, safer, and more reliable. The system includes a precision scalpel, a funnel with a needle, and an insertion tool with a needle guide. The device kit provides practitioners at any skill level with a safe and easy procedure to consistently place the pellets in the target location in the subcutaneous tissue of the upper buttock.

To attract women into the practice, many BHRT practitioners will tailor their marketing outreach to address the patient's feelings of frustration and dissatisfaction. Practitioners will emphasize the availability of options that are more personalized to an individual's circumstance and lifestyle. Short "welcome to my practice" type videos that display the practitioner as caring, helpful, and solutions-oriented can help convert website visitors into consults. A similar approach for attracting male patients has focused on low-T, or low testosterone levels.

To be successful with a BHRT program, practitioners may opt to become affiliated with one of the commercial companies. BodyLogicMD (bodylogicmd.com) offers franchised HRT programs that are accompanied by training, marketing, and practice support, as well as supplement and injectable fulfillment. Hormone Treatment Centers of America and BioTE Medical are two other companies providing packaged approaches.

Understanding the interdependence of hormones, the importance of laboratory testing, the pros and cons for treatment, as well as how to communicate all aspects of your diagnostic and treatment approach is vital to patient satisfaction. Clarifying the concept of "bioidentical" to the patient is equally important.

IV NUTRIENT THERAPY

Intravenous (IV) therapy is a method of supplying vitamins, minerals, and amino acids directly into the bloodstream. It can be used to correct intracellular nutrient deficiencies as patients can get up to 10 times the nutrients in one treatment as they could get orally in one day. The theory is rooted in the prevalence of general inadequacies in the diet, presence of chronic disease, toxins and environmental insults, and medications that deplete key nutrients.

Offering IV nutrient therapy can provide a major revenue source to your practice. It is an easy addition, and one that is complementary to most health-related disciplines. The public is placing increasing faith in this modality and seeking it out. While there are some CPT codes that can be used for reimbursement for fatigue, fibromyalgia, or chronic fatigue syndrome, this is normally a pure cash-pay service with prices ranging from $85-$200 per treatment depending upon ingredients and practice location.

Consider IV therapy as a great adjunct to wow your patients with the aesthetics of your own practice and the great customer experience you provide. Most practices include a cocktail menu, including hydration, recovery from jet lag or post partying, building immunity, or fighting colds and flu. Many of the treatments are variations of the Myers Drip named for the late John Myers, MD and include a wellness boost of vitamins and amino acids, especially glutathione, often referred to as the mother of all antioxidants. A variety of companies and compounding local and national compounding pharmacies supply the ingredients; however, we believe it is incumbent on the practitioner to put together a quality product, rather than purchase prepackaged mixes that have preservatives. These lesser-quality products often feature corn-based ingredients. Preparing sterile products requires rigorous attention to technique as well as the use of a laminar flow hood.[61] IV chelation is a unique specialty and requires advanced training.

LABORATORY TESTING

Along with aesthetics, nutritional therapy, and compounding, advanced laboratory testing makes up a big part of the what constitutes unique services in cash-pay practices. This may include laboratory developed tests (LDT), a type of in vitro diagnostic test that is designed, manufactured, and used within a single laboratory, hence the test is proprietary. Most LDTs are not insurance-reimbursable. Some have large databases of results with which to compare a given patient's measurements; others less so. We have broken out the main categories of testing and provided short descriptions of the major companies in each category. For this breakout, we have relied heavily on the guidance of Marvin Singh, MD, one of the only Board Certified Integrative Gastroenterologists in the country.

Inflammation & Cardiac Health

Many of the more advanced tests for inflammation and cardiovascular disease are being done by the larger reference labs. For example, it is commonplace to test for high-sensitivity C-reactive protein (hs-CRP), homocysteine, and even MTHFR (methylenetetrahydrofolate reductase) status as part of routine lab work. Cleveland HeartLab (clevelandheartlab.com), now part of Quest, makes their inflammation panel, TMAO (trimethylene N-oxide), omega-3 to omega-6 ratios, and NMR (Nuclear Magnetic Resonance) lipid panels, easily available. Genova also offers some of the cardiac and lipid tests similar to those offered by Cleveland HeartLab and Quest.

Gut Health

The gut is central to health and disease. Assessing gut health is key to understanding how to address underlying issues a patient may have. There are many different gut health tests out on the market that will assess intestinal permeability, vitamin & mineral deficiencies, food and chemical sensitivities, and provide basic microbiome analysis. Specimens include blood, stool, and urine. The major companies in this space include:

- Genova Diagnostics. A full-service laboratory provider, among their many tests, Genova offers NutrEval®, a urinary amino acid test for key nutritional deficiencies. GI Effects® is a comprehensive stool profile.
- Spectracell Laboratories provides micronutrient testing based on white blood cells assessment.
- Cyrex Laboratories offers testing for immune mediated reactions such as gluten and other antigens.

- Dunwoody Labs has a broad array of tests for integrative medicine practitioners, including the ability to assess blood zonulin, a marker for intestinal permeability.

There are also a variety of quick and simple tests for food sensitivities such as Everlywell and KBMO that are often used by practitioners; these tests are affordable and can be performed at home by the patient/client.

We'll discuss microbiome testing in **M**.

Brain Health

A number of companies offer dried urine testing for neurotransmitters including serotonin, dopamine, epinephrine plus glutamate, norepinephrine, and GABA. These include Labrix and ZRT. The validity of these tests has often been called into question by conventional, and sometimes integrative medicine practitioners.[62] When used as part of a complete clinical evaluation, they may be helpful in directing treatment.

Hormones

In addition to testing serum for hormones, dried fluids (blood, urine and saliva) are becoming increasingly validated as providing accurate measurements. Salivary cortisol has become a preferred mechanism for assessing adrenal function, offering both convenience and accuracy versus blood and 24-hour urine collection. Many companies offer salivary cortisol.

Dried urine provides a comprehensive look at both sex and adrenal hormones, as well as offers convenience. One of the innovators in this space is Precision Analytical (dutchtest.com). Their unique hormone testing uses the acronym DUTCH (Dried Urine Test for Comprehensive Hormones). The Dutch Complete™ provides a comprehensive assessment of sex and adrenal hormones and their metabolites. It also includes the daily, free cortisol pattern, organic acids, melatonin (6-OHMS), and 8-OHdG. ZRT also provides hormone testing.

Environmental Exposure & Toxins

We live in an increasingly toxic world. Potentially harmful chemicals are ubiquitous in our air and water, and in the products we apply to our skin. These toxins have found their way into our food supply. Given this insult, our bodies may not be able to metabolize and clear all of them, hence the need for detox programs. (See **D**) As these chemicals build up, they affect our metabolism. This is reflected in enzyme dysfunction and nutritional deficiencies, hormonal imbalances, altered brain chemistry and even cancer.

Doctor's Data offers a spectrum of tests designed to evaluate the exposure to environmental toxins, and assess the body's capacity for endogenous detoxification. Great Plains Laboratories features a full-suite of toxin testing including assessment of organic acids. They are also able to check glyphosate (Roundup®) levels. Genova and Cyrex also have tests for toxins.

Heredity Cancer Testing

Hereditary cancer testing is offered by BioReference Laboratories through their GeneDx, Inc. subsidiary. GeneDx offers a comprehensive testing menu which includes clinically relevant genes associated with hereditary cancer. Among the cancer panels they offer are tests for breast, gynecological and colorectal cancer as well as other cancers and tumor specific panels.

Taking Testing to Heart

All of these tests have a specific role in the clinical setting and may be beneficial to someone based on their symptoms, issues, and other findings. It is up to the practitioner to learn and understand these tests well to know how to best apply their utility to the particular patient.

☐   **Dr. Singh's Take Home:** *It is really important to personalize the testing modality for the patient by incorporating their desires and goals for wellness, with your particular skillset as a practitioner. You also want to take into account the patient's budget and how they are paying (cash, insurance, or both?) when making a recommendation for testing. This will not only help you optimize their health, but it will also help you optimize the relationship by showing that you understand their limitations and are trying to do the best you can for them under the circumstances.*

MICROBIOME TESTING

We are just at the beginning of an exploding body of knowledge of the microbiome—the 40 trillion bacteria, fungi, viruses, yeast, parasites, and bacteriophages that inhabit our gut, as well as those that colonize our skin and our mucosa—and how these organisms affect metabolism, brain function, autoimmune disease, skin health and beauty, and more. Compared with genetic testing, the microbiome is much more complex because after all, these 40 trillion organisms also contribute their own genetic material to the mix. Microbiome testing reports, no matter how well they are designed, still confront consumers with the science of taxonomy and long, complicated, hard-to-pronounce genus and species names. Along with genes, the microbiome is part of a diagnostic orientation, known as Precision Medicine. Spoiler Alert: Keep your eyes peeled for an explosion of cosmeceuticals featuring pre- and probiotics and other agents designed to improve the skin's microbiome.

According to Helen Messier, MD, Chief Medical Officer of Viome (viome.com), a leading microbiome testing company, "Many clinicians are not familiar with different testing methodologies, and don't understand the molecular biology, RNA and DNA that is involved." There are three different testing methods in use today.

- 16S Sequencing identifies a fraction of the gut bacteria by sequencing the DNA that comes from food and dead organisms. It is a lower resolution screening that sometimes has issues with reproducibility. It cannot identify nonbacterial organisms.
- Metagenomic analysis provides higher resolution at the species and strain level; however, it does not include RNA viruses, nor does it identify the microbial metabolites that are key for maintaining health.
- Metatranscriptome analysis provides the highest resolution of sequencing. Through the measurement of RNA, it identifies all microorganisms living in the gut, as well as quantifies their metabolic activity—the extent to which they are producing helpful or harmful metabolites. Viome is the only company presently doing microbiome analysis at this level. Other companies use a mix of 16S and metagenomics analysis.

Other organizations providing microbiome testing include American Gut.[63] This is an open platform spearheaded by UCSD scientist Rob Knight, PhD. Knight and his colleagues have combined standardized protocols from the Earth Microbiome Project and sample contributions from over 10,000 citizen-scientists from the United States, United Kingdom, and Australia. They are matching these profiles to environmental samples. UBiome (ubiome.com) offers their SmartGut™ test through healthcare providers. It links the microbiome with GI diseases such as IBS, IBD, ulcerative colitis, and Crohn's disease. Biohm Health features a test developed by noted scientist, Mahmoud (Afif) Ghannoum, PhD, who named the mycobiome, the body's native fungal community. Available DTC, the company also offers companion wellness consultation with a nutritionist. Biohm Health has developed a line of pre- and probiotics, as well to which they direct test-takers.

When it comes to the microbiome, our diagnostic capabilities are well ahead of our clinical protocols. While we are able to identify microorganisms, we are still in the infancy helping patients make sense of the results. Viome has taken an interesting approach by focusing its clinical test report around helping patients/consumers understand which foods to eat, and which to avoid based upon the metabolic activity of their gut organisms. In addition to keeping up to speed on to the latest science, physicians should:

- Hone their ability to explain the microbiome to patients.
- Stress the importance of gut organism diversity.
- Utilize the findings to encourage a more fiber-rich diet.
- Have a gut-health protocol in place and follow patients to see how it is working.
- Use the teachable moment to stress healthy lifestyle change.

MICRONEEDLING

As an alternative to cosmetic laser procedures and chemical peels, dermal needling has become a versatile option for aesthetic facilities. Spas, medical spas, and cosmetic surgery facilities are offering solutions for loose skin, wrinkles and fine lines, discoloration and scars, through one of many microneedling devices. Although medical and non-medical facilities offer microneedling, these devices and their results may vary significantly.

Microneedling can be categorized into two categories: medical needling and cosmetic needling. There are hundreds of different types of microneedling devices and brands available to the aesthetic industry. Some devices are for at-home use, while others are produced for medical offices to be used under the supervision of a medical doctor. The one distinguishing factor that separates the two categories is the length of the needles attached to the device.

Cosmetic needling treatments utilize needles of depths no greater than 0.5 mm. Such procedures are somewhat effective at reducing the appearance of fine lines and other superficial imperfections.

Medical needling treatments are intended for skin concerns that are deeper set. Acne scars, for example, require deeper penetration to break up scar tissue and stimulate collagen remodeling and production. Medical needling treatments are performed at a depth greater than 0.5 mm and up to a depth of 2.5 mm. These depths require the supervision of a licensed practitioner. The risks of medical needling when performed by a trained and licensed practitioner are low, compared to more invasive peels and cosmetic laser procedures. In addition, medical needling can improve a wider range of skin issues, such as acne scars, wrinkles, and discoloration. As of this writing, SkinPen® by Bellus Medical is the only class II needling device FDA-approved. Increasingly, medical microneedling is finding its way into combination devices which primarily use radio frequency waves to create an added heat-stimulation component.

NUTRITIONAL SUPPLEMENTS (NUTRACEUTICALS)

This category is one of the mainstays of an integrative, functional, or anti-aging practice. Increasingly other practitioners, e.g. ophthalmologists, orthopedics, cardiologists, etc., are offering selected supplements to their patients. The emphasis is on adoption of professional brands that are sold exclusively to licensed healthcare practitioners. According to Tom Aarts, Founder and Managing Director at Nutrition Business Advisors, it is estimated that supplement companies sell $1.79 billion annually in the professional channel which translates to approximately $4.0 billion in professional sales to the patient.

Become a Strong Advocate for Professional-Only Brands

Practitioners who dispense professional brands must school their staff on how to explain the value proposition versus adoption of lesser-priced supplements from mass market retailers, online sellers, or multi-level marketing programs. This rationale includes: quality, strength, purity, and known efficacy in the hands of the treating clinician. You can also point out that many are supported by clinical studies on the specifically formulated product that have been published in peer-reviewed publications. This makes for a superior product compared to products manufactured with similar, though less expensive or unproven, and even potentially harmful ingredients.[64] In addition, there is no assurance that a professional-only product offered by online retailers is not counterfeit.[65] Sharing his perspective, Tom Aarts remarked that, "The professional space, in my experience, is the fastest growing sector for a number of reasons: quality products, solid science, and great manufacturing practices."

Nate Freeman, Senior Director of Marketing for Ortho Molecular Products, notes that even among the professional brands, "Only a select few companies follow rigorous standards every step along the manufacturing process. This begins with ensuring the quality of any raw material including core testing with multiple samples taken from all levels of the container. We then do extensive sample analysis for identity, microbiology and purity. Our process even extends to extensive cleaning of the machinery after formulation. It's painstaking, but we shut down, dismantle, and scrub each part, then test for residue using black light so there is never any cross-contamination of ingredients."

Companies also differ to the extent that they are committed to the professional market. Given the larger size of the consumer market and the ease of conducting DTC via the

Internet, plus the greater margins of selling direct to patients at full retail price, many professional companies have moved to a hybrid strategy, selling products in both channels. Both Ortho Molecular Products and Xymogen are steadfast in being practitioner-only brands. Other excellent professional grade manufacturers such as Designs for Health, Metagenics, Standard Process, DaVinci Laboratories, Pure Encapsulations, and Douglas Laboratories straddle the two markets. It appears that Thorne has morphed their professional brand into a major consumer initiative, that bundled with home testing and online counseling, may increasingly compete with practitioners.

From Either/Or to Both/And.

Among the most interesting strategies is that which has been created by Designs for Health (DFH) (designsforhealth.com). Their DFH Rewards program for the practitioner takes into account sales from all channels; those that you make through in-practice dispensing, but also sales that occur from the DFH webstore and online retailers such as Amazon. The company uses sophisticated zip code targeting to credit your account for all non-affiliated consumer purchases in your territory. This crediting is based on the assumption that you are a powerful influencer of sales in your market and the company has chosen to err on the side of over- as opposed to under-crediting you. DFH provides a monthly reward to the practice based upon the total sales that are attributable to your influence. At the higher sales levels, this can amount to an additional 13-15%. Specific details of the program are available from your DFH representative.

Post a Supplement Policy

We encourage physicians to post a supplement policy that states the patient is under no obligation to purchase from you but also lists the reasons you have made these products available. Many practices will note that a portion of the profit has been designated for a charitable donation. Depending upon the type of practice, nutraceutical supplement revenue may comprise anywhere from 5% to 40% of practice revenue. In larger clinics, this can pay the salaries of the front office staff. Because there are so many individual bottles, jars, and bags of products, from multiple companies and multiple product lines available for you to purchase or recommend, keeping track of SKUs and inventory may be challenging. The number and types of products you stock and/or recommend depends upon your knowledge base, but equally important is the patient's history and laboratory results. Nutraceuticals represent an area in which practitioners may demonstrate "the curse of knowledge." The more they know, the more they tend to overprescribe, and the end result can be an overwhelmed patient saddled with a big supplement bill. Faced with what may be perceived as too extensive or too expensive recommendations, the best practitioners will pare down their recommendations and emphasize those products that are priorities.

Help Patients Cut Through the Clutter

The CRN Consumer Survey on Dietary Supplements[66] revealed that 68% of Americans take dietary supplements, a percentage that has remained stable over five years. Yet with millions of supplement takers and an ever-growing cohort of supplements, there is undoubtedly more confusion than ever before. The role of a skilled clinician is to help cut through the clutter. To effect this, many practitioners will instruct their patients to include a digital photo of all their supplements as part of the pre-visit intake history.

Have a Supplement Dispensing Rationale in Mind

There are two ways to think about supplements. The first is by category and mechanism of action. Examples include antioxidants, probiotics, Omega-3s, amino acids, digestive enzymes, phytochemicals, herbals, etc.[67] While this is a useful framework for science-oriented clinicians, a more helpful categorization is to cluster your products around the rationale for use, or the type of clinical condition you are trying to support and to have a few go-to products for each grouping. This way you won't feel so overwhelmed by all the choices. You will find a broad categorization in the box below. (Note: Manufacturers cannot make disease claims; they can make mechanism of action claims for supplements if they have evidence to support the claims. On the other hand, practitioners do not have these restrictions, although clinicians should always be guided by evidence.)

CONDITIONS AFFECTED BY NUTRACEUTICALS	EXAMPLES*
Adrenal Fatigue	Mixtures of vitamin C, B vitamins, ginseng
General Well-Being	Daily vitamin/mineral combinations
Genetic Predispositions	Folate for methylation
Gut Health	Enzymes, bovine colostrum, butyrate, zinc, probiotics
Hypercholesterolemia	Bergamot, berberine, garlic plant steroids
Hypertension	Nitric oxide
Inflammation	Products with curcumin, garlic, echinacea, fish oils
Laboratory confirmed defficiences	Vitamin D, Iron
Medication induced depletion	Example: CoQ10 for patients on statins
Memory protection	Nootropics, anti-inflammatories
Metabolic Disease	Chromium, alpha lipoic acid
Musculoskeletal/Sarcopenia	Astaxanthin, essential amino acids
Sleep Issues	Glycine, melatonin
Stress	Adaptogens such as ashwagonda, ginseng, rhodiola
Vision Support/Eye Health	Polyphenols, lutein
*For illustration purposes only	

Unlike nutraceuticals, medical foods are specially formulated and intended for the dietary management of a disease that has clear-cut nutritional needs that cannot be met by normal diet alone. Companies that provide medical foods have submitted additional documentation to the FDA to support their claims. While a prescription is not required, they must be dispensed, consumed or administered enterally under the supervision of a physician. Medical foods are not; however, covered by insurance. A number of companies, most notably Metagenics (metagenics.com), produce medical foods for a variety of conditions such as glucose response, compromised gut function, management of dyslipidemia or sarcopenia.

NUTRACEUTICAL COMPANIES by revenue
1. Atrium (Permira)
Pure Encapsulations
Douglas Labs
Seroyal
2. Standard Process/MediHerb
Standard Process
MediHerb
3. Metagenics N.A. (Alticor/Amway)
4. Xymogen
5. Designs for Health
6. Ortho Molecular Products
7. Thorne Research (Helsinn Holdings SA)
8. Integrative Therapeutics (Schwabe)
9. Apex Energetics
10. SFI
ProThera
Klaire
Complementary Prescriptions

Fill Gaps in Your Dispensary with Specialty Products

Most of us are familiar with the large nutraceutical companies. The top ten companies account for almost $1 billion of sales to practitioners,[68] and feature extensive product portfolios from 50 up to 300 SKUS.

There's a lot to be said to filling in your nutraceutical portfolio with what we call specialty nutraceuticals. In general, these are smaller companies that offer a handful of clinically tested products. These companies usually lack the big-time sales and marketing infrastructure, yet their products fill gaps, and often have a greater breadth of studies available on each of their limited SKUs.

Many of these companies are actively recruiting for speakers and key opinion leaders. Here are our top picks in alphabetical order:

- Aethern: This Barcelona-based company produces a liquid daily-shot drink for skin health and beauty. Clinical studies done by Zoe Draelos, MD and Jeffrey Dover, MD confirm positive effects on radiance, hydration and firmness. The product contains readily absorbable collagen peptides, hyaluronic acid, astaxanthin, key minerals, and over 19 phytonutrients.
- Ajinomoto: This 100-year old Japanese company supplies about 60% of the pharmaceutical grade amino acids for US hospitals. Their professional products include Capsiate Gold® a thermogenic aid for weight loss.

- Ambra Bioscience: A San Diego company, they have pioneered the science of gut sensory modulation in which non-nutrient sweeteners and bitters tickle the L-Cells in the lower GI tract to release GLP-1, PYY and oxyntomodulin, the hormones responsible for satiety. The company manufactures a variety of products under the Lovidia® brand.
- AstaMed: They produce AstamedMYO™ a blend of astaxanthin combined with Vitamin D3. The product has been shown effective in clinical studies for sarcopenia.[69]
- MitoQ: The company binds a form of CoQ10, called ubiquinone, to a fat soluble, positively-charged molecule for enhanced mitochondrial penetration. A peer-reviewed study of MitoQ® on hypertension demonstrated a 42% improvement in arterial dilation (equating to a 13% reduction in CVD risk) at six weeks.[70]
- Quicksilver Scientific: Under the leadership of noted scientist Christopher Shade, PhD, the company specializes in detox products and protocols and advanced phospholipid delivery for rapid onset and greater bioavailability
- TA Sciences: The company produces TA-65®, a patented, all-natural product that can help maintain telomere length and rebuilt telomeres through activation of telomerase.[71] The main ingredient is an extract of Astragalus, the root of which has long been used in Chinese medicine.

One company worthy of exploration is MyFormulary (myformulary.com.) This omni-channel retail facing organization helps patients find functional foods, recipes, and restaurant recommendations based upon the patient's unique needs. Consumers/patients enter health-related data into their Efficacy Engine™. The algorithm applies rigorous clinical data to identify efficacious nutrients and then scours their massive product catalogue, recipe database, and/or restaurant menus to provide personalized recommendations. MyFormulary shares revenues with their practitioner partners. Alternatively, the company can provide discounts for patients, or apply a portion of the price to other services.

OXYGEN

With the development of moderately priced, reasonably sized units, physicians can now offer the benefits of hyperbaric oxygen therapy (HBOT) in-office to patients. HBOT enhances the body's natural healing process. It involves inhalation of 100% oxygen in a total body chamber in which the atmospheric pressure is increased and safely controlled throughout treatment. Originally used for decompression sickness, and insurance-reimbursable for many types of wounds, its use as expanded off label to include a diverse assortment of conditions including traumatic brain injury, stroke, migraine, autism, and sports injuries. Oxylife Hyperbarics manufactures a HBOT device with multiple safety features.

PEPTIDES

Peptides are distinguished from proteins based upon size and structure. Traditionally, peptides are defined as molecules that consist of between 2 and 50 amino acids, whereas proteins are made up of 50 or more amino acids. In addition, peptides tend to be less well defined in structure than proteins. They can exist in a number of complex structures.

The use of peptides in the clinical realm is of growing interest for clinicians. These small molecules are finding applications in multiple treatment categories: hormones, exercise, weight loss, arthritis and inflammation, aesthetics, and wound care. There are hundreds of peptides being created in laboratories around the world. Among the more well-known are GHRH/GHRP, AOD, Melanotan 2, PCK-1, and MOTS-c.

Jim LaValle, RPh, CCN and William Seeds, MD currently lead a highly successful, well-attended peptide training program under the auspices of The American Academy of Anti-Aging Medicine. In addition, A4M has partnered with IPS, The International Peptide Society (peptidesociety.org), an excellent resource for more information.

PLATELET-RICH PLASMA (PRP) and PLATELET-RICH FIBRINOGEN (PRF)

PRP

During the past decade, platelet rich plasma (PRP) has been used in orthopedics, plastic surgery, dental practice, and dermatological clinics for its potential in wound healing and tissue regeneration.[72] These various applications have given rise to the use of PRP injections in facial rejuvenation and other aesthetic applications. PRP is a concentrated preparation of the patient's own platelets obtained by centrifugation of blood and extraction. Platelets contain a high concentration of growth factors that encourage cell proliferation, tissue remodeling, angiogenesis, and inflammatory responses. Growth factors include epithelial growth factor (EGF), transforming growth factor (TGF), vascular endothelial growth factor (VEGF), fibroblast growth factor (FGF), platelet-derived growth factor (PDGF) and keratinocyte growth factor (KGF). Once isolated, the platelets are then injected into the areas of concern and/or applied topically following a micro-needling treatment.

PRP represents a relatively new approach in cosmetic procedures.[73] Despite some positive results on studies evaluating PRP injections for facial rejuvenation and alopecia, research supporting PRP for facial aesthetic procedures has limitations.[74] These limitations include lack of standardized PRP preparation and injection techniques.

PRP is currently being used to treat androgenic alopecia, chronic wounds, acne scars, as well as for skin rejuvenation. Depending upon indications, the average patient cost ranges between $600 and $1,800 per treatment. PRP kits manufactured by RegenLab USA LLC and Eclipse are some of the most common class II medical devices FDA approved in the USA. The Amnio Genius PRP device (reviveaestheticdevices.com) is one of the fastest centrifuges on the market, capable of processing a sample in 60 to 90 seconds.

PRF

Widely documented for orthopedics and dental applications, PRF represents a new generation of blood platelet therapies in aesthetics. PRF is prepared the same way as PRP with a few differences. PRF is produced by a slow spin speed and does not require anticoagulants or any other additives making it easy to prepare. PRF contains a greater number of platelets, white blood cells, and growth factors as compared to traditional PRP.[75] Because there is no anticoagulant, fibrinogen molecules can transform into fibrin clots after injection and allow a volume effect. The platelets are retained into the fibrin scaffold and contribute to a slow release of growth factors over time for long-term benefits compared to PRP. The platelets in PRF are thought to survive better than those in PRP, and therefore promote faster healing. The platelet-rich fibrin has been used to fill in facial folds, help fat cells survive better, and promote healing. A representative manufacturer of PRF kits is EZPRF Kit.

REGENERATIVE MEDICINE

This is a broad term that primarily encompasses the use of PRP, bone-derived Mesenchymal Stem Cells (MSCs), the Stromal Vascular Fraction (SVF) of adipose, and amniotic/placental/umbilical tissue. PRP, MSCs and SVF require extraction and preparation. Regenerative treatments in the US are aimed primarily at orthopedic indications.

Bone-Derived MSCs (BDMSC) are extracted from the posterior superior iliac crest, and after centrifugation and separation, are typically injected into joints where they primarily act to downregulate inflammation. Because MSCs are multi-potent, they have the potential to transform into other types of cells in the same lineage, for example, they could transform into a chondrocyte in the knee. There is no evidence that this takes place to any meaningful extent.

Adipose tissue is a richer source of MSCs, as compared to bone. The lipoaspirate, which requires enzymatic separation frowned on by the FDA, contains other cells that can aid in jump starting healing including preadipocytes, endothelial progenitor cells, T cells, B cells, mast cells and macrocytes. The FDA is increasingly viewing the preparation of SVF as going beyond "minimal manipulation," and has concerns as to where the SVF is being injected.

While both BDMSCs and SVF involve living cells, there are also products available from tissue banks (human cell and tissue products, HCT/Ps). These are not living cells, rather they are sources for growth factors and cytokines that aid in wound healing. Placenta, umbilical, and amniotic tissue are commonly used. There is minimal preparation required.

There are many private institutions and academies that train physicians in both stem cell preparation, as well as the proper ultrasound guided joint injection techniques.

SPORTS MEDICINE

Practitioners who make sports medicine a central part of their treatment program often have dedicated staff who have been certified by the American Academy of Sports Medicine, physical therapists, or other certified sports trainers either on staff or associated with the practice. These professionals can conduct a variety of assessments including VO2 Max and resting metabolic rate. Korr is a company that provides equipment for testing both.

SLEEP

Sleep-Disordered Breathing affects 42 million American adults, and 1 in 5 of them have mild to severe Obstructive Sleep Apnea (OSA). As many as 75% of severe OSA cases are never diagnosed, in part because patients do not want to go to a sleep lab and payers are now requiring pre-authorization for sleep lab visits. The field got its jumpstart in 2008 when Medicare agreed to pay for sleep apnea treatment based on a home sleep test (HST), thus opening up reimbursement for HST. For those practitioners wed to insurance, there are now CPT codes available. Home sleep testing is approximately one-quarter the cost of a full polysomnography (PSG) in-lab test. Resources include:

- SleepView, an ultra-compact home sleep device offered by CleveMed. The company supports the practitioner by offering interpretation by a board-certified sleep MD along with treatment recommendations.
- There are also a variety of home testing wristbands that use accelerometers, skin temperature and microphones to break sleep patterns into light, deep, and REM.
- The American Alliance for Healthy Sleep (sleepeducation.org) is a good place to learn more about sleep-treatment options.
- Many practitioners will recommend nutritional aids including blends of magnesium, glycine, theanine, and melatonin to support sleep.

SEXUAL HEALTH

A number of innovative therapies are being directed toward sexual health for both women and men. PRP can be injected into the genitals in both men and women. In women, the procedure is marketed as vaginal rejuvenation. In both men and women, it is tied to sexual performance. Take note that the Orgasm Shot®, O-Shot®, and P-Shot® (Priapus Shot) are registered trademarks and cannot be used without permission.

Erectile Dysfunction (ED) requires a work up to rule out medical reasons such as diabetes. For ED, some physicians offer compounded sublingual Sildenafil or Tadalafil, the advantage being rapid onset. Shock wave therapy provided by the Gainswave (gainswave. com) device is becoming increasingly popular. The procedure is done in-office and only takes 20 minutes.

TELOMERE TESTING

Telomere testing measures current telomere status and can vary in terms of methodology and cost. The challenge is the lack of a reference standard. Telomere assessment is most valuable when done serially so the patient can learn the degree of shortening that takes place over time and how their lifestyle impacts these changes. Diseases, stress, and other factors can shorten telomeres dramatically. Many practitioners use these tests as part of a wake-up call for patients to adopt healthier lifestyle and functional programs.

There are three methods for evaluating telomeres. The first is qPCR (quantitative Polymerase Chain Reaction), used by Spectracell and Teloyears. qPCR only assesses mean telomere length by sample. It does not measure telomeres by cell, let alone by chromosomes. The second method involves flow cytometry. This does allow for mean telomere length by cell, but not by chromosome. The third method is based upon a proprietary technology known as Telomere Analysis Technology®, or TAT®, which is able to quantify and measure telomere length by chromosome. It is available from Life Length (lifelength.com), a company based in Madrid, Spain. Since it is the number of the shortest telomeres, rather than the average ones, that are most predictive of longevity, this test appears to have the greatest clinical relevance. Life Length provides an in-depth report that is available in eleven languages.

WEIGHT MANAGEMENT

This is an offering that really begs having a champion in the practice who is personally familiar with, and enthused about helping patients lose weight. The best champions have themselves struggled with their weight. Assuming you have the clientele and are marketing savvy, you have two choices. The first is to assemble your own offering that may include a combination of nutrition counseling, caloric restriction, ketogenesis, meals, bars and shakes, home delivery, body composition testing (see **B**), safe metabolic-enhancing thermogenic agents, exercise, coaching and counseling, etc. Coachcare (coachcare. com) features an easy to use standalone technology platform that integrates many of the components necessary to manage ongoing communication for better adherence to a weight management program.

A number of companies fill the need for in-office dispensed weight-related products. Among them are:

- **Ideal Protein** offers a medically developed ketogenic weight loss protocol, organized as a four-phase program. They supply a variety of foods including meal replacements that can be offered through practitioners.
- **L-Nutra** offers their Prolon® (prolonpro.com) fasting mimicking diet which provides the health benefits of a five-day fast while allowing patients to enjoy a modicum of food. The program was developed by USC researcher Valter Longo, PhD. While the program emphasizes fat-focused weight loss, patients experience other far reaching benefits including greater focus, clarity and energy; improvements in metabolic health; and the triggering of stem cell-based regeneration. This is

accomplished, in concert with autophagy which is the clean-up of aging and damaged cells.

- **The Whole30® Program** removes potentially inflammatory foods and beverages from the diet and emphasizes three "clean" meals a day, made with Whole30-approved ingredients.

Medically-Oriented Weight Loss

Medical weight loss programs, under the supervision of a physician, take advantage of compounded weight loss supplements to help patients jump start their programs. Wells Pharmacy Network (wellsrx.com), a leader in providing these compounds, offers the following adjuncts to practitioners nationwide:

- **Appetite Suppressant:** to stimulate metabolism and send signals of satiation.
- **Lipotropics/Vitamin Therapies:** vitamins and amino acids used as fat burners for weight management or to provide an energy boost:
  - o B12 injectable (Cyanocobalamin or Methylcobalamin form)
  - o Methionine, Inositol and Choline (MIC) injectables or MIC Combos, with
  - o Vitamin B12 (Cyanocobalamin or Methylcobalamin) L- Carnitine, Chromium, B-Complex
- **Human Chorionic Gonadotropin (hCG):** a hormone used as a weight management alternative. Available lyophilized or as sublingual tablets.
- **Cellulite Cream & Gel:** targeted ingredients for exfoliation and skin tightening.
- **Sermorelin:** a Growth Hormone Releasing Hormone (GHRH) analogue that stimulates the production and release of hormones by the pituitary gland. Sermorelin may improve the body's ability to burn fat and increase energy levels. It is available in lyophilized injectable form as well as troches.

Another approach is to buy into a system that offers the education, training, protocols, marketing support and products. Most are franchise or enrollment models. HealthyhabitsMD (healthyhabitsmd.com) and the Center for Medical Weight Loss are two companies that provide everything you need to develop a successful model.

Y-Lift®

Described as producing results equivalent to a mini-face lift, the Y-Lift was developed by New York-based oral and maxillofacial surgeon Yan Trokel, MD, DDS. It is an educational and training system that teaches practitioners how to strategically inject significant quantities of fillers to shape facial contours, most notably along the jawline. In addition to the training and marketing support, the company passes along significant volume discounts on Allergan and other products to the subscribing practices.

Seven Principles of Success

Launching an ancillary product or service line isn't easy. Perhaps the only "magic formula" is in having the personal resolve and the determination to successfully bring the concept to reality.

Success Principle #1 - Don't underestimate these variables:

- The learning curve *(It's always more involved than you realize.)*
- Time requirements *(Include everyone in your thinking.)*
- Capital requirement *(Include a contingency margin.)*
- Sales skills *(You may need to hire experienced talent.)*
- Marketing budget *(New services will not promote themselves.)*
- Culture shock *(Get everyone on board, aware, and supportive.)*
- Risk *(It can't be eliminated, but it can be minimized.)*
- Competition level *(Assume "the other guy" is smart, aggressive and not a push-over.)*
- Commitment level required *(Too little attention or "afterthought" promotion means DOA.)*

Success Principle #2 – It's a whole new business within your business. Treat your "ancillary" line as an independent business unit with its own goals, plan, budget, operations, resources, training, and support.

Success Principle #3 – Involve the staff early in the game. Share your vision with everyone in the office and inspire enthusiastic team support. Changes in the office routine (and culture) can be unsettling enough to undermine success. Conversely, awareness, training, and win-win compensation can inspire teamwork and create champions.

Success Principle #4 – Invest in proven elective care marketing strategies. Patients are experienced and knowledgeable consumers who respond to benefit-driven marketing. Devise a professional plan that considers:

- Internal marketing *(to leverage your existing patient base)*
- Cross promotion *(to leverage someone else's base)*
- Professional referral marketing *(when possible)*
- External advertising *(to inform and attract new consumers)*
- Publicity *(where free media opportunities exist)*
- Internet visibility *(engaging content and targeted online marketing)*

Success Principle #5 – If you build it, they may not come (without a push). If you're making a big commitment, invest in the marketing to help it succeed. To neglect the proper promotion would be like buying a thoroughbred racehorse and not planning for its care and feeding.

Success Principle #6 – Create products and packages. Consumers—especially informed patients—more easily understand and appreciate benefit-driven "products" versus less tangible "health-aware" concepts. Consumers envision their use of products and services when the deliverables are clearly defined. Consider, for example, how to productize weight loss as a program or package including physical evaluation, hypertension screening, BMI, nutrition and other support facets.

Success Principle #7 – A goal without a plan is just a wish. The successful launch of ancillary—and profitable—products and services requires a well-considered and detailed action plan with measurable goals and specific next steps.

Ancillary products and services can be an invigorating way to "step off the treadmill" without stepping away from your training and experience. What's more, it can become a rewarding path to grow your cash-pay and elective care business. But to have impact—and ultimately to be truly successful—you'll need a serious investment of time for homework, thoughtful planning, devotion of resources and budget—and the effort required to create a new business.

On one hand, it may not be easy…but if it wasn't hard, everyone would do it. And if it's done well, it will be professionally satisfying and financially rewarding.

Chapter

Where Do I Start?

Arguably, the number one factor for success in business is focus. You must decide what is essential to do now, what is nice to do—but can wait—and what to avoid. So, the answer to the question: Where do I start? is… It depends.

It depends on what stage of practice and personal growth you are in. We've gone ahead and noted four stages on our model, along with several of the key action steps that will move you to the next level. Admittedly, the lines between the stages are not hard and fast; our

PERFECTING
Become nationally known
Identify staff training efficiencies
Promote & incent staff
Consider additional locations
Extract more from vendors
Review business plan

GROWING
Carefully attend to key metrics
Focus on staff training
Add ancillary services & products
Ramp up social media
Raise practitioners' profiles
Focus on patient testimonials
Sell more existing services

STARTING
Create business plan
Engage legal, accounting, insurance
Develop website
Obtain space, equipment, products
Hire staff
Get known in community
Determine focus & financing

CONTEMPLATING
Attend conferences
Seek a mentor
Determine revenue model
Decide on services
Mitigate "cons"
Prepare to practice

distinction is a bit arbitrary, mainly for the convenience of discussion. Also, portraying an arrow moving only upward, showing unrelenting progress is a bit misleading. Every practice experiences difficulties and setbacks that slow down forward progress until the necessary corrections are made. In this chapter, we'll be looking more closely at some of the action items from this model. Others will have been covered in previous, or will be discussed in future chapters.

Procrastination Is Not the Same as Contemplation

If you want to change your practice model and embrace a more whole-person healthcare philosophy, it's important to thoughtfully prepare. The problem we have observed is that practitioners can get stuck in the contemplation stage way too long. We've seen hordes of practitioners interested in starting integrative or functional cash-pay practices attend multiple conferences each and every year (a good thing) but fail to put their new-found skills to work. They rationalize their inaction by claiming their knowledge base is insufficient and they require years more training before taking the leap. The reality is that there will always be more to learn. You will never know everything. And, the best way to learn is to do. Gain knowledge and skills in a particular discipline, e.g., gut health, CVD prevention, hormones, basic injectables, skin rejuvenation, or weight management and start utilizing your new approaches in a narrow, but focused fashion. Shilpa P. Saxena, MD, a renowned teacher of functional medicine summarizes the incorporation of new techniques in four simple, self-explanatory steps, "Nail it. Scale it. Milk it. Crush it."

Fear of change, inertia, and lack of confidence immobilize conventional primary care docs, and prevent some specialty physicians from moving ahead with membership models.

Once you've decided to start a new venture, you'll want to prepare to practice. Here are some of the steps to take:

- **Get your email database going.** We recommend you do this about a year in advance of any major move. If you are currently employed, you do not own the patient base; your employer does. However, you can direct patients to your website and blog where you offer education (not competitive services) and note where and when you will be speaking in your community. Have a simple email capture mechanism on your site.
- **Make certain you own the domain of your name.** If you don't, do this NOW, even if you don't have immediate plans for using it. While Mark operates his business through changewell.com, he has also purchased marktagermd.com. If nothing else, it precludes a competitor from taking it.

- **Get known in your community.** Take every opportunity to speak at meetings of all types that feature potential patients or influential referrers. You'll find helpful guidelines for conducting effective talks in Chapter 10: How to Get Noticed, Known & Remembered. Join and attend business-related events such as the Chamber of Commerce or local human resource meetings. See if your local natural food store, place of worship, or children's school would be open to you giving a talk. Write articles for the local free newspaper. Get involved in volunteer efforts, interest groups, and school events. The purpose of this outreach, which often doesn't come easily for tired, often introverted practitioners, is to build your database. You can start off collecting names in a simple Excel worksheet, or move to a database/mailing vendor such as Constant Contact or Mailchimp. If time and energy are limited, consider a surrogate: a spouse, partner, close friend, or potential new business associate, who will attend meetings on your behalf.
- **Always carry your personal business card.** Rather than waste the back side, consider putting a slogan or mission statement that can jumpstart a conversation or remind the recipient of your unique approach.
- **Crystalize your vision.** Here is where mentors can really be helpful. You want to know what is working and what hasn't worked for colleagues in similar spaces. One of the major advantages of attending smaller conferences in your area of interest is the ability to network and learn from speakers and colleagues. You might even ask a colleague you admire from a different locale whether you could visit their practice and shadow them for a moderate fee.

Making the Leap from Thinking to Doing

Just as you would construct your new home on a solid foundation, so too must you provide a solid cornerstone for your business. This cornerstone is a legal framework that will let you sleep well at night. We've reached out to our favorite national and international healthcare attorney, Kristen Montez, JD (globalhealthcarelaw.com) for her top ten legal tips. You'll also find a few war stories to drive home the importance of some key points.

Top Ten Legal Points of Advice
1. **Create the best team.**
   a. Accountant: Your accountant should be well-versed in healthcare practices, including which expenses can be write-offs and employing best business valuation strategies.
   b. Lawyer: Engage a lawyer who supports your business model and vision. You should not be reluctant to ask questions for fear of receiving a bill.

    c.   Insurance Broker: Make your broker your friend. Insurance brokers are on the front line when it comes to lawsuits. They often know what types of lawsuits are being brought before a lawyer will. Have your broker review your consent form, especially if you are practicing integrative medicine. Run business and treatment ideas by your broker. Have him/her confirm in writing (email should be fine) that your specialty, or your new treatment modality is covered by your insurance.

2.   Operate under the appropriate corporate entity.

    a.   While operating as a corporate entity does not shield you from medical malpractice claims, it does protect you and your assets from other liabilities, i.e. medical equipment leases and rental space leases. Your lawyer and accountant should provide you with the best guidance for practice structure (C or S-corporation, LLC, Professional Medical Corporation, Sole proprietor, etc.) based upon State regulations and your personal financial situation.

3.   Have the correct insurance in place. This is another great opportunity to engage your broker for guidance.

    a.   Professional liability (medical malpractice) insurance.*

    b.   General liability insurance.

    c.   Worker's compensation insurance.

According to Ed Kuhn, a liability specialist with WMPG Insurance, "medical professional liability insurance for healthcare practitioners in cash-based, elective procedures is no longer considered high risk. These doctors are now covered in the standard malpractice market. Procedures like HRT and aesthetics have not resulted in any large negligence settlements or judgements. Good coverage at competitive prices is much easier to procure now."

4.   Always create a medical chart—even if you're just giving your friends Botox®!

    a.   The chart must be comprehensive. Document consent, patient phone calls, treatment options, and when patients do not comply or do not show.

    b.   Do not lie in the chart.

War story: *I represented a patient against a dentist who removed twelve of her upper crowns during the initial patient exam. The dentist then removed all nine of her lower crowns two weeks later. Within six months, the crowns were cracking apart and my client developed, among other things, jaw issues. For months, my client returned to the dentist for adjustments. Every time she presented for an adjustment, the dentist would say "left happy." Yet, my client would return one week later with the same complaints. During the deposition, the dentist testified she did not recall the patient having any complaints of the treatment. We settled out of court after her deceitful deposition and false patient chart.*

5. **Always obtain consent.**
   a. Make it your custom and habit to always obtain verbal consent in addition to written consent. Then document verbal consent in the chart.
   b. However, a patient never consents to medical malpractice. Just because a patient "consents" to an experimental procedure, does not absolve you of all potential liability. Therefore, even if you obtain written consent, you must practice within the standards of care of your medical community.
   c. Be confident that your patient has the mental capacity to provide consent.

6. **Maintain patient privacy.**
   a. If you are a cash-pay practice, you may not be subject to HIPAA. However, certain State laws have similar patient privacy requirements even if you are cash-pay. Bottom line: it is just best practices to safeguard your patient's private health information by creating physical, technical and administrative safeguards.

7. **Avoid fraud and abuse.**
   a. When partnering with other healthcare providers, remember this: everything in writing, and nothing for free.
   b. Agreements and relationships should be in writing and at fair market value. Have an attorney review all relationships before finalization.

8. **Understand the legalities of employment.**
   a. Be sure to confirm with your State employment laws before you terminate an employee.

   War Story: *A medical group fired a long-term employee within one hour after she reported to work for the day. They did not pay her for that hour. The ex-employee knew she was legally entitled to that hour of pay. She also knew the state imposed waiting penalties for each day she was not paid, up to 30 days. On day 31, she submitted a demand letter to the medical group for the unpaid one hour and the waiting penalties. She was entitled to the $15.25 (her hourly rate) as well as over $3,000 in waiting time penalties. Had the medical group consulted a lawyer prior to letting her go, they would have avoided the $3,000 fine.*

9. **Leave your practice on the right terms.**

   a. Review your employment agreement with an attorney prior to leaving. You may benefit from a separation agreement. Ask how you should continue your patient relationships based on your employment agreement and your State's laws.

10. **Stay on your licensing board's good side.**

    a. Do not make outlandish marketing claims, e.g. you "cure" incurable conditions. This is a big red flag for licensing boards (and the Federal Trade Commission).

    b. Use Laboratory Developed Tests as support for a comprehensive history and physical examination. Don't rely solely on the tests.

    c. For innovative procedures that are not yet mainstream, have substantial supportive medical literature on hand. Consider getting fellowship-trained in these upcoming, but less broadly acceptable areas, of non-conventional medicine.

Learn the Easy Way from Practitioners Who Have Learned the Hard Way

We have had the pleasure of teaching and training with Rebecca Hunton, MD and her practice manager Lorin Carpenter from Radiantly Healthy (rh-md.com) in Indianola, FL. Hunton brings a unique perspective to her teaching, born of three ingredients: a good number of years in practice, an early background as a CPA, and finally some painful lessons that have led her to create systems for practice efficiencies. We've summarized some of the lessons Hunton and Carpenter have learned along the way:

On Hiring

- Insist on a cover letter. Summarily reject any resumes without one. Reject candidates with typos in their resume.
- Bring candidates in for a working interview. Have a simple contract that allows you to pay them as a 1099 employee (assuming they are compensated less than $600) for a day or two.
- Contract with the employee for a three-week trial period. You want to make certain they are professional and get along well with your team. You should know this after three weeks.
- Hire for attitude. You can always train them or get the necessary training for them.
- Speaking of attitude, be on the alert for entitlement. If you get a whiff of it during the test period, don't hire the person.

- Don't waste time trying to make someone fit.
- Make certain you have an employee manual. You can download generic ones from the Internet and modify accordingly.
- Do a background check. While a background check won't pick up everything, you'll feel really stupid if you miss a major red flag.

On Managing the New Hire
- Give staff the ability to voice their opinion during the trial period.
- Remember, your young children may be your dependents, but your employees should not be.
- Let new hires know they should not mistake your kind and caring demeanor (assuming you have one) for someone who will allow inappropriate behavior to jeopardize the business.

On Space Utilization
- You must know what is making you money versus what is costing money.
- Factor in revenue per square foot and overhead per square foot.
- On a monthly basis, evaluate the return and costs of your space to include:
  - the average monthly payroll
  - payroll per square foot
  - payroll as a percentage of revenue
- Purchase "shiny new objects" with care.
- Beware: If the new things require you to take time away from what you are doing that's making you money, that's not good. Take into account what you are losing on the other end.

On Tracking the Business
- Shoot to keep overhead at less than 40%.
- Hire a new practitioner when you are 30% busier than you want to be.
- Keep close tabs on the basic metrics. These include:
  - Revenue per week and month, compared to previous or last year
  - Payroll/revenue each month
  - New patient enrollment by week and month
  - Number of patient follow-ups
- Overhead is best tracked quarterly as some costs are variable.

Consider Bringing in a Consultant

There are individuals and companies that specialize in setting up practices and improving those that are underperforming. This work almost always requires on-site evaluations and hands-on training. Hunton and Carpenter offer their services to a few very select practices. Other highly-regarded consultants in alphabetical order include:

- Beautiful Forever: This is an aesthetic business consulting service built by Cheryl Whitman. For more than three decades she has helped hospitals, spas, anti-aging centers, and physician practices to achieve dramatic results.

- BeWell Alliance Inc.: This is the brainchild of Toni Lyn Davis who has over 30 years' experience building high-end wellness centers. She specializes in helping clients create and launch "signature programs" that support their brand, as well as provide staff with the tools to monetize them.

- Collabrant Health: This practice development consulting business was created by Tim Patel, who previously performed this service for Cenegenics. Patel has both the knowledge and experience to help practices in the private-pay, concierge, age management, and integrative medicine models.

- FON Consulting: Run by Glen Sabin, FON ("Force of Nature") is the preeminent source for staying abreast of opportunities for growth within integrative medicine. Sabin takes on a limited number of clients. We highly recommend his informative blog on integrative medicine.

- Freedom Practice Consulting: One of the largest firms, Freedom has been used by hundreds of physicians to increase profitability. The company provides an intense and comprehensive curriculum in all facets of practice transformation and improvement. Practices can explore their system during their discovery days.

- Lisa P McDonald: In addition to running Integrative Connections, the IFM job board, McDonald also does consulting to help practices better manage their Human Resource functions.

- Practice on Purpose: This is a consulting business run by Pattie Ptak, with whom we have worked for several years and highly recommend. Ptak personally works with you and your team to create the protocols, systems, and procedures that allow your staff to run your practice efficiently, generate numerous referrals, and give you more personal time and financial freedom.

- Practice Profitability: This is the brainchild of Richard Castellano, MD, also known as "The Smile Doctor." A high-energy, focused, and skilled trainer, Castellano conducts large-scale events for clinicians where he introduces them to his model and tools, and provides an impactful experience. Attendees can follow up with his online coaching and educational programs.

- RejuvMedical: Located in St. Cloud, MN, the company has a consulting arm, as well as hosts an annual conference that draws hundreds of practitioners to learn about their system. Created by Joel Baumgarter, MD the center features a 28,000-sq. foot clinic focusing on reversing chronic disease.

- Shorr Solutions: A father-daughter practice management team with years of experience in the aesthetic world, Shorr specializes in increasing practice profitability. Jay Shorr had been the practice administrator for his wife's South Florida dermatology practice. He was joined in his consulting work by his daughter Mara, following the death of his wife.

How to Successfully Add Ancillary Products & Services

As you grow your practice, you will invariably seek to take on ancillary products and services to grow your top line revenue. No matter which new products and services you decide to adopt, you'll want to answer the following:

- Is there sufficient market demand for this? Speak with business owners in practices similar to yours and make certain the products/services are profitable, efficacious, well received by patients, and safe.
- Are your patients asking for these products or services?
- Are these products and services directed toward your existing patients, or designed to attract different types of patients?
- How important is it for you to be an early adopter in your market and to capitalize on first mover advantage? Or would you rather wait till the product or service is more well established?
- What's the current level of competition? Consider the number of competitors, their skill level, and their apparent commitment.
- Does the opportunity support your business and personal objectives?
- Do you have (or can acquire) the requisite skills? Delivering new services may require additional clinical, sales, business, or other capabilities.
- What's the learning curve and do you have time for it?
- Who will be doing the actual work? If you need to hire, what skill sets are required?
- Are you and your staff able—and willing—to sell the product or service?
- What are the capital requirements?
- How much additional marketing support (and budget) is required?
- Will you feel comfortable with the risk of a new endeavor?
- How important is this to you? What is the priority and the timetable?

- Will this be cash or reimbursable? How does that impact cash flow?
- If you decide to bring in a product or service, to what extent can you count on the vendor to help you market the product?
- For the costlier products, have you spoken with your accountant re: IRS Section 179, and explored the monthly leasing cost?
- Do you have the space for your new product?

Invest in People

At the most basic level, each one of us who is employed, has a giving-getting contract in our minds and hearts. We give a modicum of our effort, enthusiasm, skills, and commitment, but what do we want in return? If you answered, "money," you are only partially correct. Money does motivate people, but it is definitely not the only motivator. All the studies on motivation can be summed up by a simple statement, "What motivates people is what motivates people." In other words, there are many motivators. As a leader, or a boss, the key to performance is to identify subordinate's motivators. This varies both personally and generationally. Millennials seem to want two things—to grow their skillset and to have more control over their time. When faced with the choice between time off and money, many younger employees will opt for the free time. Other employees will value tangible evidence of accomplishment, plaques, gift cards, or better parking spaces.

One of the most dominant motivators for the driven, high-performance employee (and really all employees) is obtaining feedback. Not just the "atta boy" or "atta girl" kind, but feedback that is specific, timely, and more positive than negative. The best bosses strive to catch employees doing something right and praise them on the spot. Employees also want to know that their work makes a difference and they are contributing to a larger mission of helping people get well and stay healthy.

The best incentives are team incentives. This requires that the practice owner share goals and some key metrics with the team. As your staff become increasing competent and confident in their roles, they should have more say in decision making. You can also groom them to take on additional responsibility.

Become Nationally/Internationally Known

We encounter many practitioners who run successful businesses, but who also have larger aspirations. Not content to just be well known and recognized in their local communities, they want to take their knowledge and experience and share it on a national or international stage. This is often the time at which they start considering public relations (PR). It is also the time that a host of questions start to surface:

- Do I need to hire an agency?
- What can I do myself?
- What do PR agencies really do?
- Is it worth the money?
- How do I evaluate their results?

We asked Nancy Trent, of Trent & Company, Inc. (trentandcompany.com) to weigh in on these questions. Trent notes that public relations is the key to getting more media coverage. In addition to generating more business, PR can:

- Allow you to charge more for your business
- Pre-sell your services to patients and minimize the sales cycle
- Help your patients sell your services to their friends
- Attract the very best sales staff
- Generate more research requests
- Become a platform to sell your books, research, endorsements, products, or equipment.

Trent notes that starting a PR campaign can be challenging and exciting for a medical practice, but it can generate great results if it is strategically planned.

Whether you decide to hire an agency, or not, there are many things that you can do yourself to boost your media presence.

1. **Develop your news instinct.** You'll want to stay on top of the current health-related stories to see if and how you might contribute.
2. **Create a local media list.** Have your staff scan for contacts in the media that reach your audience. You can grab the names of the editors, producers and contributors from websites, mastheads or social media. Some websites will have calendars of topics they feature throughout the year, so see which months apply to you.
3. **Develop a press kit.** This is simpler than it seems. You should pull together your background information, biography, fact sheets and story ideas, along with images for editors, reporters and producers. Include any statistics, case studies, photography and video that can be used for "b-roll" for TV. You can use this to approach local journalists, which we will discuss in greater detail in the next chapter.
4. **Get media trained.** There are many local resources for this. Media training is different from speaker training. It is more focused on how you portray your brand, and how to respond to interviewer's questions.

5. **Leverage up your major suppliers.** See what they might be able to offer in terms of co-op money or other resources. If you are a big customer, they might work hard to keep you happy. Plus, your success is theirs as well.

What to Look for in a PR Agency

It is important to distinguish between effort and results. You want results. This means placement in the outlets that will help grow your business. The challenge is that developing a PR strategy implementation plan does take time, and has an associated cost of someone's time, energy and experience. Ideally, you might be able to arrange to lower the monthly fees and replace some of their monthly retainer with bonuses, based upon success. For example, placement on a national TV show, or in a national publication would trigger the bonus. Most agencies will insist on a minimum six-month commitment.

If you have the time and energy, you can send out a Request for Proposal, and meet with a handful of agencies. If you want to go national, then take a trip to New York City or Los Angeles. Let these agencies pitch you. Look eyeball to eyeball with the person who is responsible for your account. How senior or junior are they? Who will be assigned to your team? What is the plan? How often will you be hearing from them? What else do they need from you? What is a reasonably good measure of success they think they can obtain for you?

Good, strategically placed PR, delivered by a professional agency with a strong track record in your space, can help you enhance your presence and take your talents to a larger audience.

We'll discuss the concept of presence in detail in Chapter 10: How to Get Noticed, Known & Remembered, specifically detailing how to give better presentations both live and on video. To conclude this chapter, we will address the question that practitioners who have well-functioning businesses often ask us:

Should I Write a Book?

There comes a point in the lives of many healthcare professionals when they decide they need a book. They believe they have a story to tell. Or they hope, as many of the marketing gurus note, that a book will help get them "out there." For those who have success on the speaking circuit, it's a great feeling to autograph your book so attendees can take a little piece of you home with them. A quick word of caution: please do not entertain the notion that you will get wealthy with your book. At best, you may make a modest amount and at worst, you will have the equivalent of an upgraded business card or company brochure.

Driven by technology, book writing, publishing, and distribution is easier than ever before. Once the purview of large, primarily East Coast publishers, self-publishing and self-promotion is an expedient way to move your ideas into words, and your words into pages. But, if you retain the hope of having a major publisher produce and distribute your work, there are a few things you should know.

- You will need to retain an agent and produce a book proposal that outlines why the book is perfect for the market; why you are the ideal author; why you can and do write well; and why you will be wildly successful in helping the publisher get the book widely known. The book proposal will include the book outline and one or two sample chapters. In addition to receiving a percentage for putting the deal together, your agent may also get a percentage of your speaking fees.

- If you don't have a solid database of approximately 100,000 names in your mailing list, a large social media following, and a track record of speaking at major conferences, or otherwise being distinguished, chances are good that a publisher will not be interested.

- It will usually take about 18 months from the time you submit your manuscript for the book to come out. This depends on timing for the fall and spring seasons.

- Major publishers place their promotion bets on the books for which they have provided major advances. They pick a few potential winners and put dollars behind them.

- Depending upon your negotiations, you will purchase your own book at between 40-50% off retail price. The publishers are counting on you to drive promotion and sales.

- The advantage of a major publisher is the possibility of getting an advance against royalties which you can also use to hire any resources you might need to get the book completed. Don't count on receiving any monies beyond the advance.

Getting a major publisher to accept your work is like getting into a great fraternity at an Ivy League college; however, it's no guarantee of success. Just as many non-fraternity, non-Ivy league graduates succeed equally well based upon skills and perseverance. In the book world, this is the path of self-publishing.

How to Write & Self-Publish a Book

This is Mark's tenth book, three of which were done with major publishers, and seven, including this book were self-published. Many would-be authors think that writing is a creative endeavor. If you are writing health-related non-fiction, it's 5% inspiration and 95% perspiration. It takes time, energy, and mastery of the writing process, something that doesn't always come easily. Let's start with how to write a book. Here are some of Mark's tips:

1. **Create an Engaging Title.** This is harder than it seems. You want to visualize your readers and see if you can come up with a title that will pique their interest. Short and snappy is better than long and tedious.

2. **Overcome Writer's Block with—Dare I Say it— "Diarrhea."** Every writer gets stuck from time to time. Every writer prematurely judges his or her work way too early. My answer is diarrhea. Just get the words out of your brain and through your fingers or mouth (dictation) onto your document. Write in phrases, partial sentences, and jump around as ideas come to you. Don't feel the need to organize or prioritize, or even create finished prose. Get in the habit of jotting down book ideas as they come to you.

3. **Dictate and Polish Later.** I am fortunate in that I took a typing class in 8th grade, and it has served me remarkably well. I like to see the words on the page as I write. Many people are much better at dictating their thoughts. In fact, if you are ever called upon to give a talk remotely on the subject of your book, audiotape it on your mobile phone. Then upload it to an automated transcription service called Temi (temi.com) and you will have your audio converted into text in minutes. This will help you get started. The current price is $6/hour. You can also upload videos for transcription.

4. **Start Generating the Organizing Principle for the Book.** This is where Stewart and I have somewhat different styles. I don't feel the need to have the organizing principle for the book in place before I start writing. Why? Experience has told me that I will most likely reorganize the outline a half dozen times before landing on the final one. I keep producing chunks of content and move them around as I progress through the manuscript. Stewart is more linear and keeps pushing for the final outline. I like to think of this as dynamic tension.

5. **Bring Your Main Points to Light.** This is where most first-time authors fall down. They usually write a me-centered stream of consciousness, highlighting only their first-person experience and how events affected them. If you are the Dali Lama, the Pope, a famous rock star, or a top fashion designer, this can work. Or, if you have gone through a transformational experience that is so profound that you believe you can hold the reader's attention for 40,000-60,000 words (120-240 pages, depending upon type size, leading and margins), then go for it. For the rest of us, a better approach is to consider how to bring our key points to life. You can do this by mixing things up: interweave a personal story (keep it short, and focused) with a statistic, an interview with an authority, a quote, a graph, a chart, or a picture.

6. **Get Writing Help.** In 1979, I typed (on a manual typewriter with carbon paper) a double-spaced 400-page manuscript entitled "Growing Older Gracefully" cataloging my work teaching yoga and tai chi to seniors. I sent the manuscript to a friend who was a book agent. He pulled out 26 pages he thought "might make it." He had drawn big red diagonal lines across the remainder. How and where do you get writing help? I started working with and learning from my first co-author Charles Jennings who wrote for a local magazine. Later on, I took a few classes. Don't have time for classes? Don't know a writer? Simple, do what I do now. Go online with your local or national university and post that you have a writing intern position available. Note that you are looking for an English or Creative Writing major; or if your work is more research oriented, select an intern in a health-related discipline such as public health, neuroscience, or behavioral sciences. Ask to see writing samples. You should be able to hire someone for $15-$20 an hour.

7. **Seek the Services of the Professionals.** Even if you have the ability to put together a decent manuscript, the work is far from over. You have to get your book designed, laid out, proofed, illustrated, and put into the appropriate formats for paper and electronic editions. Then you need a strategy to launch the book, and generate a good buzz. This is where you need professional help. This is in fact, where Stewart and I sought professional assistance.

We turned to Doug Crowe (dougcrowe.com) who has built a unique team over the years. Doug offers a "100% done for you" service (authoryourbrand.com) where he takes your ideas and unique voice, and captures it in a series of journalistic interviews. He then edits, publishes, launches, and markets your book for you… so you can run your business. We engaged Doug after completing the manuscript and turned to him for design, layout and help getting the book printed and put into an electronic version. Doug's company has successfully launched over two hundred #1 Best Sellers on Amazon, so we hope we'll be counted in this number. His promotion process is somewhat counter-intuitive. He works in reverse by first building a community of readers before creating the book, therefore assuring a solid launch. He offers a free eBook on the steps involved which can be found at https://storyselling.me.

Moving into Marketing

At this point, we hope you have achieved a measure of clarity: where you want to put your clinical focus, the products and services to integrate into your offerings, and the reimbursement model that's right for you. With this in mind, it's time to turn to the tools you need to get noticed, known, and remembered. This begins with strategic marketing.

PART 2

Practice Enhancement

CHAPTER

HOW TO PROFIT FROM SCIENTIFIC MARKETING

After working with thousands of doctors and other practitioners over the years, we understand you likely have some burning questions and misconceptions surrounding the subject of private practice marketing. In this chapter, we will answer your most pressing questions and set the record straight once and for all.

Let's start with the two biggest fears that prevent many doctors from even trying marketing—the fear of hurting their reputation and the fear of losing money.

"Won't marketing make me look cheesy, needy, greedy, or sleazy?"

Things have certainly changed a lot since 1993 when I (Stewart) first began teaching doctors how to market their practices. Healthcare, technology, insurance reimbursement, competition, and healthcare business models have, of course, entirely changed.

However, one thing that hasn't changed for many doctors is the nagging fear that marketing would ruin their otherwise stellar reputation. After all, "Isn't marketing just for *bad doctors who need patients?*"

We understand your concern. Ethics have a proper and special place in healthcare, dating all the way back to Hippocrates. What's more, doctor marketing was actually illegal in the US until the 1977 Supreme Court case Bates v. State Bar of Arizona. Today, while younger doctors often embrace marketing, many Baby Boomer doctors still express reservations (or outright hostility) toward the entire topic.

To be clear, you *could* damage your reputation by resorting to cheesy or misleading marketing. We strongly advise you to steer clear from going down that path. However, the

155

good news is that you can actually *enhance* your reputation through compelling, ethical marketing.

Moreover, bad doctors aren't the only ones who market.

What do Mayo Clinic, Cleveland Clinic and MD Anderson have in common? Of course, they are among the most clinically respected healthcare providers in the world. However, in case you haven't noticed, they are also among the savviest and most aggressive marketers in healthcare. Their highly sophisticated marketing executives lead teams of professional marketers to promote their respective institutions. While we are not privy to the specifics of their multi-million marketing budgets, Spyfu.com estimates each spends the following pay-per-click advertising budgets just to drive more traffic to their respective websites ALONE.

Pay-Per-Click Advertising Budgets

MayoClinic.org $148,000 per month ($1.78 million annualized)
MDAnderson.org $79,800 per month ($957,600 annualized)
ClevelandClinic.org $153,000 per month ($1.83 million annualized)

Source: SpyFu.com, August 5, 2018

Of course, each institution's overall marketing budgets are far greater. Clearly, the world has changed and respected institutions (and practices) *do* market.

So, it's not a question of whether healthcare marketing is inherently good or evil. It is all in how you do it. And yes, you can actually improve your reputation with *effective* marketing while attracting the patients you want.

"Isn't marketing a total waste of money?"

You may be surprised to learn we categorically agree: Yes, it is possible to lose a ton of money on ill-conceived, improperly executed marketing. The most common cause? Spaghetti marketing. That's where you throw a bunch of stuff up against the wall to see if anything sticks.

However, it is also possible to make a lot of money by following scientific, evidence-based marketing methods. In our seminars, I (Stewart) reference our model, the *Scientific Method of Marketing.* Follow this model to minimize financial risk and optimize your chances of success.

1. Proven Strategies

The idea of learning from the experience of others should be self-evident. After all, you didn't start treating patients until you had successfully completed years of education and training based upon the experience of countless practitioners before you. So, when it comes to marketing, it certainly makes sense to understand what has worked for others in the past.

Practitioners face a nearly infinite number of potential marketing choices. While many ideas have a near zero chance of producing a trackable, positive return on investment, others work over and over again. Some of our favorite best-practices marketing strategies (which we will expand upon later) include paid search advertising, paid social media, doctor referral building, patient referral building, phone skills, and direct response advertising.

2. Marketing Plan

We'll provide you the instructions you need to create an effective marketing plan later in this chapter.

3. Effective Implementation

When you launch your marketing plan you'll need to consider the following:

- While you as the practitioner should probably lead the effort, who should coordinate the details, and how will you hold them accountable?
- Who will do the creative work?
- Who will buy your media?
- How will you handle marketing approvals? Hint: marketing by committee does not work. Everyone seems to have an opinion about marketing, including employees, partners, spouses, friends, and the person who cleans up the office. Resist the temptation to listen to them, or else your marketing will default to the least common denominator and grind to a halt.
- How will you track results?
- What is your timeline? How will you make adjustments over time?

4. Evaluate Results

This is arguably the most crucial step. To maximize your return on investment, you'll need to test, track results and adjust.

Some tips:

- Today, technology exists so you can track every single phone call to your practice. The secret is to use unique, "tracking phone numbers." These local or 800#s will be used only in specific ads, so you will know the source of each inquiry. All kinds of data will be captured, including caller ID, time of day, length of call, and even outcome.
- Similarly, website calls and form fills can be rigorously tracked, so that you will know the source of all web leads.
- You also have the option to record phone calls from your marketing. The greeting must say, "This call may be recorded for quality assurance," and the recordings must stay in a HIPAA-protected platform.
- Based on your tracking and the "marketing math" outlined on th following pages, you will be able to estimate the return on investment for each campaign.
- Over time you will "double down" on the winners, and cut out the losers. That's how you optimize your ROI.
- Better still, with experience you can create ongoing marketing systems that work.

Profit from Marketing Math 101

The following variables define the success of any given marketing effort:

- How much money did you invest?
- How many people inquired as a result?
- Of those, how many came in for a first appointment?
- Of those, how many converted into paying patients?
- What was the average revenue per patient?

Let's take for example marketing strategy X.

Investment: $10,000
Number of inquiries: 100
Number of first visits: 40
Number of new patients: 25
Average case size: $2,000

Note: Because you will often need to make marketing decisions quickly, we recommend you calculate the "average case size" for your most important service lines. This is the total average revenue you will collect during the first year from patients. Take the records of patients who have been with you for a one-year period and do the math. Remember, case size is not your office visit fee. We often treat the money patients spend in subsequent years, along with their referrals to others, as "gravy." Thus, the case size is a very conservative measure from which to calculate return on investment (ROI).

Was that a successful marketing effort? Well, let's do the math.

- $10,000 / 100 inquiries = $100 per inquiry
- 40 visits from 100 inquiries = 40% phone conversion rate*
- $10,000 / 40 visits = $250 per visit
- 25 new patients from 40 visits = 62.5% sales conversion rate*
- $10,000 / 25 new patients = $400 per new patient

*Implement staff training to improve both of these metrics over time

"$400 per new patient? That's outlandish, right? How can I ever spend that much money?" But wait, you forgot to calculate the ROI.

- 25 new patients x $2,000 = $50,000!
- $50,000/ $10,000 = 5:1 ROI

We love 5:1 ROIs. We like 3:1 ROIs. We are ecstatic about 20:1 ROIs. We don't like 0.01:1 ROIs.

"Wait, what about overhead?"

In most private practices, the vast majority of costs are fixed. Within reasonable limits, your big costs like salaries, rent, utilities, device leases, and the like are stable each month. The variable costs are easily identifiable and can be factored in. So, even a 2:1 ROI is usually worth doing as it profitably builds up your patient base.

How to Create Your Marketing Plan

"Ugh. Do I really have to write (or get) a marketing plan?" No, you only need a marketing plan if you want to be successful!

But let's clarify something. By marketing plan, we don't mean an academic exercise. We also don't advocate spending $100,000 with one of the big consultancies to receive a 100+ page technical document. Rather, we mean a well-thought-out roadmap to promote your services ethically and effectively. It can be as short as 3-5 handwritten pages if it is well-thought-out. (Unless of course you want to raise capital, in which case you will need a more formal document.)

Your marketing plan should typically include the following sections: Objectives, Budget, Target Audience, SWOT Analysis, Competition, Positioning and Key Strategies. The rest of this chapter will provide insights and instructions to writing a successful plan.

Your Objectives

This is the most critical section of your marketing plan. We encourage you to open your laptop or take out a piece of paper now to do some brainstorming. Don't worry about getting your objectives 100% right yet. Start by answering the following questions:
- What would be your ideal mix of cash versus insurance-based cases?
- Do you want more patients, better-paying cases, or both?
- Which service lines do you want to promote? Approximately what percentage of overall revenue will be attributed to each?

- What is your conservative overall revenue trend for the next 12 months? (Most people confuse this number with their goal, which is the next step. Beware of assuming too much "natural" growth.)
- What do you want your gross revenues to be over the next twelve months (compared to the trend)? Therefore, about how many new patients will you need for each service line?
- Do you want to create a "brand" where most people in your city or town know your practice's name?
- Do you need to match or exceed the marketing from (aggressive) competitors?
- Do you have specific providers, locations, or technologies that you'd like to promote?
- Would you like to become a recognized leader in your field?
- Would you like to increase your doctor referrals?
- Would you like more referrals from existing patients?
- Would you like more patients from the Internet?
- Do you want to enhance your reputation?
- Would you prefer to work less?
- What else would you like to do with your time over the next 12, 24 and 36 months?

Next, start separating your initial thoughts into goals and objectives. Remember: goals are usually long range and broader, e.g., "I want my practice to become THE premier provider of facial aesthetics in my town." Or, "I want to help our patients build a healthy brain." Or perhaps, "We help people with autoimmune diseases live better lives."

Objectives are more specific. They break your goals down into concrete steps. Whenever possible, make your objectives SMART.

Specific. Be very clear what needs to be achieved.
Measurable. How much revenue? How many patients?
Achievable. Make sure your goals are realistic; otherwise you are likely to quickly lose heart and stop.
Relevant. Are your goals relevant to your deeper values?
Time-bound. What are your deadlines? One, two, or three years?

Here are some sample objectives:
- Generate $2,000,000 gross revenue in the coming fiscal year.
- Bring in an additional $500,000 in cash business over the next 12 months, breaking down approximately into 1/3 laser hair removal, 1/3 tattoo removal, and 1/3 injectables.

- Grow Dr. Smith's practice to the point where it is profitable by year-end.
- Grow new patient volume in our Springfield office from 100 new patients per month to 200 new patients per month.
- Generate 100 new patients from the Internet each month.
- Generate at least $15,000 a month from CoolSculpting®.
- Generate $100,000 in new, recurring revenue this year.

From these numbers, you can break down your objectives into smaller Key Performance Indicators (KPIs) if you like. For example, if you want 100 new patients a month from the Internet, depending upon how effective your staff is, you will likely need at least twice that number of phone inquiries per month (200 inquiries).

Also, while SMART objectives are crucial, you may want to mix in a few broader goals too. Inspirational goals can keep you motivated. After all, you need to know "Why am I doing this?"

Why You Must Grow Your Practice to Survive Ever-Increasing Competition

Healthcare used to be a fragmented industry, populated with countless small providers who were artificially protected from the rigors of competition in the marketplace due to regulations, generous insurance reimbursements, a "clubby" healthcare culture, and the difficulty consumers faced (pre-Internet) in comparing providers.

"Competition" was a word rarely heard in polite company within the healthcare community. You didn't have competitors. You had colleagues. Almost all doctors and other healthcare providers were single practitioners. Virtually no one spent any real money on marketing, and nobody had a recognizable brand. Few doctors thought much about attracting cash or elective cases, either.

Today, of course, everything has changed. Healthcare (like other industries) is consolidating at an astonishing rate. Practices have become groups which have become supergroups. Hospitals are buying insurance plans and vice versa. Meanwhile, private equity companies are now rolling up hundreds of private practices. Well-funded retailers like CVS and Walgreens have stormed into primary care. Finally, business-savvy practitioners have learned the marketing game, built local brands, and often "own" their market.

If you want to foretell the future for your specialty, you only have to look at the cautionary tale of LASIK (laser-assisted in situ keratomileusis). I (Stewart) began my healthcare marketing career back when LASIK was just getting started. Most of the ophthalmologists I met then were understandably conservative about embracing the then radical new technology. I distinctly remember conversations that included, "I will try it out with a few patients," "I don't want to spend much money on marketing," and "I am going to share a laser with some other doctors to keep my costs down."

Meanwhile, a tiny percentage of more forward-thinking ophthalmologists understood the incredible business opportunity LASIK presented and told me that they were willing to "go for it." These "renegade" doctors embraced marketing long before others even knew what was happening. To understand what happened next, let's take a moment for a brief lesson in economics.

The Pareto Principle

In 1896, Vilfredo Pareto published a theory which became known as the Pareto Principle, or the 80/20 rule. Pareto noticed that in Italy (and other countries) 80% of the wealth was held by the richest 20% of the families. What's more, the top 4% of families (20% of 20%) held about 2/3 of the wealth (80% of 80%), and the top 1% of families (20% of 20% of 20%) held about HALF the wealth (80% of 80% of 80%).

This "law of the vital few" is extremely powerful and applies to many facets of life. For example, the top 20% of insurance salespeople sell 80% of insurance policies. The top 20% of beer drinkers consume 80% of the beer sold. The top 20% of your referring doctors almost certainly generate 80% of your doctor referrals (we'll talk more about that later). And, 20% of your employees likely cause 80% of your employee problems. In the United States, the top 20% of families enjoy 80% of the wealth, and the top 1% control half the wealth.

So, what happened when a few ophthalmologists "broke rank" from their colleagues and began marketing? These ophthalmologists tapped into a huge pent-up demand and were able to command $6,000 for a surgery that lasted only a few minutes for both eyes. LASIK was so profitable that the savviest doctors immediately began marketing more aggressively and refining their operations.

Flash forward a year later, and let's pretend two excellent ophthalmologists were competing for LASIK cases in your town. One was conservative and performed only 20 surgeries last year. The other was aggressive and completed 1,000 cases. Ask yourself:

- Which doctor has the most marketing experience?
- Which doctor has built up a huge base of satisfied patients who can make referrals?
- Which doctor earned $6,000,000 from LASIK procedures in a single year?
- Which doctor can afford to spend even more on marketing?

- Which doctor has built an enviable brand as THE leading LASIK provider in town?
- Which doctor has the most experience doing LASIK surgeries?
- Which doctor would you likely see? (Be honest, these are your eyes we are talking about. One doctor has done 1,000 cases, the other 20.)

Did you notice the darker side of the Pareto Principle? If 20% of doctors win 80% of the cases, that means the lower 80% are left to fight for only 20% of the pie. In case you are wondering whether this phenomenon still holds up today, you will notice in most cities, a handful of ophthalmologists have created strong brand names and dominate the LASIK market. I can also tell you that a few years ago I (Stewart) spoke at of the annual meeting for the American Academy of Ophthalmology and asked a crowd of about 200 people, "How many of you are doing a meaningful number of LASIK cases each year?" About five surgeons raised their hands.

Maybe your specialty will not evolve in the same way, but remember, graduate and undergraduate business courses are replete with case studies of fragmented industries which eventually became consolidated into the hands of a few "superpowers." Think cars, cell phones, computers, retailers, movie studios… The list goes on.

What should you do? Develop a winning mindset and, if you haven't already, start marketing. We aren't asking you to take foolish risks. Rather, we are recommending that you learn from this book (and other sources), dip your toes in the water, and eventually get in. If you follow the principles outlined in this book, you will minimize your risks and maximize your opportunities.

Of course, doing nothing is still an option. It just isn't a good one.

How to Define Your Marketing Budget

Hopefully you are excited by the goals and objectives that you just set for yourself. That's a good thing. Now we have to talk about spending money. (Are your good feelings beginning to fade?)

Before we define your marketing budget, let's set the record straight on one of the most essential concepts in this book:

Marketing is an INVESTMENT, not a cost center.

Private practice is typically an economically challenging service business, and one of the keys to success is minimizing expenses. Why would you pay more than you have to for gloves, electricity, rent, tongue depressors, tables, chairs, etc.? Every dollar wasted is a dollar less profit for you.

Marketing, on the other hand, is an investment. When it works, it generates more money than you put into it. We promise that marketing is a lot more fun when you receive a profitable return. When you invest $1 and it returns $3, you will likely want to try that again. Spend a little more to make more. When you find a real winner, you just may want to spend a lot more.

Establishing a Marketing Budget

You'll want to first come up with an annual marketing budget. You can break the annual budget down into specific strategies and tactics later. How do you calculate a marketing budget? It turns out there are a variety of ways, some being better than others. You can also combine methods, similar to how real estate appraisers value houses with the Sales Comparison Approach, the Income Approach, and the Cost Approach.

1. **SWAG Budget** (aka Strategic, Wild-Ass Guess). This is the method most practices use to come up with their budgets. We do not recommend the SWAG budgeting method, nor its closely related cousins the, "How much do I want to spend?" budget and the "How much did we spend last year?" budget.

2. **Competitive Spending.** If you are working with an ad agency, ask their media buyer to review your competitors' advertising. Through his or her media relationships and various proprietary third-party services, your media buyer should be able to give you a sense of your competitors' advertising spend including estimated budget, media choices, audience reach, and ad frequency. More sophisticated marketers (including some hospitals) also hire marketing research firms to quantify brand awareness and loyalty among the various players in the marketplace. You can also estimate how much your competitors are spending on pay-per-click advertising by referencing Spyfu.com. Once you have data, you can determine competitive budgeting goals. For example, do you want to outspend your competitors and if so, by how much? Or, do you want to build your brand awareness to the point where it eclipses your competitors? As you probably have guessed, the competitive spending approach is generally most appropriate for providers with expert advisors and larger budgets.

3. **Equity Protection Budget.** Many practices have little reoccurring revenue (e.g., surgeons, tattoo removal, hair restoration) and therefore need to rebuild their patient base every year. Other highly successful practices recognize they have a lot to lose, and therefore want to invest in marketing not so much to grow, but to protect what they already have. We'd argue these practices should invest a certain percentage of revenues to ensure long-term viability.

4. **Percentage of Sales Budget.** This is still widely used by Corporate America, although this method is certainly not without its flaws. Consider the premise: How much you spend is determined by how much you make…which is determined by how much you spend….which is determined by how much you make. It is a paradox with no independent variable. Also, there is no single percentage-of-sales figure that applies to all circumstances. A new, small, consumer direct healthcare provider (like a medspa) could easily spend 15% of sales on marketing or more. A $30 million, doctor referral-based gastroenterology group in a smaller market could do a lot of excellent marketing with a 2% budget. Of course, we understand that you still want a range, so without knowing the specifics of your practice, goals, market, services, competitive situation, patient base, etc., many practice marketing budgets fall between 5% and 10%.

5. **Return-On-Investment Budget.** ROI-based budgeting is based upon where you want to go, versus where you have been. Let's say Doctor A wants $1 million in real growth over next year but is only willing to invest $10,000 to achieve it. He has a small practice, few referrals, and no marketing experience. Hmmm… he is betting on a 100:1 ROI. Yeah, good luck on that. Meanwhile, Doctor B is more realistic. Her practice already brings in several million in annual revenue, enjoys a good reputation, garners many professional referrals, and through successful marketing has built a brand. Based upon some of Doctor B's past marketing experiences, she hopes to achieve somewhere from a 3:1 to 5:1 ROI on marketing. Doing some quick math, $1 million in growth divided by an estimated 4:1 ROI goal divided by 12 months would roughly be $20,000 per month. If that budget turned out to be beyond her comfort zone, she would simply cut the budget and likewise reduce her goal.

Most of the above methods have their merits, and every practice situation is unique. Marketing, like virtually any meaningful activity, has risk. However, we'd argue your choice to own a private practice in the 21st century is an even bigger risk. Doing nothing is perhaps the biggest risk!

Whatever budget you choose, be sure to come up with a number you can live with for the entire year. While you need to be realistic, a lot of doctors need some urging to "think a little bigger." What's more, just like a jet requires twice as much thrust to get airborne as it does to stay there, your marketing needs a certain critical minimum budget for it to become airborne at all.

Have you come up with a number, even if you feel a bit tentative? Great. Let's proceed. (Don't worry, you can always come back to this section later with a more conservative goal and budget.)

How to Choose Your Target Audience

Another essential concept in marketing is to recognize that your practice is not for everyone. While it sounds counter-intuitive, you will be far more successful by focusing your efforts on the subset of the population who will be most inclined to appreciate what you do and pay for it, while virtually ignoring those who are not the right fit. Put another way, if you try to be "everything to everybody," you will be "essential to nobody."

You can start by reviewing the demographics of your area. Start by simply going online and searching your town name(s) combined with the word "demographics." From there, you can easily create demographic profiles such as "married women, between 35 and 55, with household incomes of over $75,000 per year."

To go a step further, you can utilize our favorite free online tool for US-based practices, i.e., the Zip Code lookup tool by Claritas.[76] Start by entering the zip code for your office(s), and then expand to neighboring relevant zip codes. Beyond the typical age, race, language and income data, Claritas' Prizm breaks the entire United States down into 68 "clusters." Clusters have cute, descriptive names ranging from "Upper Crust," to "Kids & Cul-de-Sacs," to "Pickup Patriarchs," to "New Melting Pot."

Carefully read the descriptions for each of the top 5 clusters for each of your primary zip codes, and choose the ones that best fit. From there, along with your experience, you can create "personas" to guide your marketing efforts. Personas go beyond mere demographics by adding "psychographic" or lifestyle traits into the mix. We recommend you add stock photos and descriptive names to help you create "real people" that your marketing will speak to.

For example, "Brooklyn Beth" is white, female, and 30. Though engaged, she and her fiancé both tell her mother that they are "far too busy to get married." A registered Democrat, Beth lives in Brooklyn and commutes via subway to the "City" for her marketing director job at an insurance company. Beth earns over $90,000 per year and spends money on personal luxuries like massages, spin classes, handbags, fine dining and cosmetics. Her expensive tastes and urban location cause her to secretly worry about money. She would benefit greatly from financing her elective care.

"Suburban Ally" is 47, Jewish, married, lives in Connecticut, volunteers, and has two teenage daughters who keep her extremely busy. Ally loves commuting into Manhattan for just about everything, including

her healthcare. However, lately she feels unfulfilled by conventional medicine. She chose her doctor in part because she is a woman, but feels dissatisfied with the amount of time she receives from her. Ally complains that she hurts and feels tired all the time, but her doctor only tells her, "that's just a normal part of aging."

Can you see how personas can help you focus your efforts? We recommend you develop 3-5 key personas, based upon your experience with patients and the types of people who live in your community. This is a fun exercise to do with your staff.

Also very important, Do not overlook the opportunities within your own patient base. How many patients do you have that might want your elective or cash services? Which patients are likely to make referrals to you?

Perform a SWOT Analysis

A SWOT analysis is a classic business tool that can help you evaluate your "Positioning" in the marketplace (more on that later). SWOT stands for Strengths, Weaknesses, Opportunities, and Threats. Let's begin.

Strengths - What are the strengths of your practice? For example:
- Board certified doctor(s)
- 15 years' experience
- Great bedside manner
- (Mostly) friendly staff
- Easy parking
- Central location

168

Weaknesses - What are the weaknesses within your practice? Examples might include:

- No coordinated marketing efforts or marketing budget
- "Curmudgeonly" office manager who is in over her head
- New to the specific cash procedures you want to promote
- Poor online reviews
- Poor search engine optimization
- Outdated website that doesn't represent the quality of care you can provide
- No way for patients to communicate with you online
- Run late often (always?)
- Poor case conversion (sales) skills for elective care
- Limited hours, e.g. open only 9 to 12 and 2 to 5 pm on weekdays, closed weekends
- Outdated building, inside and out
- Lots of staff turnover
- Front desk is poor at converting inquiries to new patients

Opportunities and Threats are often (though not always) external to the practice. These are things you cannot control. Examples include:

Opportunities

- Breakthrough technology
- A competitor is retiring or giving up and leaving town
- No one in your marketplace is doing a good job at online marketing
- A physician liaison could boost doctor referrals for medically necessary cases
- Extenders could increase your bandwidth
- Growth in a nearby neighborhood

Threats

- A new, marketing-savvy competitor arrives on the scene
- Private equity roll ups
- Your primary hospital has a new CEO who wants to take your most important services in-house
- Changes in the economy
- Decreasing insurance reimbursements
- Increasing regulations
- A patient has a terrible (and public) outcome
- Three competitors buy precisely the same six-figure aesthetic device you just purchased
- Regulatory changes

Evaluate Your Competition

Chances are you already know who your primary competitors are, but when was the last time you seriously studied your competition's marketing efforts?

Take some time now to Google various keyword phrases for the services you want to provide. You will likely find that some names come up over and over again, while others are nearly invisible. Take note of who shows up at the top in the pay-per-click ads, who shows up in the "map pack," and who shows up in the organic search results.

In Chapter 8: How to Get Patients from the Internet, we'll tell you more about how to evaluate their search engine positioning and websites, but for now, jot down some notes about your first impressions. As objectively as possible, determine who (from a patient's point of view) looks like a leader, and who doesn't. Remember, patients do not have the same insider's viewpoint that you do.

Write a bulleted summary of each of your major competitors in your marketing plan. To the best of your knowledge, rate their strengths and weaknesses regarding patient experience, clinical skills, customer service, marketing prowess, search engine positioning, website, pricing, online and offline advertising, etc.

Positioning: What Makes Your Practice Special

Marketers define positioning as "the position in the mind of the consumer that your practice occupies relative to competitors."

We define your positioning as the answer to "Why you?" Why should the patient choose you over anyone else? Put another way, "What is the one thing you want people to remember about you, if they can only remember one thing?"

Your positioning statement needs to be:

1. **True.** This should of course, go without saying. Don't say you're convenient if you're not. Don't say you're board certified if you're not. Don't say you're friendly if you're not.

2. **Differentiating.** How are your services different than your competitors? If you find this question difficult, take heart. Even elite packaged good marketers struggle with this issue. After all, how would you differentiate a new product in a mature and highly similar category like sodas, coffee, toilet paper, or detergent? A bit of

good news: even if your prospective positioning is similar to what a competitor could say—but isn't—you could seize the positioning first and aggressively. Then, if they were ever to try and duplicate your positioning, it would look like a copycat effort.

3. **Memorable.** If your positioning is hard to remember, it will be hard to promote.

4. **Compelling.** It is possible for a positioning to be true, differentiating and memorable, but not persuasive. For example, you could be the only left-handed surgeon in town, but so what?

Once you have defined a positioning, you may want to hire a creative person or agency to refine that positioning into a tagline. Similar to a slogan, a tagline "tags along with your logo." Remember however, that a positioning is not synonymous with a tagline. The tagline translates the positioning in a consumer-friendly way.

For example, while many dentists hate this, consumers strongly prefer dentists who are gentle. If a dentist were practicing in an area where none of her competitors were effectively saying "gentle," she could move aggressively to own that positioning. However, the "G-word" is bland, generic, and certainly overused in dentistry.

So, word crafters might translate the "gentle" positioning into a tagline like "Whisper soft dentistry." The next step would be to hire an attorney to see if the proposed tagline is legally defendable in your state, as well as investigate legal options like getting a sales mark or trademark. You can also do a quick online screening yourself by going to the United States Patent & Trademark Office (uspto.gov).

Your positioning will also be the unifying theme of all your branding efforts (more on that later).

The 6 Vital Marketing Strategies

Now that we have done all the prerequisite homework, it is finally time to start choosing the strategies that will make up the core of your marketing plan. Before we go any further, know that there are six—and only six—marketing strategies pertinent to your healthcare practice.

1. Branding
2. Doctor Referral Building

3. Traditional Advertising
4. Public Relations
5. Patient Experience *
6. Digital Marketing *

* Note: because patient experience and digital marketing are so important to your success, we are going to explore those topics separately in the following three chapters.

Each of those six categories contains a nearly infinite number of options. We will summarize those strategies which are generally the most effective for most practices.

#1. BRANDING

Is your logo the same thing as your brand?

If you are not sure, don't feel bad. A lot of marketers confuse branding with a practice's logo, fonts, graphic design, and colors. Those things are part of your brand identity. The brand identity represents your brand and is only a portion of your brand.

Regarding logos, there are several things to remember. First, do not let the creation of your logo become a never-ending project. We've seen practitioners fret for years before finally settling on a logo. Second, it's okay that your logo will never become famous like Nike's design-based logo. You don't recognize Nike's logo because it is so good or creative. Instead, you recognize their logo because Nike invests over $3 billion a year on marketing.[77]

Since we can safely move forward with the assumption that a $3 billion annual marketing budget is out of reach for your private practice, we will instead recommend that you hire a graphic designer and create a marketing-based logo. A marketing-based logo includes the practice name, a unique visual element, and the aforementioned tagline which "tags along with the logo" and summarizes your positioning.

Also, we usually recommend providers create a unique practice name rather than the use the founding doctor's name, though there are exceptions to the rule. Here are some thoughts regarding both approaches:

Unique Practice Name
- Strive to come up with a memorable name
- Can include a benefit or keyword in the name
- Be careful to not chose a generic name that is too similar to competitors' names

- While geographic identifiers can be beneficial in the beginning, they can handcuff you if you expand into new regions
- Generally requires an attorney to make sure your practice name is both properly registered and defendable

Doctor's Name
- No need to trademark, but make sure you claim the URL for your name
- May be unique and easy to remember (or not)
- Difficult for competitors to copy
- Can capitalize on a strong professional reputation
- Could be turned into a "method," e.g., the Smith Method
- Has no inherent benefit to people who don't know you
- Recruiting could be more difficult, as new providers may not want to appear subservient to the founder

The Many Facets of Your Brand

Your brand is the sum of the experiences that people have with your practice. While the positioning statement is a rational argument, your brand is your larger reputation, and more emotional.

Your brand includes things like the cumulative effect of all of your past marketing; your professional reputation; your doctor and staff manner; patient outcomes; how people dress; whether there is litter in the parking lot; length of wait times; convenience; office decor; how patients are treated on the phone and in person; sick people in the waiting rooms; blood on the floor (yes, we've seen this); and more. Most practices already possess some form of a brand. It is just that some brands are far stronger and more favorable than others.

Here are some of the benefits of having a brand:

- People know you have something to lose, so they trust a brand more.
- People are more likely to try a brand they have heard of.
- People are willing to pay more for a brand.
- Your brand creates real value that you can sell someday.
- Having a brand makes it easier to attract top talent.

What makes this topic exciting is that you can actively shape your brand by design, rather than leaving your brand (reputation) to luck and happenstance. Most importantly, you need to start building your brand by delivering a superior and consistent product. Far too many doctors and amateur marketers jump into promotion before they have created a great product. That's a costly mistake, because all the great promotion in the world won't help if you don't have the right product, which is largely comprised of the patient's experience (see Chapter 7: How to Create the Ultimate Patient Experience).

Once your product is ready, you should weave your brand through all your marketing efforts (ads, your website, brochure, collateral, etc.). Your thoughtful, purposeful marketing campaign will then enhance your reputation with patients, doctors, and (over time) the public.

#2. DOCTOR REFERRAL BUILDING

Professional referrals are often associated with primary care doctors referring medically necessary, insurance-based cases to medical specialists. However, all kinds of cash-based healthcare practitioners can enjoy referrals from like-minded professionals.

For example, a hair restoration practice could court hair salons, retailers, gyms and even noncompetitive medspas. We've met chiropractors who do an excellent job getting referrals from MDs by positioning their practices as a conservative treatment for chronic back pain. Integrative medicine MDs generate referrals from like-minded alternative care practitioners, rheumatologists, and endocrinologists. Physical therapists in direct access states can woo referrals from fitness instructors.

Still, while some practices do an excellent job of building doctor referrals, many others do not. The following are some of our favorite secrets to building and growing professional referrals.

- **The surprising secret to winning more doctor referrals.** When it comes to doctor referrals, while critical, clinical competence is typically presumed. What's more, differences between providers are often difficult for referring doctors to judge. We can summarize the surprisingly vital secret ingredient to your professional referral success in one word: relationships. People refer to people they like, people they trust, people they believe are competent, and people they think are successful.

- **How to build powerful (and profitable) relationships.** If you are serious about growing doctor referrals, you will need to commit to a *long-term series of positive, consistent contacts.* There are countless ways to do that, but some of the most well-known include informal "drop-bys," provider-to-provider meetings, referral seminars, CME courses, lunch and learns, holiday gifts, and case studies. When you constantly bring value to your referral sources you'll be perceived as a *partner,* not a *pest.*

- **Prioritize your list**. Start by auditing the number of referrals and corresponding dollar values from your referring base. Check both by individual doctors and by practice. Some practice management software programs are better at reporting this data than others, but make sure you follow through on this step even if you have to do it manually. We suggest the following categorizations:

  - **A Referrers:** These are the 20% of doctors who refer you 80% of your doctor referrals. Take excellent care of them.

  - **B Referrers:** These are people who already refer to you, but have the potential to become "As."

  - **C Referrers:** These doctors have the potential for growth, but are not currently referring.

  - **D Referrers:** These doctors could refer from time to time, but are unlikely to ever become big referrers due to their hospital affiliations, existing relationships, insurance plans, geographic location, or specialty. That said, they are still worth touching periodically; for example, via occasional letters or emails.

- **Remember to protect your most essential referral sources first!** Make sure you secure your A referrers first, before worrying about building up the Bs and Cs. If your best referral sources are important to you, we guarantee they'd be important to your competitors. What's more, given today's highly competitive environment someone else is probably already whispering in their ear.

- **Referring doctors' staffs often hold the real power.** In the real world, referring doctors' staffs yield an incredible amount of unofficial power over referral patterns. When I (Stewart) speak to this concept at our live seminars, I usually hear a nervous giggle from some of the staff in the audience. After an awkward silence, an office manager or referral coordinator typically gets up the courage to admit something like, "Nobody who is rude to us gets *our* referrals."

Referring doctors often want to be fair and ask staff to split referrals among a shortlist of trusted doctors. But in the real world, patients often ask, "Which one is best?" The coordinator whispers, "Well all of these doctors are capable, but this one over here is *really nice.*"

Exactly Who Is Going to Do All of This?

While some doctors are excellent at building their own relationships, for most, the idea is simply impractical. Maybe 1% of doctors have the aptitude for it, and of those, few are willing and able to devote the time and energy required to lead the charge on referral building. Most doctors will tell you, "I am just way too busy," or "I became a doctor so that I don't have to be a salesperson."

For the 99% of you who are unwilling or unable to build doctor referrals, we recommend you consider investing in one or more physician liaisons. This concept is not new. Hospitals have been using physician liaisons for years, and liaisons are now pretty common in a lot of medical specialties including radiology, orthopedics, and oncology.

Here are some best practices to get you started:

- Determine who will serve as your physician liaison. While it would be a home run if you already have an existing employee with both the time and ability to act as your physician liaison, that almost never happens. Therefore, you will likely have to recruit someone from the outside. Remember that while clinical skills are beneficial, sales skills are even more critical. If you have to choose between the two, err on the side of sales experience. (Hint: While former drug reps seem like the obvious choice, they often do not work out.)

- Before you begin recruiting, write a detailed job description that outlines the qualifications, duties, expectations, and objectives of the position.

- Make sure you hire at the right level and invest enough money into the position to be successful. You are looking for someone who has the rare ability to influence both doctors and their staffs. Remember: Corporate America is willing to pay a great deal for people who can do that.

- Avoid the incredibly common mistake of asking your physician liaison to also handle your marketing communications. Marketing and sales involve entirely different skill sets. You are setting your liaison up to fail if you ignore our advice here.

- Make sure you manage and oversee your liaison. Make sure your liaison has a goal for every meeting. Build communication over time. Track progress. The liaison's goal should be to build relationships and protect your loyalists, encourage "splitters" to refer more, and convince non-referrers to try you.

- Be sure to arm your liaison with powerful brochures and collateral that will compare favorably with your competitors' efforts.

Use a Database

Your physician liaison should use a Customer Relationship Management (CRM) program to keep track of her efforts. There are many choices out there, including Sugar, Salesforce and Marketware. Designed for physician liaisons, Marketware offers premium options including claims data from CMS and commercial insurers. Using that data, you and your physician liaison could see precisely who is referring to whom in your marketplace, and by how much.

#3. TRADITIONAL ADVERTISING

While it may seem that doctor advertising is everywhere, the reality is that only a small percentage of practitioners dare to regularly advertise in traditional media. Many practitioners have never even tried because they assume the effort would be an expensive failure. Others fear advertising would reflect poorly on their professional reputation. Still others may have once tried an ad or two in the newspaper, but "headed for the hills" when their nascent efforts were not immediate, runaway successes.

On the other hand, some practices blindly invest a great deal of money into external advertising, without any evidence at all that their efforts are working.

Despite all the confusion, a tiny number of the savvy practitioners quietly clean up through smart, science-based advertising. Given the right circumstances, consumer-direct traditional advertising has the potential to grow your practice, build your reputation, and profitably bring you new patients.

What Makes for Great Advertising Creative?

While each medium brings with it its own unique characteristics, some common elements are critical to success in all of them. There are infinite numbers of variables, but here are some of the most important for traditional (and digital) marketing.

- **You are not the target audience.** If you create ads according to your own tastes and knowledge, your advertising is certain to fail before you even begin. Whenever a doctor tells us, "Well I wouldn't respond to that ad," we remind them, "You have had countless years of education, training, and apprenticeship. The average patient had one semester of health class in the eighth grade. Patients look at things entirely differently than you do."

- **Sell from the heart, not the head.** While practitioners like to focus on making compelling rational arguments, that's just not how patients buy. Patients buy emotionally and then justify rationally. While your ads need to appeal to both sides of the brain, emotions trump rational thought. On that note, many types of emotional appeals can work, including vanity, sex appeal, fear, social acceptance, empathy, fear of loss, and pain.

- **Copy is king.** In 1906, one of advertising's pioneers John E. Kennedy said famously, "Advertising is salesmanship in print." While the public and amateur marketers notice design the most, the under-appreciated copy (words) does most of the heavy lifting when it comes to persuasion.

- **KISS your copy.** When it comes to copy, keep it simple. Long flowery prose and multi-syllable words are guaranteed to fail. Show off your fantastic vocabulary and advanced literary composition techniques elsewhere. What does work are things like:
    - Short words, short sentences and short paragraphs
    - Easy to read copy
    - Simple vocabulary (8th grade level)
    - Active voice (not passive)
    - White space
    - Strong benefits
    - Calls to action
    - Urgency
    - Bullet points

- **Design.** While we just expounded on the virtues of great copy, that doesn't mean design is not essential. Great design is attractive, builds the right image, captures attention immediately, and strategically controls eye flow.

- **Offers.** Offers are designed to give consumers a low-risk, time-limited incentive to act now. Examples include a free seminar, a free consultation, a discounted entry-level service, etc. Offers are fundamental to direct response, which is the school of advertising focused on getting people to take action, (as compared to name awareness or building a brand). Direct marketers sometimes joke about the three rules of direct response marketing, i.e.,

  1. Always use an offer.
  2. Always use an offer.
  3. When an offer seems difficult or impossible, see rule #1.

Consider engaging a media buyer.

If you are buying media on a minimal basis, it is fine to purchase from the media outlet directly. However, if you are purchasing substantial amounts of media, you really should consider hiring an ad agency or independent media buyer. That's because a qualified media buyer will:

- Represent your interest, not the media's.
- Recommend a media mix that is strategic, based upon your market's unique media characteristics.
- Do all the legwork of planning, buying, auditing, billing, and reporting.
- Negotiate better rates, packages, and added value incentives.
- Analyze and compare the Cost Per Thousand (CPM) of various media choices. Choosing media with a lower CPMs will statistically translate to higher ROIs.
- Correlate spikes in website traffic with broadcast media spots to demonstrate the impact of traditional media on digital marketing, and better represent the true ROI.
- The best part? The media buyers' 15% commission is typically paid by the media, and their negotiations should actually save you money.

Which Media Options Are Best for You?

Newspaper

While newspaper advertising remains popular with inexperienced advertisers, most practitioners should simply pass. Still, there are exceptions. For example, while the Internet has hit newspapers hard in recent years, some potential patients (mainly seniors) read the newspaper daily, and will likely continue for life. What's more, some newspapers allow advertisers to target select audiences very precisely.

If you are considering newspapers, you have a variety of options. First, there is usually a metropolitan newspaper which offers varying days of the week, sections and geographic zones. There are also specialty papers, like free family newspapers, free weekend newspapers, niche papers (e.g., Jewish, Korean), weekly community newspapers, regional editions of USA Today, and college newspapers.

Magazines

Here are some of your options:

- **City magazines.** These are the prestige glossy magazines that you see at the checkout counter at the grocery store. In our experience, they work best for cosmetic and other high-ticket advertisers who are willing to commit to a large ad every month.
- **In-flight magazines.** These can work, but would only make sense to test this market if you (1) Offer high-end services that people would travel for; (2) Your practice is located in the magazine's hub city; and (3) You are an experienced marketer, willing to take financial risks.
- **Regional editions of national magazines.** These may offer limited opportunities, but are generally for experienced marketers. Fewer and fewer publications are offering this option due to declining circulations.

Outdoor (Including Billboards)

Outdoor advertising (also known as out-of-home advertising) primarily consists of billboards, but also includes movie theater screens, bus station shelters, benches, ads in taxis, pharmacy bags, subway stations, moving billboards on trucks, and bus wraps.

Billboards may be worth considering when branding or name awareness are the goals. Billboards are also good at supporting other more direct response media as an added layer. While billboards usually require a substantial investment ($3,000-$10,000+ per four-week period), they can be inexpensive on a cost per exposure basis. Of course, one big limitation is that you only have room for about seven words on a billboard.

Radio

Broadcast advertising (TV and radio) typically requires sizable investments, yet can be very cost effective on a cost per exposure basis and a return-on-investment basis. Let's start with radio:

- Length of spots: Can be 15-seconds, 30-seconds, 60-seconds or even 120 seconds.
- Repetition works: We recommend at least 60 exposures per month per station.
- Flights: We recommend running in flights, e.g., two weeks on, two weeks off.
- Formats: The format should be consistent with your ideal demographics. You can choose from stations that emphasize sports, talk, cool jazz, soft hits, pop, classical, NPR and more.
- Radio remotes can build interest for special events.

Television

While many doctors fear TV, it is often our big gun of choice. It can work incredibly well under the right circumstances.

- TV options include network affiliates and cable.
  - Usually with network TV, we recommend buying spots based on specific programs.
  - Cable viewership tends to be highest in the evening. Usually you would buy combinations of networks, depending upon your target audience (e.g., Bravo, E!, Hallmark Channel).
  - From an ROI point of view, network will usually out pull cable.
- Length of Spots: Can be 15-seconds, 30-seconds, 60-seconds, 120 seconds or even half hour infomercials.
- Repetition: Like radio, we usually recommend at least 60 exposures per month per station.
- Flights: Like radio, we often recommend running in flights, e.g., two weeks on, two weeks off.
- Production for TV is more complicated. Sometimes you can ask the station to do a simple voice over and graphics spot, maybe adding in B-roll. The trouble is, the stations are not healthcare marketing experts, so your spots may prove ineffective or come across as cheesy. Because consumer expectations are high with

TV, when possible we recommend hiring an expert help to write and produce the commercials.

Yellow Pages

A couple of decades ago, the Yellow Pages were highly profitable for some specialties, including dentists and veterinarians. Today, of course, most prospective patients skip the Yellow Pages and go straight to the Internet. Unless you have a healthy budget, target seniors, and can negotiate guarantees from the publisher, you should usually invest elsewhere.

Direct Mail

The most significant advantage of direct mail is that you can rent a mailing list and target precisely the people you want. You can select names based upon various criteria, including age, sex, estimated income, race, and geography (down to the neighborhood level). You can also mail to new movers, opt-in "ailment lists," and your patient base (so long as you remain HIPAA-compliant).

You can mail direct mail in an envelope, as a postcard, or even as a self-mailer. Surprisingly, lots of copy usually works well in direct mail. "The more you tell, the more you sell."

The biggest downside of direct mail is its cost. Traditional all-in costs for direct mail (creative, printing, envelopes, mailing costs and especially postage) range from a minimum of 50 cents per person to over a dollar.

Co-op direct mail (like Val-Pak) offers advertisers the chance to target prospective patients much less expensively, generally about 5¢ per person. So, depending upon the zone, you might be able to target 10,000 households for only $500. Most doctors dismiss Val-Pak and similar advertising offerings as cheesy. However, from an economic perspective, co-ops can sometimes make sense. If your response rate was only 1/10 of 1% (10 inquiries), and half of those became patients (5), that means your cost per new patient would only be $100 each. Depending upon the specialty, co-op offerings can be highly profitable, even if the ads feel a little low brow.

#4 PUBLIC RELATIONS

This is the last of the six Vital Marketing Strategies we will discuss in this chapter. PR includes:

- Publicity and media relations
- Community events
- Crisis management

- Shareholder and stakeholder communications (large institutions including hospitals)
- Employee communications (large institutions like hospitals)

In Chapter 5: Where Do I Start?, PR expert Nancy Trent shared some great advice regarding how to use public relations to become nationally or even internationally known. For our purposes here, we are going to share some additional ideas for publicity, community events and also touch on crisis management.

Publicity

What exactly is publicity? Publicity usually means working to get favorable free press coverage. You can easily distinguish publicity from advertising by whether you have to pay for it. If the newspaper writes a story about your practice for free, that's publicity. If they charge you to run the same article, it is advertising.

Here are some publicity tips:

- To get publicity, you'll need to pitch an idea to the press that is newsworthy! Reporters are skeptical and 100% disinterested about helping your business. Rather, they are focused on reporting news that is helpful to their readers, viewers, or listeners.
- Healthcare is a category that reporters like to cover because human interest stories, tearjerkers, and new technologies often get attention. Sometimes you can make yourself available as an expert resource, and then translate a national news story into what that means, "Here in River City." In addition to topical health issues, there are always classic storylines such as managing holiday stress, diet tips, sun protection, etc. and you can always pitch your unique approach to these topics.

  - You cannot control publicity.
  - Reporters may not even speak with you at all, and even if they do, they have no obligation to cover your story.
  - A reporter may ask your opinion on something you are excited about, but then find five other experts who say you are not only wrong but on the verge of malpractice.
  - Reporters sometimes get the facts wrong.
  - Some reporters act as if they were Woodward and Bernstein, and approach every interview with thinly veiled hostility. "Tell me, how many people have died from this new procedure…"

- You can do some research to find and approach local reporters yourself. Send an email or press release to whoever covers the health beat. However, if you are committed to a long-term strategy to garner press, you should consider finding a professional publicist. Rates vary of course, but professional publicists usually require a monthly retainer starting around $4,000 per month.
- Over time, press coverage can build your reputation, especially with patients but also within the healthcare community. Make sure you leverage your publicity wins in your marketing. For example, you could create a press page on your website or include a video of your best television interview on your home page.

Community Events

Some practices and a lot of hospitals like to participate in community events. Most are free or can be sponsored at low cost. If you are looking to attract patients from community events, you'll want to follow these tips:

- Prioritize events based upon location, likely attendance, and especially your interests. Only support events you legitimately care about. The experience will be better for you, and your passion will come through in the marketing.
- Make sure you have great signage.
- Make sure one or more doctors attend.
- Ensure there are friendly, outgoing staff in your booth to engage passersby.
- Try to have something interesting and eye catching in the booth. One of our clients had great success at a community event by featuring an EMG and a sign that said, "Discover the hidden cause of your back pain." As a result, some people stood in line for up to an hour to get a free exam.
- Make an offer when possible.
- Encourage patients to stop by, through word of mouth, posters, flyers and emails.
- Take lots of pictures for social media.
- Set appointments with a calendar book or iPad.

One of the best approaches to getting known in your community is to take every opportunity to give talks and seminars. We've devoted the better part of Chapter 10: How to Get Noticed, Known & Remembered to providing you with tips to become a more compelling speaker.

Crisis Management

Large institutions like hospitals should plan ahead for crises. Hopefully you will never have to deal with an ugly news crisis in your practice, but if you do, consult with your attorney and also find a qualified PR crisis management specialist. Jay Geer (MillerGeer.com) is a PR specialist who does a lot of this kind of work.

Read the Following Chapters, Then Be Sure to Complete Your Marketing Plan

In this chapter, we explained how to follow the Scientific Method of Marketing to reduce your risk. We also provided you with a blueprint to create a marketing plan. Finally, we have covered four of the six essential healthcare marketing strategies, i.e., branding, doctor referral building, advertising, and publicity.

Because they are so important, patient experience and digital marketing (including social media) are covered at length in the following three chapters. The final chapter includes additional advice on how to build your professional presence.

As you read the remaining chapters, be sure to include all the appropriate recommendations into your marketing plan. When you are finished with the first draft of your plan, we recommend you go back and reread everything you have written to make sure it all makes sense together. If not, make appropriate revisions.

Your marketing plan is your roadmap for your successful future, for the next year, and beyond. While you need to stay committed to the results, be open to necessary changes that may arise.

If you don't have time to create a marketing plan yourself, or if you need help creating one, be sure to seek out expert advice. In any event, remember, your marketing plan is a key component of your success. Your bottom line is worth the effort.

CHAPTER

HOW TO CREATE THE ULTIMATE PATIENT EXPERIENCE

A Journey in Time

What is the Patient Experience? It is their (not your) perception of how you represent your brand at every touchpoint in their dealings with you. It's the feeling they get from your advertising and website; the friendliness and helpfulness of the person answering the phone; the quality of your signage and lighting in your parking lot; the encounter with your front desk staff; the time spent in your reception room; the cleanliness of your facilities; the quality of your consult; and the competence and caring of everyone who interacts with them on their way back to their car. It is a gestalt phenomenon.

The patient experience comprises a multitude of small, but meaningful impressions that come together to help the patient answer the final question of every survey: Would you recommend this practice to your friends and family? We're here to help make certain the answer to this question is affirmative. To do this, we will not just emphasize what you should do, but more importantly, we'll examine the gaps where you are losing patients due to flaws in your process, and yes, your people. The good news is these leaks can be plugged. Doing so improves both patient satisfaction and practice profitability. To begin our journey, we will introduce you to the Conversion Cascade, a concept that Mark developed with noted Toronto-based plastic surgeon Stephen Mulholland, MD.[78]

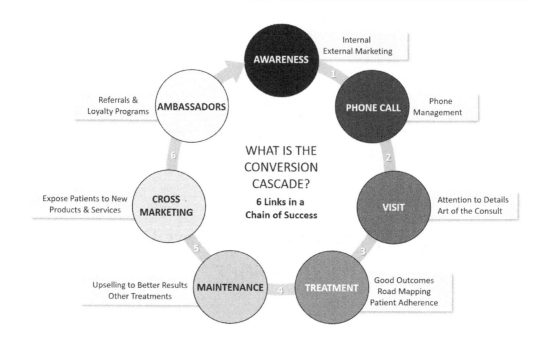

The Conversion Cascade

There are six links in a chain of success that begin with the patient becoming aware of you and your services. They are shown on the diagram above in which your great marketing and word of mouth entices prospects to contact the practice. You convert the phone call (and increasingly online scheduling) into a visit. You use the phone or text message to make certain the patient keeps the appointment. When the patient shows up, the office is as presentable as possible; so too are the staff. You "wow" the patient with your great diagnostic, educational, and treatment skills as well as the personalized, caring service of the entire team. You craft a treatment plan that lays out the frequency of visits and the adherence regimen. You provide a mechanism for patients to continue communication with your office between visits. When the patient comes back for follow-up visits, you introduce additional appropriate services and products. You routinely ask the satisfied patients to give you an online testimonial, perhaps shooting a video right in the office, or you inquire about referrals. You do something really nice for the 20%, or sometimes 10% of patients who make up 80-90% of your revenue.

Sounds simple, right?

By the way, you track and monitor conversion at every step of the way. This means you know:

- How many calls/online inquiries you received each day/week, and their source
- What percent of calls turned into visits

- What percent of visits turned into treatments
- The average treatment price patients paid
- The number of times the patient came for treatment
- The sales performance of your staff
- Who, by name, are your most important patients and what you've done to show them some love

Your business suffers whenever there is an interruption, leak, or hang up in the smooth flow between the steps. We have identified six major gaps that break the chain of involvement: bad branding, the leaky phone, the callous consult, the compliance conundrum, lack of selling skills, and fear of asking for testimonials and referrals. We'll address how to close these gaps as we go forward.

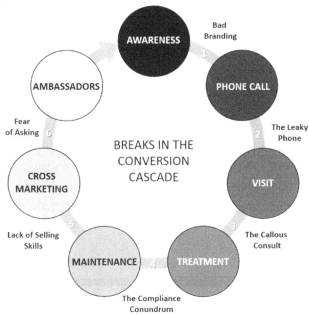

It All Begins with Getting Noticed

A prospective patient may learn of your services by word of mouth. Increasingly, however, your online presence and the strength of your brand play a key role in the first step on conversion.

Awareness → Call/Contact

Even with the most glowing referral recommendations in hand, today's prospective patient is going to check out your web presence. This will certainly include a perusal of your website. It may also include a glimpse at your Facebook Page or Instagram, or a quick look at your LinkedIn profile. Their investigation may also include checking you out on the popular rating sites such as Vitals, RateMDs, or Yelp. Your website is an opportunity to establish your brand in the consumer's mind and heart. It should help distinguish your services and set you apart from the competition.

It is at this stage that "bad branding" and poor marketing planning and execution can eat up your dollars and yield poor results. We'll have lots more to say about this because this topic is so important. We've devoted two entire chapters to digital marketing beginning with Chapter 8: How to Get Patients from the Internet, followed by Chapter 9: How to Make Social Media Work for You. The goal of your entire marketing effort, whether based on traditional advertising media, digital media, or a combination is designed to encourage the patient to contact your office by phone or online scheduling.

Call → Visit

The Leaky Phone

About 90% of the practices we come across do an abysmal job handling their incoming calls. Whenever we "mystery shop" doctors' practices, our patient experience typically begins with "Doctor's office, please hold." This is followed by transfers to nowhere, long wait times, being forgotten altogether, or hung up on by obviously harried receptionists. We often get polite but confused responses, rude responses, or even the front desk person's diagnosis. What's more, virtually no one asks us if we'd like to make an appointment.

Remember when new patients call your office, it is their first experience interacting with your practice. Beyond what callers say verbally, they are judging your practice and looking for clues about how they will be treated if they decide to come in. For example, if your receptionist seems harried and unfocused, the caller may conclude your practice must be harried and unfocused. The caller will then decide whether or not to come, primarily based upon this first critical encounter.

Worse yet, poor phone experiences aren't just a customer service problem. They are an incredibly expensive problem. Here's why:

Say for example, a given practice is investing $5,000 a month on marketing, and that the marketing generates 50 qualified new patient inquiries ($100 per inquiry). Because the front desk staff has never been trained on how to deal with these calls, they will lose half of them unnecessarily due to lack of skill, apathy, being closed at lunch, a misunderstanding of the importance of callers, etc.

You could argue that they wasted half of their $60,000 annual marketing budget, which equates to $30,000, and that's undoubtedly expensive. The trouble is, this cost is minuscule compared to the real loss, which is the opportunity cost.

Let's say the average case size for this practice is a modest $2,000. Twenty-five lost calls per month times 12 months times $2,000 equals $600,000 in lost opportunity!

Poor phone skills can quietly kill a great marketing program and even cause a practice to fail. The seemingly unimportant task of handling new patient inquiries turns out to be one of the most critical success factors in your marketing plan.

So why do most practices do such a terrible job handling phone inquiries?

- Because practice owners usually underestimate the importance of the position, they tend to hire inexperienced, poorly paid people.
- Team members are rarely trained on phone skills and how to deal with new patient inquiries.
- Phone problems can compound when a "communication gap" occurs between a millennial employee and the practice's older patients.
- Let's face it, even with training not everyone should be on the phone. When practices make a mistake, they often are utterly oblivious to the problem and fail to correct it
- Finally, practices often set their receptionists up to fail by giving them too many competing tasks, e.g., data entry, filing, checking people in and out, etc. When that happens, overwhelmed receptionists tend to become very efficient at getting patients off the phone as quickly as possible.

Please note that new patients who find you from your marketing efforts or from the Internet tend to be more challenging to convert than patients who were referred to you by friends, family, or other doctors. Therefore, it is easy for uninformed staff to conclude these callers are bad people or cheapskate "price shoppers." Then, it becomes a self-fulfilling prophecy.

But, the real issue is that marketing-generated patients have no prior relationship with the practice, so they are naturally going to be a little more hesitant and skeptical. Nobody taught prospective patients how to shop for professional services, but once your skilled team reassures them, they will go on to become great new patients like everyone else.

So how can you turn things around? While optimizing your front desk is a never-ending job, here are some strategies you can follow to make a significant impact quickly.

- Teach your team that there is nothing more important than a new patient inquiry, and then reinforce that concept at least weekly. That realization alone will help your organization improve.

- Set your front desk up to succeed by eliminating unnecessary distractions. If possible, nominate your most skilled person to handle new patient inquiries. (Routine calls can go to anyone.) Tell inquiring callers something like, "Hi Mrs. Jones, welcome to our practice. Tell you what, Mandy is our New Patient Ambassador and she can answer all of your questions." Then, Mandy should take the call in a quiet spot, free of distractions. Her job is to focus and get the new patient to commit to an appointment.

- Speaking of which, we need to underscore a critical point. When a prospective new patient calls your office, your Ambassador's objective is not to educate the patient, ask a bunch of routine questions, or (this happens a lot) diagnose the patient over the phone. Your Ambassador's job is solely to get the patient to commit to an appointment and come in. When your team truly understands this distinction, calls will become easier, and patients will appoint more frequently.

- Look at your New Patient Ambassador position as a sales position. If you practice in a very retail specialty like aesthetics, you should look for sales experience when hiring for this role. Depending on the practice, your Ambassador may also do the case presentations (selling) when patients come in. (More on that later.)

- Hire right, and pay right.

- Hire a professional phone skills trainer to educate your team and create systems. The ROI should be enormous.

- Be sure to have someone mystery shop your office on a regular basis.

- Remember, patients who call and speak to a live person will be more likely to show up as compared to patients who schedule online. The phone and a real person forge a human connection, so take every advantage of that.

- Create a call outline (or script), that incorporates the following critical steps:

1. **Perfect greeting.** For example, "Hello and thank you for calling Salt Valley Wellness Clinic. This is Shannon. How may I help you?"

2. **Probe for the reason for the call if necessary.** Your Ambassador needs to understand each patient's needs.

3. **Establish value.** Most practices miss this critical step. For example, "Mrs. Jones, I am so glad you called, and you found the right place. Our practice's mission is to help people like you, who feel traditional medicine has failed them. Dr. Smith is a board-certified medical doctor, who specializes in integrative medicine. She loves helping patients with chronic fatigue, even when they have failed everywhere else. In fact, she speaks to other doctors about the topic. But the best part, you are going to love her. She takes care of my mom."

4. **Ask for the appointment with a dual alternative close.** "Now let's see, I have Monday morning or Tuesday afternoon." (Either answer is a yes!)

5. **Be prepared to answer any objections.**

6. **Track the source of the call.** "Whom may we thank for referring you?"

7. **Gather all the information you need in a patient-friendly way.** Schedule patients to come in as soon as possible, especially Internet or advertising generated-patients. The longer the gap, the higher the likelihood the patient will cancel or not show up. Be sure to enter your new patient info into your automated systems, which we will discuss next.

Utilize Appointment Reminders, Recalls, and Patient Emails

While dentists have used appointment reminder systems for years, an amazingly high percentage of other healthcare practices continue to lag far behind. That's a shame because the costs of not having a recall and appointment reminder system can be enormous. We know of one dermatology practice that procrastinated forever, but when they finally got around to implementing a recall system, they grew a million dollars in annual revenue almost instantly.

Today's automated appointment reminder systems have moved far beyond postcards and time intensive staff phone calls. The best systems, such as Solutionreach, instead use a combination of templated emails, texts, and automated phone calls. Patients can quickly respond to confirm or reschedule. Of course, these systems can be used for monthly promotional emails as well.

Some practice management systems come with these communications programs built in. There are other standalone scheduling, reminder and retention systems that you can easily and immediately plug into your workflow. If you don't need a recall feature but want to send promotional emails to, you might consider simple tools like Mailchimp or Constant Contact. If you're going to get sophisticated, you can consider robust marketing automation platforms like Hubspot. Always be sure to get an opt-in from patients before subscribing them; every email sent must include your address and an opt-out option. Of course, whatever you do, be sure to remain HIPAA-compliant, and check with an attorney for details.

Visit → Treatment

The Visit as Viewed by the Patient

You may well be inured to the ambiance of your practice. After all, you are there constantly. There are things you may well take for granted or just not notice. Your patient, however, is not so forgiving. She is seeing your clinic for the first time and her senses may be highly tuned due to anxiety about the visit. This means that the reception area is not a waiting room, but a comfortable receiving area. Coffee, tea, or water should be readily available. The bathroom(s) is pristine. The music is tasteful, not off-putting, and at a pleasing volume. Give some thought to the magazines you want to have in your reception room. Offer a broad variety based upon the demographics and interests of your patients. Many practitioners will steer clear of any that involve politics.

The major tone of the visit is really set by the person who greets the patient and welcomes the patient to your practice. The reason you hire for attitude is for this very purpose: the power of the first impression. A true story that drives this point home: Mark was recently in Cleveland and noted a Medical Dermatology and Aesthetics Clinic near to where he was staying. He decided to check it out, as his host, had asked him if he knew of any good cosmetic doctors nearby. He opened the door into the reception area, only to be met by the receptionist sequestered behind a glass partition. She was looking down at a chart, and head down, without making eye contact, uttered one word, "Name?" The upshot: not a practice that deserves his friend's hard-earned cash.

Waiting time can be a major turn-off for patients. If you are running an elective cash-pay practice, try to organize the booking process so that no more than one or two patients are in your reception room at a time. Private pay patients hate to feel "herded" and do not like to wait. In fact, their time may be more economically valuable than your own.

Treatment → Maintenance

Perfect the Art of the Consult

There have been many surveys done on what patients are looking for in a doctor. Our favorite is a University of Chicago assessment that asked patients what factors go into making a "high-quality" doctor (in the conventional setting). As you look over the chart below, you'll notice that the most important factors are the people-centered ones such as listening, caring, communicating, and spending time. In the cash-pay era, a callous consult just won't cut it.

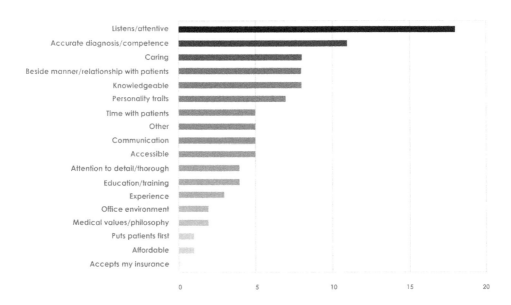

What do patients want?

Most important factor that makes a high-quality doctor

Source: NORC Center for Public Affairs Research, University of Chicago, July 2014   Percent volunteer most important factor

The consult is where the clinician has to be at his or her best. There are five elements to a great consult:

- **Time:** Adequate time for the patient to tell her story, and for the practitioner to demonstrate listening and comprehension skills. You refrain from interrupting.

- **Presence:** Body language, eye contact, and voice tonality demonstrate that you are with the patient at this moment in time, without distraction. Your body is relaxed. You sit eye-level with the patient, arms uncrossed. You lean slightly forward for better engagement. You are mindfully attending to the patient.

- **Inquiry:** You ask open-ended questions and surface the patient's ambivalence around health behavior change ("I know it's important for me to lose weight, but..."). You actively search for the patient's intrinsic motivators and tie your treatment to the outcomes *they* want to occur.

- **Empathy:** You know how important empathy is to the patient and how it contributes to adherence and better outcomes,[79] so you actively listen to see if you can reflect how patients are feeling about their condition. You make an attempt to understand what they have gone through. You paraphrase and then point to hope: "Sounds like you've had a really rough week. Let's see if we can't get you feeling better."

- **Road mapping:** You get commitment to a treatment plan that the patient has bought into. When in doubt, you ask patients to rate their commitment, and rework goals so they can be successful. You also layout in detail the time-based course of their treatment plan.

Putting It All Together

To demonstrate the power of these five ingredients, we turn to one of our favorite citations, a sham acupuncture study done by Ted Kaptchuk, MD reported in the *British Medical Journal*.[80] The study was designed to test the therapeutic ritual. Kaptchuk broke a group of irritable bowel syndrome patients into three groups—an untreated control group and two sham acupuncture treatment groups. One group received the standard short visit with limited patient engagement; the other group had an augmented visit. The study measured global improvement, symptom severity, adequate relief, and quality of life. In each case, the limited group did better than the control, and the augmented group did better than the limited. So, what did the clinicians do differently in the augmented approach?

- First, they asked probing questions regarding symptoms. They inquired not just about physical symptoms, but also how irritable bowel syndrome related to the patients' relationships and lifestyles.
- They asked patients about the "cause" and "meaning" of their conditions.

o   Practitioners in the augmented group displayed a warm friendly manner. They used active listening, repeating patients' words and asking for clarification.

o   They displayed empathy with statements like, "I understand how difficult this must be for you."

o   They also communicated confidence and a positive expectation, saying something like, "I've had great success using acupuncture with IBS, and I look forward to demonstrating this to you."

o   These are all the components that one would expect in a great clinician-patient relationship…but they did one more thing. They invoked 20 seconds of thoughtful silence while feeling the pulse or pondering the treatment plan.

Addressing the Compliance Conundrum

Treatment → Maintenance

There is a big disconnect that exists in every practice. Ask the practitioner how many times Mrs. Jones has come in for her treatment (average number of visits) and the practitioner will throw out a number ("Let's see, I recommended she come in every quarter, so I'd say four times a year."). When they then dig into their EHR and address the same question, the answer is twice during the year.

In the world of aesthetics, the effects of treatments last for a known length of time. To keep wrinkles at bay, patients will require neurotoxins every quarter and filler twice a year. Microneedling, hair removal, or hydradermabrasion should ideally be done every 3-6 weeks for a course of 4-6 treatments. This equates to seeing the patient at least every other month. Yet surveys have shown that patients are often not compliant with these treatment regimens, and they fall through the cracks.

Vojin Kos, and Aubrey Rankin, founders of HintMD (hintmd.com) sought to solve this issue for the aesthetic practitioner. Their technology platform addresses the issue of retention through a personalized membership model tied directly to the specific practice. Once the practitioner and patient agree on a treatment plan, the system translates this into simple monthly payments for the patient, which makes it easy for a patient to commit to their plan. The patient can track their membership, including upcoming appointments or product shipments through the HintMD app, again encouraging treatment consistency.

The biggest challenge that Kos and Rankin had to overcome, and the brilliance of the system, lies in the ability to modify the treatment plan, and hence, the monthly payment. For example, if the patient has been routinely getting 30 units of neurotoxin per quarter, but after consultation, decides to purchase only 20, the membership fee is lowered accordingly. HintMD has also added a cosmeceutical direct-ship model for patients in which the practitioner gets the full (usually 50%) margin. Here again, HintMD had to overcome the major problem patients have with direct ship: the inability to change delivery frequency. Their model accounts for this, and they are enrolling the major cosmeceutical manufacturers in the plan.

While HintMD is focused exclusively on retention issues in the aesthetic market, Coachcare (coachcare.com) addresses this problem more globally, focusing their technology platform on communicating with and managing the patient between visits. Their target customer is the "coach" —basically anyone and everyone who is trying to get patients to improve their health. The system is used by medical practitioners, nutritionists, sports medicine professionals, trainers, and yes, health coaches. Coachcare has been adopted by organizations both large and small. Originally focused on weight management, they have broadened their scope to other health specialties including pain management and chiropractic care. The system is remarkably flexible, so practitioners can choose how they want to communicate and what they want to track with patients. They can support an expansive library of content that practitioners can digitally distribute to their patients. Initial customization is included in the monthly subscription fee. An example of their schema (in this case focusing on weight and pain management) is shown below.

FEATURES

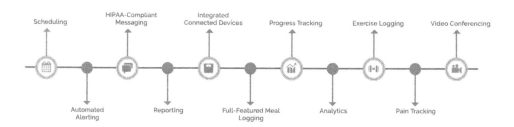

There are many practitioners who continue to opt for high-touch, traditional methods to stay in touch with their patients. Examples include sending hand written notes and cards to patients, or personally calling patients post procedure or in response to texts.

Maintenance → Cross Marketing

Selling Sometimes Sucks (But It Doesn't Have to)

We routinely do a fill-in-the-blank exercise during our workshops. We ask participants to complete the following. When it comes to healthcare, I think selling is _____.

You can just imagine the descriptors we get. Most of the audience members are negative about the whole concept (selling sucks). They say it is "undignified," "improper," or "sleazy." Then there is a smaller group, who note that selling can also be "necessary," "fun," or "essential." For the naysayers, we then go on to advance a simple argument:

1. Selling is an exchange of value.
2. Your patient wants a result.
3. She is willing to pay for the chance to achieve it.
4. Your job is to help her get what she wants.
5. If she does, you have facilitated a "win-win" value exchange.

Sometimes this progression gets a few heads to nod. More often, we have to reframe the entire act of selling as the act of *influencing*. Anytime you make a treatment recommendation whether it be prescriptive, e.g., antibiotics for a sinus infection, a drug for metabolic syndrome, a steroid for a rash—or lifestyle-related, e.g., lose weight, start exercising, be mindful, take this supplement—you are attempting to influence the patient to adhere to your recommendation. They want a result, are willing to pay for it, and you utilize your knowledge and positional power to help them get what they want.

In our society, physicians have great "positional power." Along with nurses (number one), military officers, grade school teachers, and pharmacists, they are rated as among most honest and ethical of professionals.[81] Most doctors are held in high esteem; their knowledge and opinions are valued. Hence the importance of remaining ethical in making your "selling" recommendations. In our workshops, we frequently ask the audience if they know what this late 18th century medical device is.

Can you identify this medical device?

If you guessed that this is a tobacco insufflator, a bellows-like device that was used along with tobacco smoke to help resuscitate drowning victims in the late 1700s and early 1800s, you are quite the medical historian. Ultimately, as more data came to bear, doctors realized that the tobacco was not helpful to the patient's recovery. What has remained in our lexicon, however, is the methodology whereby the tobacco was insufflated, as shown in this picture.

This is where the expression, "blowing smoke up someone's butt" comes from. Just image how great the positional power of the physician must have been. A cold, wet patient, newly pulled from the river would lie quietly and compliantly while the physician administered this treatment. We bring up this analogy as a reminder that with power comes responsibility—ethics is paramount in all healthcare dealings.

How to Ethically and Successfully Sell Your Professional Services

Professional selling is a big enough topic for its own book (or two). Still, in this section we can certainly help you with some of the most important points.

Start with the right system. Successful salespeople and their managers start by creating a sales system. In a previous section, we recommended a phone inquiry sales system that starts with the New Patient Ambassador. As we hinted, she could do a lot more than simply handle phone calls. In a cash-pay practice, she could lead the entire sales process. While every practice is different, we hope you can apply some of the ideas from the following sales system.

1. The New Patient Ambassador follows the process we previously outlined for the phone inquiry. She keeps her notes in a database and reviews them just prior to the visit.

2. Upon arrival, the Ambassador personally greets the new patient moments after she steps through the door for her appointment. The Ambassador makes the patient feel comfortable by offering water, coffee, or snacks, and meets briefly

with the patient to discuss her goals for the visit, establish rapport, and to set expectations. The Ambassador can also help with any paperwork or insurance issues (if applicable). Pro tip: Include an authorization for patient financing among the paperwork, in case it is needed. More about that in a moment.

3. Just before the examination, the Ambassador should brief the doctor on the essential things she has learned so far about the patient. While examining the patient, the doctor should listen to the patient's needs and build rapport. At the conclusion of the examination, the doctor should make clear recommendations. When questions come up about money, the doctor could talk broadly about treatment options and costs, but usually should avoid discussing financial details. Also, avoid giving the patient too many choices, as that can confuse patients to the point where they do nothing.

4. The Patient Ambassador (not a finance person) could then meet again with the patient to talk about the benefits of treatment and get her excited about moving forward. By this meeting, the Ambassador should already have a strategy to discuss money. For example, "Well, I have some great news for you. While insurance won't cover this procedure, we do have some affordable payment options for you. We could run your credit card $250 for each of the next six months, sign you up for a no-interest, 12-month payment program through CareCredit, or you can pay upfront with a check and save $100. Which sounds best for you?" Of course, the Ambassador needs to handle objections and work to gain commitment. If the patient does not commit, the Ambassador will need to follow up as appropriate.

Find the right person. Contrary to popular belief, there is no one magic ingredient that all successful salespeople share. However, we'd feel a lot more excited about a prospective salesperson who is a good communicator, has successfully lived on commission in a past life, has completed one or more professional sales training programs, fits the target audience profile, knows and believes in your services, can adapt to various personality styles and is fearless talking about money. Great salespeople are proud of what they do, and not at all nervous to ask for a commitment. In fact, more than one Patient Ambassador has boasted to us, "They call me the Closer!"

Select the personality best suited for the job. You may be familiar with one or more of the various behavioral style models out there with personality classifications such as Controller, Promoter, Analytical, and Supporter. The best salespeople understand these models, know how to communicate with patients in each category, and give them what they want. For example, Analyticals want lots of information, so provide it to them. Controllers want to be in charge, so give them options. Promoters hate details, so stay focused on the big picture and keep things light. Supporters want to feel heard and be loved, so do that for them.

Ask questions and listen. The key to professional selling is not clever tricks or high pressure. Instead, it is all about asking the right questions to discover the patient's needs, uncover objections, and build rapport. Remember, it's all about them! The best salespeople do 30% of the talking, while the prospect does 70%.

Some of our favorite "magic questions" include:
- What were you hoping we could do for you?
- Why are you interested?
- How long have you considered this?
- If you had a magic wand, what would it change, and what would it do?
- What's most important to you about....?
- What concerns do you have?
- If there were one thing that would hold you back from moving forward, what would it be?
- What research have you done?
- Why haven't you done this in the past?

Speak their language. Use the words patients choose. Talk about benefits, not features. Avoid technical jargon. Dress and act appropriately for your role. Tell stories anonymously about other patients' results (facts tell, stories sell).

Sell to the heart, not the head. People make decisions emotionally, then justify rationally. Remember emotional appeals like altruism, pride, fear (pain), vanity, the desire to be healthy, etc. The above magical questions can easily get them talking and emotionally involved.

Provide financing options. Patients focus less on how much the overall price is, and more on what the monthly cost is. Realtors and car salespeople famously know this, because they like to talk about payments per month. So, when possible, offer credit cards, automatic debit on checking or credit cards, and patient financing programs.

Cross Marketing → Referrals and Ambassadors

Once the patient has enjoyed your professional services, they are of course more likely to refer their friends and family to you. Some will do so on their own, while others may need a little nudge. When you encounter highly satisfied patients, you can just ask them for referrals.

We find that many doctors understandably feel reluctant to ask because they fear rejection, or they are worried about looking "needy," or they simply don't know how to ask. At the same time, we know it works. It brings in new patients with zero cost, and most patients are happy to refer—some even feel honored to help.

The secret to getting a positive response without looking and feeling like a needy salesperson is all in how you do it. Here are some tips:

- It is best when the doctor or lead practitioner does the asking, though staff can help too.

- Since timing is everything, ask at the peak of their experience. Be alert for unexpected compliments or expressions of satisfaction.

- Be sure to note it in the chart whenever you ask patients for referrals so that they don't get inadvertently requested by you or staff multiple times.

- Script and practice. You can use any of the following scripts as starting points:

  - "Mr. Jones, how are you doing?…. Great, glad to hear it. Tell you what, I'd like to ask you a favor. If you liked what we have done here, I'd like you to send us someone else we can help too. I am sure they'd be pleased, and we'd appreciate it too. Would you do that for them?"
  - "Mrs. Smith, we love it when you come in. Do you have any friends just like you that we can help too?"
  - "Something happened the other day that concerned me. A patient came in for a well check and asked if we knew anyone we could recommend for weight loss for her husband. I was shocked because I thought she knew that medical weight loss is one of our favorite areas of expertise. So, I am making it a point to get the word out to all of my patients, just in case you know someone who could benefit from our help."

Of course, once patients refer, you should acknowledge them in some fashion—a simple email, thank you note, or a kind word the next time you see them. You can call the patient and leave a voicemail if you really want to wow them. Some practices give small thank you gifts, discounted or free services, or host patient events. Of course, be sure small gifts are legally permissible in your state. Also, when you thank referring patients be sure not to use the referred patient's name—for HIPAA reasons.

In conclusion, while it's no secret that today's patients demand a better patient experience than their parents were willing to accept, that is especially true for cash-pay healthcare. When patients pay you their own hard-earned money, they instantly transform beyond mere patients and become your customers instead.

While in the past, your "patients" may have been willing to endure little annoyances like long waits, messy waiting rooms, or rude staff, today's "customers" won't. The bar continues to rise, and consumers have a plethora of competitive practices from which to choose.

Savvy, successful practitioners are entering the market and building huge businesses by scaling patient experience and caring. Richard Park founded CityMD with that principle in mind, and today his New York chain of urgent cares has grown to over 100 locations.

If you are already delivering an excellent patient experience, congratulations.

If not, we respectfully suggest you and your team take on an entirely new mindset when it comes to delivering a superior patient experience in the cash-pay world. We hope the principles we have shared will help you do just that.

Chapter

How to Get Patients from the Internet

Do you want to attract more new patients from the Internet? Of course, you do. (Who doesn't?)

Our goal in this chapter and the next is to answer your most pressing questions about digital marketing and social media. Because you face an infinite array of digital marketing options, we are going to focus on those strategies most likely to work.

You'll find that some of the tactics we share are ideally suited for "do-it-yourself" efforts by doctors or internal staff, while others require the expertise of people who live and breathe digital marketing every day. Some of the tactics require only time, while others will require an added financial investment. Along the way, we will point you toward some additional resources to further help you with your digital marketing.

Your Website: The Epicenter of *All* Your Marketing Efforts

"OK, we just got our new website built. Now we are finally ready to begin marketing."

"Arrrrgggghh!" We cringe every time we hear those words because the underlying assumption is all wrong. You don't begin marketing after you have a website. Your marketing starts with your website, and it is *the* most crucial component of your marketing plan. A weak website can cripple all your subsequent marketing efforts, and sadly most of the new websites we see lack some or all of the best practices we are about to share.

Sometimes the problems can be solved with extra money, time, and effort. However, many of the websites we see are so inherently flawed that it is actually easier and less expensive to simply start over. That can be true even when the doctor believes the new website is "pretty."

We liken these sad scenarios to revision surgery. No one wants to go through the pain, time, effort, and expense of new website (or surgery) again. But when a new website is botched so badly that subsequent marketing efforts are doomed to flatline, a complete redo is often the only logical course of action.

Key Website Objectives

Before we consider website best practices, let's take a moment to define the objectives of a healthcare website (in rough order of priority). Your website must:

- **Attract new patients.** The number one priority of your healthcare website must be to attract new patients. To do that, your website needs to first show up high in search results when prospective patients look for a provider and then compel them to inquire. Most websites fail either or both of these requirements.

- **Facilitate patient due diligence.** Today many patients will check you out online prior to calling, even when they were originally referred by a trusted doctor, friend or family member. Your website must "have them at hello."

- **Compare favorably to your competitors.** While it used to be nearly impossible to compare providers, today the Internet makes it seem easy. Your fiercest competitors are always just a click away, and a lot of patients will shop around before making a decision. Does your website fairly represent your practice compared to your competitors?

- **Support your brand image.** Your website is the first experience many patients will have with the brand you are trying so hard to create. Does yours enhance or detract from that brand?

- **Facilitate patient communication.** Whenever we talk with patients about what online features they'd like most from their providers, they tell us they'd love the ability to make online appointments and communicate via (secure) email. Meanwhile, most doctors tell us these are precisely the two features they'd like to avoid. To remain competitive, we recommend you listen to the marketplace, just like the savviest healthcare retailers are already doing. Fortunately, many practice management systems and EHRs with patient portals include these features. Doctors just have to agree to use them.

- **Educate patients.** This topic is a little tricky. Yes, you need to educate patients enough to convince them to call you, but you do not want to try and replace WebMD, NIH or Mayo Clinic. In fact, too much information can actually overwhelm patients and *decrease* the likelihood they will call you.

- **Additional objectives.** Large group practices and hospitals may require websites that also support employee recruitment, act as a portal for admitting doctors, woo donors, and more.

Secrets to Successful Websites

We talked about why websites are so important to your marketing and what goals your website should accomplish. Now let's drill down about what makes some websites more successful than others, particularly from a patient-generating point of view.

- **Headline.** Your website needs a differentiating headline that clearly distinguishes your practice from the competition and answers the question, "Why you?" Amazingly, most doctor websites fail this easy, fundamental test. Make sure you (or your marketing people) spend the time required to come up with a powerful headline based upon this concept.

- **Benefits.** Benefits answer the question, "What's in it for me?" For example, when the *feature* is minimally invasive surgery, the *benefits* may include reduced pain, fewer complications, less downtime, etc.

- **Superior Design.** Yes, your website needs to be attractive, but that's not sufficient. It should also look up-to-date, reflect your brand, create a great first impression, and build trust. Great designers know how to achieve these objectives and lead the eye to where they want it to go-via attractive type fonts, colors, graphics, etc.

- **Content Management System (CMS).** We recommend you choose a website built on a CMS such as WordPress, so you can make minor updates on your own.

- **Superior User Experience.** One of the famous marketing books from the early days of the Internet was entitled *Don't Make Me Think*.[82] Almost twenty years later, users have become even more impatient and lazy when it comes to browsing a website. They expect a positive interaction with your website, and if it doesn't deliver, they will move on to another website (and another practitioner); this is referred to as "bouncing." Some of the most important user experience traits include:

- o   Intuitive and easy navigation.

- o   Follows Internet conventions. For example: the logo should appear on the upper left-hand side of your website and be clickable to the home page.

- o   Mobile responsive. Since most healthcare practice websites receive about 2/3 of their traffic from mobile devices, savvier website developers think mobile first when they approach a new project. Mobile responsive websites provide great user experiences by rearranging themselves visually for virtually any type of device, including big screen TVs, desktops, laptops, tablets, and smartphones. To see mobile responsiveness in action (or not), simply grab the side of the browser window on a desktop and squeeze it in. A mobile responsive site will rearrange itself as you shrink the viewing space, ultimately ending up with a mobile display.

- o   Fast load times. Users absolutely *hate* slow loading websites, and the data proves it. According to Google, "As page load time goes from one to five seconds, the probability of a bounce increases by 90%."[83] Beyond user friendliness, both site speed and mobile responsiveness matter a lot for SEO (search engine optimization) too. More on that later.

- o   Above the fold. A nod to the early days of newspaper publishing, "above the fold" refers to the top of a webpage which is immediately visible when viewed on a laptop or desktop. Because it is responsible for many visitors' first impression of your practice, the above the fold portion of your home page requires special attention during the design process. (Note: above the fold's importance has diminished somewhat in recent years due to the rise of mobile and long-form home pages.)

- **Calls to action.** It's amazing, but when you place the word "call" in front of your phone number, your website visitors will be more likely to call you. Likewise, if you add an intake form to your site with a subjective command like, "Contact Us," visitors will be more likely to comply. "Book an Appointment" buttons are especially preferred by busy, upscale patients. Calls to action are powerful sales tools—make sure they are prominent on your website.

- **Click to call.** In our increasingly mobile world, patients love the convenience of being able to click your practice's phone number to call you without the hassle of dialing numbers. Your click to call phone numbers should reside at the top right-hand side of every page of your website.

- **Offers.** Likewise, offers can dramatically increase your website inquiries. Think of offers as a way for prospective patients to take "baby steps" toward becoming a patient. Some excellent offers include free seminars, webinars, eBooks, video series, free screenings, free phone consultations, newsletter sign-ups, open houses, etc. Sometimes the goal of the offer is to get people to call your office, but other times the goal is simply to trap their email address so that you can market to them over time.

- **Photos.** Most people are highly visual, and photos can have a dramatic impact on a website's effectiveness:

  o   Home page photos can set the mood for an entire website. In fact, when people show us websites they like, their opinions are heavily based upon the attractiveness of the main home page photo. Ideally, your website photos will wow visitors and differentiate your practice from competitors.

  o   Target audience photos should represent the people you are trying to attract. In most instances, they should be diverse by age, ethnicity, and gender. Try hard to choose photos that look authentic rather than corny. Some leading online paid stock photo libraries include Shutterstock, iStock by Getty Images, and Adobe, while free resources include Unsplash, Pixabay, Stockvault, and Pexels. Depending upon your state and specialty, you may need to include disclaimers when using photos of models who are not actual patients. Speaking of which,

  o   "Real patient" photos can really help your website stand out from the crowd. While some specialties are more challenging than others to use real patients (e.g., addiction treatment), getting patients to say "yes" is typically easier than you might expect. Your patient photos will look especially credible when you include captions with the patient's name (or just first name) and the words, "actual patient." Make certain to get releases to use the photographs in your marketing.

o   Before and after photos are vitally important for aesthetic practices. Use your own photos whenever possible (versus from the manufacturer), and make sure they are well lit, clear, detailed and most importantly, show substantial improvements.

o   Regarding doctor and team photos, make sure everyone is well groomed, well-lit, and shot against similar backgrounds. Definitely avoid the usual hodgepodge of mismatched photos. If you have a large practice with busy doctors, you may need to schedule several days to work around their schedules. Because some people are naturally more photogenic and comfortable in front of a camera than others, take as many photos as necessary. That holds especially true for those providers who are "stars of the show."

o   Prospective patients like to get a sense of what doctors' offices look like before they visit, so when possible include inviting interior and exterior photos of your facility.

o   If you want to use custom patient photos or office photos on your website, make sure you invest the time and money to hire a professional photographer.

- **Video.** By offering your website visitors the chance to experience your practice through sight, sound, and motion, video provides a great way to distinguish your practice from its competitors. While many of the tips we shared in the photography section also apply to video, here are some additional thoughts:

o   Practice overview videos are just that. These professionally produced videos are typically several minutes long and can be narrated by a doctor, voice-over narrator, or a professional spokesperson. The script should be replete with benefits that promote the primary service lines. Typically filmed at the practice's office, these videos can include comments from doctors, staff, and patients. Resulting footage should be then edited into a final video, complete with music, graphics, transitions, and titles.

o   Patients love "Meet the Doctor" videos since they allow them to experience the provider without the cost, inconvenience, awkwardness, and the commitment of an office visit. Since many doctors are not comfortable on camera, we usually recommend shooting each doctor "interview style," where the subject looks slightly off camera at the unseen interviewer. See Chapter 10: How to Get Noticed, Known & Remembered for more tips about video.

o   Patient testimonial videos are very convincing to would-be patients. When possible, use a professional videographer to shoot multiple patients in one day. Going forward, you should capture patients at the peak of their satisfaction—before their excitement subsides. Some savvy practices find a quiet, attractive setting in their office where they can easily video patients on-the-spot with an inexpensive lighting kit, microphone, and video camera or smartphone.

o   Virtual tour videos offer another way to make patients feel comfortable before they visit. One great and little-known idea is to hire a Google-approved videographer.[84]

- **SEO friendly.** While search engine optimization is an ongoing activity, your website should incorporate essential SEO On-Page attributes from the start. Sadly, as we mentioned above, most web designers do not have a clue about SEO. Likewise, very few copywriters have the knowledge and skill to write copy that motivates humans, but works for search engine spiders. So, you may find yourself in the unenviable position of paying other people to deconstruct and rebuild your brand-new website. That is like buying a new car and paying someone else to rip the top off to install a convertible roof. It's far better cheaper and better to buy a car with the convertible roof included in the first place.

What Are Some Options When Buying a New Website?

There is a bewildering variety of website options from which to choose. Do-it-yourselfers like to choose offerings such as Wix.com, where they can create their own website and write their own words for next to nothing. Alternatively, graphic designers will often work for a few thousand dollars, though typically you will have to write the copy and find someone else for SEO.

Today, many doctors want to trade up to online marketing systems that include affordable websites with increased functionality such as local SEO, reputation management, and appointment reminders built in. Expect to pay between $400 and $900 a month.

Custom websites are a completely different category. While templated websites can launch in a month or less, custom websites usually require at least three months from start to finish. Prices vary widely based upon the amount of labor needed to complete it, copy (words), features, the expertise of those who are doing the actual work, where the work is done, the number of pages, whether it requires e-commerce, etc.

Note: More than 100 companies create websites for doctors. Stewart's agency HealthcareSuccess.com creates custom websites, while its subsidiary PatientFetch.com offers affordable website and marketing combinations.

Rise to the Top with Search Engine Optimization

Search Engine Optimization (SEO) refers to the art and science of rising to the top of organic search results on Google, Bing, and other search engines. While some people refer to SEO as "free search" (as opposed to digital advertising), it isn't truly free. While you won't have to pay money to Google, true SEO will cost you time, money, or both.

With over 2/3 market share, Google has risen to become the "undisputed heavyweight search engine champion of the world." Your primary goal should, therefore, be to advance to the top of page one on Google's search engine results pages (SERPs). When we say the top, we mean that literally. According to Advanced Web Ranking (August 2018), organic (natural) click-through rates for search by position on Google are:[85]

Desktop Page One	**Mobile Page One**
Position 1 - 32.73%	Position 1 - 23.57%
Position 2 - 13.44%	Position 2 - 12.26%
Position 3 - 8.74%	Position 3 - 8.23%
Position 4 - 5.53%	Position 4 - 5.27%
Position 5 - 3.82%	Position 5 - 3.62%
Top 5 positions on Google's first page - 64.26%	Top 5 positions on Google's first page - 52.95%

Our Favorite Internet Geek Joke
Question: "Where's the best place to bury a dead body?"
SEO Geek Answer: "Page 2 on Google"

Before we go any further, let's make sure we are all on the same page regarding the most common search results on Google.

1. Most often you will see that ads dominate the top of the page, especially for highly searched phrases in competitive markets. Google allows up to four of these pay-per-click ads in the top position. (Much more on that later.)

2. Beneath the ads, you will usually see Google's local results, also affectionately known as the "map pack." These three listings are pulled from the Google My Business directory. (More on that in the coming section on Local Search.)

3. Beneath the map pack, you will find the organic (or natural) listings. This section makes up the bulk of the page.

4. At the very bottom of the page, you will often find more pay-per-click ads.

While you will see the same basic layout with desktop and mobile results, due to the limited size screen size the ads appear much more prominently on mobile. We suspect that's why the first position of organic listings on desktop garners 33% of all organic clicks, while the first organic position on mobile garners only 24% of organic clicks.

Also, according to Google, unique to mobile, searches for terms like, "near me," "can I buy," "to buy" have grown by over 500% over the last two years.[86]

Google   plastic surgeon near me   🔍

All   Maps   Shopping   News   Images   More   Settings   Tools

About 84,600,000 results (0.31 seconds)

Affordable Financing - Plastic Surgeon Near Me
Ad www.orangecountyplasticsurgery.com/ ▾
Dr. Bunkis is a Board Certified plastic surgeon with 35+ years of experience
View Our Procedures · Our Practitioners · Reviews · Dr. Bunkis

CosmetiCare Plastic Surgery - Voted "Best of OC" - OC Weekly
Ad www.cosmeticare.com/plastic-surgery/orange-county ▾
Financing Available. Free Consultations. Award Winning Surgeons & Staff. Over 30 Years in Practice.
Board Certified Surgeons. Live Chat Support. Brands: BOTOX® Cosmetic, JUVÉDERM VOLUMA® XC.
KYBELLA®, Restylane®.
📍 1101 Bayside Dr #100, Corona Del Mar, CA

Michael Omidi Md FACS - Top 5 Plastic Surgeon in CA
Ad www.michaelomidi.com/ ▾
Tummy Tuck | Face Lift | Nose Surgery | Hair Restoration. Call Us Today! Schedule A Consultation.
Real Self top 100. Services: Mommy Makeover, Breast Augmentation, Vein Treatments, Rhinoplasty.

JC Plastic Surgery - Joon Y. Choi, MD
Ad www.joonchoimd.com/ ▾
Board Certified Plastic Surgeon Call for Free Cosmetic Consultation. Face Surgery. Liposuction.
Breast Surgery.

Rating ▾   Hours ▾   Your past visits ▾   ⋮ ⋮ ⋮

Dr. James F. Coleman, MD   🌐   ◈
5.0 ★★★★★ (2) · Plastic Surgeon   WEBSITE   DIRECTIONS
2.4 mi · 12791 Newport Ave · (714) 508-2105
Closed · Opens 9AM Wed

Coastal Dermatology and Plastic Surgery   🌐   ◈
2.3 ★★★☆☆ (3) · Plastic Surgeon   WEBSITE   DIRECTIONS
2.4 mi · 12721 Newport Ave · (714) 838-5680
Closed · Opens 9AM Wed

UCI Plastic Surgery   🌐   ◈
5.0 ★★★★★ (1) · Plastic Surgeon   WEBSITE   DIRECTIONS
1.9 mi · 1451 Irvine Blvd #441 · (714) 456-3077
Closed · Opens 8AM Wed

☰ More places

The Best 10 Cosmetic Surgeons in Tustin, CA - Last Updated October ...
https://www.yelp.com › Tustin, CA › Health & Medical › Doctors › Cosmetic Surgeons ▾
Best Cosmetic Surgeons in Tustin, CA - Kyle R Song, MD, Devine Image, Donald ... Tariq Ali Khan ,MD
- Orange County Concierge Doctor, Jeffrey Lee, MD DMD, Dr. Jay's ... Dr. Haddad did a GREAT job not
only with me but with my friend.

UCI Plastic Surgery: Cosmetic & Plastic Surgery Orange County CA
https://www.uciplasticsurgery.com/ ▾
UCI is Orange County's premier plastic surgery and laser treatment practice with 3 convenient
locations in Orange, Tustin, and Costa Mesa.

Plastic Surgery Cosmetic Reconstructive Surgery Beverly Hills Los ...
www.colemanplasticsurgery.com/ ▾
Plastic Surgery, , Aesthetic Surgery, Cosmetic Surgery and Reconstructive Surgery in Beverly Hills,
Los Angeles, Tustin Orange County and San Fernando ...

Find a Cosmetic Surgeon in Your Area | American Board of Cosmetic ...
https://www.americanboardcosmeticsurgery.org/find-a-cosmetic-surgeon-near-you/ ▾
Find A Board Certified Surgeon Near You. Choosing a cosmetic surgeon is one of the most important steps in your decision to have cosmetic surgery.

Find a Plastic Surgeon Near Me | ASPS - American Society of Plastic ...
https://find.plasticsurgery.org/?gclid=CN_wkoCow6wCFUbf4AodLBexpg ▾
Find information on board-certified plastic surgeons in cosmetic and ... FIND A PLASTIC SURGEON NEAR ME. ZIP or City, State or Country. Doctor's Name.

Find a Plastic Surgeon Near Me | ASPS
https://find.plasticsurgery.org/ ▾
Find information on board-certified plastic surgeons in cosmetic and reconstructive surgery. Use our free Find a Surgeon tool to get started, or call ...

Cruise Plastic Surgery
https://orangecountycosmeticsurgery.com/ ▾
Board certified plastic surgeon, Dr. Joseph Cruise is a recognized leader in Orange County breast augmentation, facial rejuvenation, and body ... Welcome to Orange County Cosmetic Surgery, where we ... Take a look around to learn more

South Coast Plastic Surgery - Irvine & Orange County CA
https://www.socoplasticsurgery.com/ ▾
Dr Song and staff at South Coast Plastic Surgery located in Irvine in central Orange County welcome you to the practice that cares!

Dr. Daniel Reichner | Orange County Plastic Surgeon
https://www.drreichner.com/ ▾
Reichner Plastic Surgery. As an experienced provider of plastic surgery in Orange County, Dr. Reichner's highest priority is complete patient satisfaction.

Facial Plastic Surgery Orange County Newport Beach CA Dr Ali Sepehr
https://www.orangecountyfacialplasticsurgery.com/ ▾
Look more youthful and refreshed with Facial Plastic Surgery at our Newport Beach and Orange County, CA practice. Dr. Ali Sepehr offers Facelift, Rhinoplasty, ...

AMCC Medical & Cosmetic Center - an award winning clinic
[Ad] www.amccbeauty.com/ ▾
offering the latest medical, cosmetic, laser, skin care treatments and more. Pigmentation Removal. wrinkle-removal. Skin Care. Facial Sculpting. Body Contouring. Services: Restylane®/Juvederm, Ultherapy, DermaShine.
Hot Deals · Restylane®/Juvederm · Dao Acupuncture
♀ 1317 S Baldwin Ave, Arcadia, CA - Closing soon · 9:30 AM – 6:00 PM ▾

OC Dermatology | Liposuction to Remove Fat
[Ad] coolsculpting.ocdermatology.com/ ▾
Easy, safe, and successful way to reduce fat without surgery. Call us today. 60+ Years of Experience.
Book an Appointment Today
♀ 22032 El Paseo #220, Rancho Santa Margarita, CA - Closed now · Hours ▾

JC Plastic Surgery - Joon Y. Choi, MD
[Ad] www.joonchoimd.com/ ▾
Board Certified Plastic Surgeon Call for Free Cosmetic Consultation
Directions · Services
♀ 1310 W Stewart Dr #606, Orange, CA - Closed now · Hours ▾

Searches related to plastic surgeon near me

board certified plastic surgeon near me	uci plastic **surgery** clinic
plastic surgeon near me **free consultation**	plastic **surgery** before and after
uci aesthetic and plastic **surgery institute**	plastic **surgery** prices
uci plastic **surgery** orange ca	uci plastic **surgery specials**

Goooooooooogle ›
1 2 3 4 5 6 7 8 9 10   Next

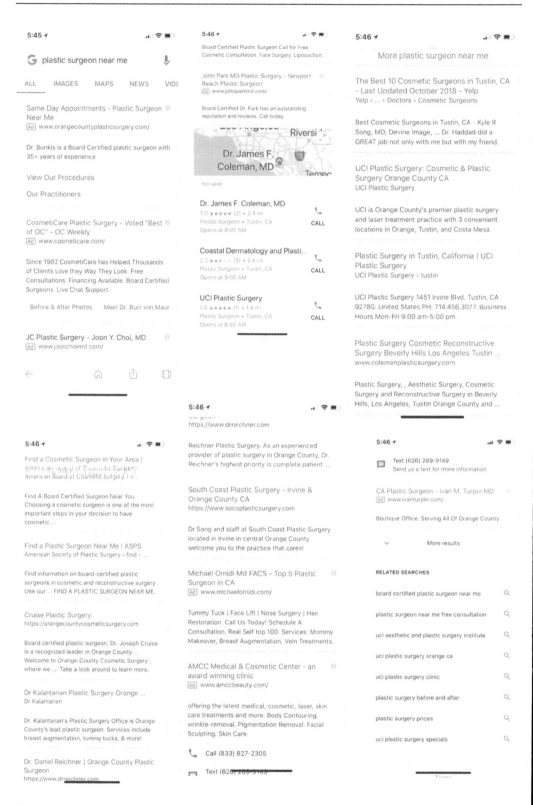

Google and the Google logo are registered trademarks of Google LLC, used with permission.

SEO Buyer Beware

Like many industries, search engine optimization firms vary widely in both approach and competence. While some firms are ethical, highly professional, and extremely competent, others fall into the "not so much" category.

Sadly, at least half the websites we audit lack any search engine optimization. That's not surprising because many website developers know little to nothing about SEO. Just because you bought a new website does not mean that it is search engine optimized. Much worse, we often encounter clients who have been paying someone for search engine optimization for years, yet their sites do not follow even the most basic "SEO 101" techniques. These cases are often so egregious that we can only conclude that their "SEO expert" is either incompetent, a thief, or both.

Finally, we would be remiss if we did not raise the topic of "black hat" SEO. Black hats will tell you they have secret tricks to get you to the top of Google. However, Google's Search Engine Spam team is comprised of PhDs who have seen every trick in the book— continuously refining their algorithms to thwart and penalize black hat SEO techniques. A black hat SEO could gravely damage your website's reputation with Google, and inadvertently cause its rankings to plummet.

3 Primary SEO Strategies

The three main SEO strategies are On-Page SEO, Off-Page SEO, and Local SEO.

On-Page SEO
These strategies allow you to improve your website's rankings through the code, images, and words that make up your website. Because clients directly control their websites, On-Page techniques can yield quick wins. Therefore, we typically start there. Some of the most important techniques include:

- **Optimize tags.** Tags are snippets of text placed within a website's code that help Google and other search engines understand the contents of the page. Even though they are mostly hidden from the user, tags are vitally important. In fact, websites without these essential tags fail the remedial SEO test. Some of the most prominent are:

  - **Title tags** serve as the title for each web page and sometimes appear on browser tabs. Make sure every page's title tag is unique, contains (at this writing) about 70 characters, and includes relevant keywords that describe the page.

- **Description tags** describe the page with a couple of sentences. The description tag includes the text you hope Google will include on its SERP. Be sure to include both keywords and sales copy.
- **Alt tags** are meant to help people with visual disabilities, because they describe the contents of each photo. Alt tags may help the page rank overall, and sometimes help the image itself show up in search. Alt tags appear to users when they hover over photos.
- **Header tags** help Google understand the relative importance of headlines, by assigning priority, i.e., H1, H2, H3.

- **Site loading speed.** While site speed matters a lot to the user experience, it also matters considerably to Google. Google has long penalized slow websites for desktop searches, and beginning July 9, 2018, it changed its algorithm to penalize slow mobile experiences as well.[87]

- **Mobile responsiveness.** On April 21, 2015 (sarcastically known as Mobilegeddon), Google changed its algorithm to penalize websites that do not display well for mobile searches. Note: Google prefers website owners commit to one website and make it mobile responsive, versus creating a second mobile-only site.

- **Content, content, content.** Google continually encourages website owners to avoid worrying about SEO techniques and instead focus on creating great content. Great content means:

  - Well written, free from grammatical errors, easy-to-understand copy.
  - Meaningful. Google hates thin, low-value content.
  - Authoritative. Over time, your goal is to create such good content that Google will recognize you as an authority in your field.
  - Original content. Google strongly prefers original content and views duplicated content as plagiarism (even when doctors don't realize the copy was stolen). About half the websites we come across suffer from duplicate content. Check for duplicate content on your own website at copyscape. com.

- **Blogs.** These are a great way to add content over time. Most practices should start with a website that has all the necessary pages (e.g., About Us, Insurances, Services, Team, Locations, etc.), and then build out blog posts over time.

- **Keywords.** While Google's algorithm has gotten smarter at distinguishing meaning, it is still important to include the keywords you want to rank for in both headlines and copy.

- **Sitemaps.** Typically found in the footer, HTML sitemaps are essentially tables of contents created for users to find their way around your website. XML sitemaps, on the other hand, are code-based indexes designed to help search engines navigate your site.

- **URL age and history.** Because Google favors URLs that have a strong history, optimizing a website with a brand-new URL is especially challenging.

- **Secure domain.** You may have noticed that some website addresses begin with HTTP, while others now start with HTTPS. Websites with HTTPS (Hypertext Transfer Protocol Secure) are more secure than HTTP because the information transmitted back and forth from their servers is encrypted. If you don't see HTTPS in front of your URL website, you should hire a web developer to convert to an SSL (Secure Socket Layers) server. As a reward, you will get a "security certificate," savvy website visitors will feel more secure, and your Google SEO rankings may improve.

- **URL name and structure.** Keywords in a URL can give a minor boost to search, and building out URLs with logical, non-spammy structures can help. For example, SpringfieldWomensHealth.com/aesthetics/botox.

For free tools to audit your website for SEO, mobile responsiveness, and site speed, go to CashPayResources.com.

Off-Page SEO

In the early days of the Internet, search engines were terrible at providing relevant results to users. That is until Larry Page and Sergey Brin came up with the brilliant insight that spawned the Google fortune. In summary:

"The most important academic research papers are cited often by others."

Looking at it another way, "It doesn't matter that YOU think you are great. It matters if OTHERS think you are great." So, building upon that idea, websites that are linked to by many other websites must be more important than sites without any "backlinks." Best of all, the breakthrough thinking worked!

Of course, the scammers soon came along and tried to ruin the party. You may remember the emails, "If you link to me, I will link back to you." Soon, link farms grew rampant, with networks of websites tied together through complex backlink structures. So, Google looked beyond the *quantity* of the links, and began to assess the *quality, relevance, and age* of the links:

- **Domain authority.** Backlinks from websites that Google deems credible and authoritative are more powerful than ordinary links. Thus, a link from the *New York Times* is better than a link from Billy Bob's BBQ.

- **Domain suffix.** The .edu and .gov suffixes carry higher authority than other suffixes.

- **Reputation.** Similarly, links from trusted sources like universities are far, far better than links from porn sites. Links from disreputable websites or "bad neighborhoods" can actually hurt you.

- **Relevancy.** The more relevant the link, the better. For practitioners, that means local and healthcare related links.

- **Age.** Over time, even high authority links decay, meaning you always have to seek new links to stay relevant.

Because you can't control the websites you don't own, link building is difficult, complex, and time-consuming. SEO pros have access to tools and techniques far beyond the scope of this book. However, here are some achievable tips and ideas, assuming you have the time, desire, and ability:

- Create really useful health-oriented eBooks, white papers, infographics, videos, and slide decks. Post these on your blog or a resources page on your website. Use these resources as "bait" when you reach out to owners of local websites and blogs.

- While links are ideal, mere online mentions of your name or practice name from credible sources like media outlets help. These are called "citations."

- Web directories organize and categorize websites so that users can find and compare similar websites relevant to their needs. Think of them as a massive list of websites, organized into an outline by topics. There are countless directory sites out there, so make sure you consider every opportunity. For example, if you are a public speaker, you could request inclusion into public speaker directories. For practitioners, however, the best opportunities come with healthcare and local directories, which we will cover next.

Local Search and Directories

Google Map Pack

As we have seen, when patients search Google for local providers they typically will find the "Map Pack" on the first page of results, just below the ads and above the rest of the organic search results. Since the Map Pack features only *three* providers on the most heavily trafficked search engine, it is by far the most essential online directory for you to optimize. Because many of the principles that work for Google will also work for your Facebook Page, Bing Places For Business, and many other local directories and health directories, we will start there.

- Your first step to appearing (correctly) in the Google Map Pack is to claim the Google My Business page for your practice. Start by logging into (or creating) the Google email account that you want to associate with your business. Then go to google.com/business and follow the prompts. Be sure to add as much detail as possible.

- After you have entered all the necessary data, Google will need to verify your account. Sadly, this step almost always requires you to wait for a postcard from Google before you can confirm the listing and move forward. Be sure to alert your staff to stay on the lookout for a postcard from Google; most staffs mistake the postcard for junk mail and toss it. When that happens, after a lot of waiting you'll have to request another one. This frustrating process becomes a nightmare for large, multi-location practices.

- Once your listing is verified, you'll need to complete your listing. Be as thorough as possible! The game is largely won and lost here, so include all the details like address, days and hours, primary phone number, website URL, amenities (e.g., free WIFI), etc.

- According to Google, "Businesses with photos receive 42% more requests for driving directions to their location from Google users, and 35% more clicks through to their websites than businesses that don't have photos." So, it's pretty clear you'll want to include excellent (and current) photos in your listing.[88]

- Google also encourages you to respond to any reviews you receive.[89] Your responses will not only improve your online reputation but will probably improve your search results as well. (Look for much more about reviews in the following section.)

- According to Google, the primary factors that determine local rankings are:

  - "Relevance refers to how well a local listing matches what someone is searching for. Adding complete and detailed business information can help Google better understand your business and match your listing to relevant searches."
  - The distance between the searcher and the business.
  - Prominence refers to how well-known a local business is, such as local landmarks or prominent brands.

- The number and quality of your reviews will improve local rankings as well.

More Directories

After optimizing your Google My Business page, your next priority will be to claim, update, and optimize your Yelp, Facebook Page, and Bing Places For Business listing in a similar fashion. Once "the Big 4" are complete, you'll want to optimize many of the remaining directories out there for three crucial reasons:

1. You will receive visitors and patients from many of the directories you optimize.

2. Many online directories feature patient reviews and star ratings.

3. Consistent, updated directory listings will improve your website's overall search engine ranking. Here's why:

First, as you might imagine, multiple directories result in numerous backlinks to your website. Second, consistent information across the web will help Google ascertain what is happening concerning you and your practice.

The fact is, most practices and doctors do a terrible job of keeping their name, address and phone numbers (NAP) consistent across the Internet. Practices can change addresses; doctors sometimes switch practices; practice names can change; doctors can leave a practice and forget to update their online profile; well-meaning consumers can suggest incorrect information on unclaimed listings; and doctor names can have multiple variations and even misspellings. For example, the following names could all represent the same person, who meanwhile practices at several locations in the same city:

- Dr. Jonathan Smith
- Dr. Jon Smith
- Dr. John Smith
- Dr. Jon Smith, MD
- Doctor Jon Smith
- Jonathan Smith, MD
- J.D. Smith, MD

Your own disparate listings can similarly confuse the heck out of Google, which obviously is not a good thing for you or your website. So, you'll need to optimize the many other directories out there beyond Google, Bing, and Facebook. Note: many directories feature online patient reviews and star ratings. We will cover reputation management in the next section.

Examples of leading healthcare directories include:

- AMA Doctor Finder
- Castle Connolly Top Doctors
- CMS Physician Compare
- HealthFinder.gov links to other medical specialist search sites, like the AAFPRS, AAO, and OMA
- HealthGrades
- National Committee for Quality Assurance
- RateMDs

- RealSelf
- US News & World Report
- VeinDirectory.org (and many other similar paid directories)
- Vitals
- WebMD
- Wellness.com
- ZocDoc

Examples of leading local directories include:

- AngiesList
- Apple Maps
- Better Business Bureau
- Business.com
- Best of the Web Local
- Citysearch
- FourSquare
- Indeed
- LinkedIn
- Local.com
- MapQuest
- SuperPages
- TrustLink
- Trustpilot
- WhitePages.com
- YellowPages.com
- YP.com

Claiming, cleaning, and optimizing listings for individual doctors and practice locations can be a tedious, time-consuming, and frustrating experience, especially if some of the listings were created long ago by someone unknown or unavailable. What's more, well-meaning consumers can suggest edits to your listing on some sites, including Google. Those changes can compound the inconsistency problems.

A variety of affordable online resources are now available to help you update most of your directory listings. To get our latest recommendations, check out CashPayResources.com.

Reputation Management

Practitioners have expressed concern over online reviews ever since they first burst onto the scene in the mid-2000s. Doctors rightfully point out some of the potential problems including unfair complaints, non-patients posting false reviews (including competitors), employees airing dirty laundry, problems beyond the doctor's control, etc. One doctor we know summarized it well: "I have saved thousands of lives over the past twenty years. Yet I only have two online reviews, both extremely negative, one of which is from someone who was never even a patient."

We understand how you feel. Reviews can be inaccurate, biased, and sometimes downright cruel. The trouble is, patients love reviews, and Google loves reviews. Here are some important statistics to understand the world of patient reviews better.

According to Reed Mollins, Co-founder of Doctor.com, "Patients are looking to pick a provider who has social proof. Fifty percent of practices have no reviews, and of the 50% who do, the average is 2.4. We have found that practitioners who have reviews get five times more clicks than those who do not, even if they only have one star."

What's more, according to a recent Bright Local online ratings survey:[90]

- 33% of people have read online reviews for healthcare professionals, making healthcare the third most popular review category (behind restaurants and lodging).

- 93% of consumers read online reviews to determine whether a business is good or bad.

- 85% of consumers trust reviews as much as personal recommendations.

- 73% of consumers said positive reviews make them trust a business more, while 50% reported negative reviews make them trust a business less.

- 68% of consumers said they are more likely to use a local business based upon positive reviews, while 40% reported negative reviews would influence them to not use a local business.

- 87% of consumers said they require a 3-5 star rating before trusting a business.

- The most trusted consumer rating websites are Facebook (20%), Yelp (20%), Google (16%) and BBB.org (15%).

- The average consumer reads 7 reviews before trusting a business.

- 63% of consumers have left positive reviews, while 35% have left negative reviews.

- 74% of consumers have been asked by a business to leave a review, and 68% of them complied.

A quick glance at rating sites will confirm that patients highly value "the soft stuff," like how much time you spend with them; how your office looks; how your staff treats patients on the phone and in the office; convenience of both schedule and location; insurances accepted (or not); how long it takes to get an appointment; in-office waiting times; etc.

So, while we assume you'd prefer patients rate you and your practice based upon the merits of your expertise, the good news is: (1) You can take steps to improve the patient's experience so that they will rate you more highly going forward, and (2) You can take additional steps to improve your existing online reputation and generate more (positive) reviews.

Here are some key strategies to improve your online reputation:

Start by Auditing Your Online Reviews

You can't fix problems you don't know exist. So, as a first step, we recommend you take a moment to Google your name, your other doctors' names, and your practice name. Make careful notes about the website listings which appear on the first page. Then do the same thing including the word "reviews." Repeat the process on Bing. You'll probably see common rating sites in your searches. Google's search results are always changing, but your results will likely include sites such as:

- Google My Business
- Facebook
- Yelp
- Bing Local
- Healthgrades
- ZocDoc
- Vitals

Dominate the First Page of Search Results for Your Name

One of our favorite reputation management strategies is to work to dominate "page one" of searches for your name with properties you can control, at least to some extent. Hopefully, these efforts will push other websites onto "page 2." These could include:

- Twitter profiles for your business and doctor(s)
- YouTube channel for your business
- Videos tagged to individual doctors' names on YouTube
- Single page websites for each doctor, with keyword driven URLs, e.g., SeanWhiteMD.com
- Glassdoor (assuming you have happy employees willing to give you excellent reviews)
- Indeed (ditto)
- Facebook
- Google My Business for each practice location
- Google My Business for each doctor (this is now permitted by Google, though claiming and optimizing listings for 10 or more doctors can be a nightmare)
- And from the directories you previously claimed and optimized
  - Articles
  - Interviews
  - Speeches
  - Association memberships
  - Media appearances

How to Respond Appropriately to Reviews

Of course, nothing is guaranteed and despite your best efforts, it is probable that at least one of the rating sites will remain stubbornly on the first page of your results no matter what you do. So, in this section we'll cover how to respond to the reviews that are already out there.

- First, people reading reviews think more highly of businesses that respond to their reviews. Second, patients who write reviews often hope to hear from you (more on that in a moment). Third, as a reminder, the visibility of your Google My Business listing will likely increase if you respond to its reviews. Therefore, you should usually respond to your reviews. The only exception we can think of is that you may not want to respond to a "rogue" rating website, for fear of raising its visibility in the search engines.

- To avoid HIPAA violations, your responses should NEVER disclose a patient's identity.

- When responding to positive reviews, be sure to thank them generously. When possible, write longer responses for positive reviews, in the hope the extra content will raise them in search results. Sometimes you can include some appropriate keywords in your response.

- When you can identify the patient responsible for a negative review, we recommend you (or someone from your office) contact them directly and try to solve the problem offline. Sometimes patients will be so happy with your efforts to resolve their issues that they will either take down or at least amend their negative review.

- If a patient refuses to take down a negative review, or if you don't know who the reviewer was, you or someone from your team (depending upon circumstances) should typically respond with a sincere, specific response. Make sure patients know you take their concerns seriously; note that you are disappointed they did not have a great experience; let them know that you did not intend to inconvenience or offend them; and invite them to reach out to you offline. Here is a sample response:

  > "We are very sorry we kept you waiting. We know our patients lead busy lives, and we value your time. We do work very hard to stay on time, and most often we are successful in reaching that goal. However, sometimes emergencies or other issues happen that are beyond our control. Please call our office to discuss your experience further, and we will do what we can to resolve it. Also, if you like, we can schedule your future appointments during slower hours when emergencies are less likely to arise. We do hope to see you again. Best wishes,"

- When a review is especially critical, try to stay calm and do NOT respond angrily or impulsively. Online wars can quickly spiral out of control and could significantly damage your practice. Think of the old metaphor about wrestling with a pig. You'll both wind up muddy, but the pig will enjoy it.

- If a review is factually wrong, or if the review is in extremely poor taste (e.g., vulgar language, racist, hateful, sexually explicit), the rating site may honor your request to take it down. Most sites including Yelp have policies and processes posted on their websites.[91] However, be forewarned that rating sites generally favor the reviewer, and in most cases will deny your request.

- While there are rare exceptions, it almost never makes sense to sue a patient (or website) over a bad review. Court cases are typically a matter of public record, and if the press picks up the story, the problem could grow exponentially worse both online and offline. If the problem is so egregious that you feel you must take legal action (e.g., the patient wrongfully accused you of cutting off her leg), then by all means, seek legal counsel. Generally speaking, patients can express their opinion in the United States very freely without fear of legal consequences. (E.g., "He is a terrible doctor.") However, if the patient posts a review that is both harmful and factually incorrect, you may be able to sue for libel. If you are a public figure, you will also have to prove malice. Of course, lawsuits can become very expensive very quickly, and you'll have to weigh the risks versus the advantages.

- Also, you should know that the Consumer Review Fairness Act prohibits you from contractually barring patients from reviewing you.[92]

- If a common theme emerges from negative reviews, consider that there may be an element of truth to them. Your patients are giving you honest, valuable feedback, so please listen. For example, we know of one LASIK provider whose patient reviews consistently express a dislike for the practices' "hard sales" approach. An aesthetic practice we know gets lots of negative reviews about long wait times. A functional medicine practice has many reviews that say they just want to push expensive supplements. Where there is smoke, there is often fire.

How to Generate More Positive Reviews

Once you have followed the preceding steps, your next goal will be to generate a higher percentage of positive reviews going forward so that your good reviews will eventually overwhelm any negative reviews. There are a number of ways to do that, and of course, some are better than others. Also, you need to know that each rating site has its own review solicitation policy.

- First, refrain from encouraging friends, relatives, and employees to rate your practice (with the possible exception of employee sites like Glassdoor). Likewise, you shouldn't pay directly for positive reviews. Not surprisingly, virtually every rating site prohibits these practices and besides, there are better ways to improve your online reputation without resorting to fake reviews.

- Alternatively, some rating sites allow you to offer small incentives to patients who review your practice—so long as you reward all reviews, not just the positive ones. Ideas include nominal gifts like $5 Starbucks cards, donations to charities, or save-the-planet ideas like, "We'll plant a tree in your name."

- Some practices go a step further and ask patents about their experience before they leave. While everyone gets a "thank you" for their feedback, happy patients receive a business card that asks them for a review on whichever sites the practice prioritizes. You can shorten long ratings listing URLs with bit.ly. Alternatively, your web developer could create custom "301 redirects" from your website domain, e.g., HoustonSmileCenter.com/Yelp.

- It is worth noting that industry leader Yelp prohibits businesses from actively soliciting reviews from customers at all.[93] However, you have some other more indirect options; here are some helpful tips:

    - Yelp allows and can send you a "Find us on Yelp" sticker (aka window cling).[94]

    - You may have seen the "People love us on Yelp," sticker, which Yelp awards to qualifying businesses who have claimed their listing and have lots of positive reviews. (Though more than a few websites sell knockoff stickers.)[95]

    - Likewise, if you garner enough positive reviews, Yelp may offer you a Yelp Review Badge for your website, which automatically updates itself as new reviews become available.

    - Yelp uses a proprietary algorithm to evaluate reviews and filter out reviews it suspects may not be legitimate. While Yelp is, of course, secretive about its algorithm, industry pros have observed some common themes as to the reviews which wind up disappearing as, "not recommended."

- Practices that suddenly get many positive reviews.
- Multiple reviews come from the same WIFI network.
- Reviews from people who rarely use Yelp at all, have never searched for a business on Yelp, or have written only one review.
- Incomplete reviewer profiles, especially those with no photo.
- Reviews that are strongly slanted positively or negatively.
- Reviews that are short and lacking details.
- Reviews from a geographic location other than where the business is located.

- Some practitioners angrily accuse Yelp of filtering out most of their legitimate, positive patient reviews, while approving and posting virtually all of the negative ones. We recently looked at one doctor's Yelp dashboard and confirmed that over 70 positive patient reviews were "not recommended," and almost all of the denied reviews were positive. For its part, Yelp denies that it manipulates listings or extorts businesses.[96]

Multiply Positive Reviews Through Reputation Management Automation

While the aforementioned building techniques can help, a variety of vendors offer automated systems to generate more reviews. While specific offerings differ, the reputation management systems tend to share some common characteristics:

- The first step is to encourage all patients to provide their feedback directly to the practice through a simple survey.

  - By far the best way to get patient feedback is to ask them to complete a simple electronic survey before they leave; provide them with a tablet, laptop computer, or kiosk to do this.

  - The second-best way to solicit patient feedback is to text them your request and survey link soon after their departure.

  - You can also email patients, ideally as soon as possible following the visit. While response rates for emails will be much lower than for in-person requests, automated systems can send several emails over time to non-respondents.

- Finally, you can send emails to large numbers of past patients. Response rates will predictably decline as the amount of time since the patients' last visits increases.

- The next step in this process is to separate positive survey responses from neutral and negative survey responses. This can be done through a method known as the Net Promoter Score, or NPS. According to the Harvard Business Review, the following single question is an ideal indicator of overall consumer satisfaction:[97] *"How likely is it that you would recommend [our practice] to a friend or family member?"*

  Most often respondents are asked to respond on a scale of 0 to 10, with 10 being the highest satisfaction. Respondents are categorized as follows based on their rating:

  - Promoters - 9 and 10
  - Passives - 7 and 8
  - Detractors - 0 to 6

- Promoters are encouraged to elaborate with comments and are asked for permission to share their responses on the practice's website. When patients agree, their comments and NPS (translated into a 5-star rating) automatically appear online. Almost immediately following this step, patients are then encouraged to share similar comments on whichever ratings websites the practice desires. Everything is automated and incredibly easy for the patient. Of course, you must take proper precautions to avoid running afoul of HIPAA laws.

- Passives and Detractors are likewise asked to elaborate on their experience, but their input stays with the practice. Their feedback is not shared on the practice website or rating sites. This process allows unhappy patients to blow off steam before they go online to complain. It also allows the practice to learn from its mistakes, and privately circle back to the patient and attempt to resolve the problem.

- Reputation management programs also provide online dashboards that allow you to: (1) Manage the program; (2) Customize surveys, emails and texts; (3) Enter patient email addresses and mobile numbers; (4) Track both positive and negative responses; and (5) Monitor review sites and alert you when new reviews are posted.

As you can imagine, these programs offer a compelling way to generate lots of high-quality reviews, while mitigating the risk of bad ones. Please note that Yelp warns businesses using these highly effective automated programs that they run the risk of seeing their listing drop within the Yelp platform.[98]

Should I Advertise on Rating Sites?

Our answer is, "If at all, be selective." On the one hand, some sites offer excellent opportunities. For example, Google is a powerhouse, and ads that show up on Maps can be useful. ZocDoc sometimes shows up well in searches and also offers some unique features. On the other hand, a lot of doctors have a hard time feeding "dogs that bite them." We usually recommend different, better ways to invest in your digital marketing budget. Speaking of which,

Digital Advertising

Over the years we have learned to accept the fact that most doctors don't care all that much about websites, SEO, directories, reputation sites, and social media. Those are all great features, but in the end, the doctors we know want the ultimate benefit, i.e., more new patients and more revenue.

Putting all the great techniques we've discussed aside, if most doctors had a single marketing wish, they'd opt for a magic box where you could drop $100 in, and $500 would pop out. In all our travels over the past two decades, digital advertising is the closest thing we have found to that magic marketing box.

Digital Advertising is Predictable, Profitable, Passive and Scalable

- **Predictable.** One of the most fantastic things about digital advertising is that you can begin with a relatively modest investment, make decisions based on best practices, test various hypotheses, and track results. Over time, digital advertising campaigns can be optimized by cutting the losers and investing more into the winners. Within six months, results usually become predictable.
- **Profitable.** While nothing works 100% of the time, digital advertising typically has the highest direct ROI of any marketing strategy you can choose. Given the right circumstances, digital advertising will usually be profitable, and sometimes very, very profitable.
- **Passive.** While it takes a lot of work (and expertise) to set up and run digital advertising campaigns, that doesn't mean you have to do the work yourself. In

fact, you shouldn't. While many ongoing marketing strategies must be done at the practice level and are time intensive (e.g., doctor referral building, internal marketing strategies, answering phone inquiries, closing cases, and organic social media), digital advertising is something that you can and should delegate to outside experts. More on that topic later.

- **Scalable.** The tech industry does a very great job at "thinking big," and one of the words they use all the time is "scalable." That kind of thinking applies to your private practice as well. While it's nice when you find something that works for one office, it's a lot more exciting when it works for 20. Digital advertising scales exceptionally well, whether you have 20 locations to promote, or you want to have 20 locations to promote.

Pay-Per-Click Advertising (PPC) Targets Patients Who Are Actively Searching For Your Services

While almost everything we have discussed in this chapter will directly or indirectly improve your search engine rankings, the fact is that SEO takes time, and in some cases, a lot of time. What's more, even if you follow every best practice we have discussed, you cannot control Google's algorithm, and it continually changes. So, while we love SEO, we think it is time to let you in on an industry "insider" joke.

You can *pray* for clicks, or you can *pay* for clicks.

Actually, we recommend you do *both*.

We understand that many doctors steadfastly prefer to solely focus on SEO and organic social media because they assume these are both "free." However, by now you have learned these strategies are never really free. Even if you don't write many checks for SEO and organic social media, you and your staff will instead need to spend a lot of time.

Time? Who precisely in private healthcare practice today has extra time?

Of course, spending money doesn't sound very appealing either. That is unless you think back to return on investment (ROI). Just like the magic box, pay-per-click (PPC) can often—not always—give you a positive return on investment where you put in $100, and $200 pops out. Sometimes even $500 or $1,000 pops out.

What Is Pay-Per-Click Again?

Do you remember what you see at the very top of search engine results pages? That's right, the pay-per-click (PPC) ads.

It's no mistake that Google's PPC ads enjoy the best possible real estate on the Internet. What's more, over time Google has made its PPC ads graphically look more and more like the organic search results. As a result, about a billion Google users worldwide click those PPC ads billions of times each year, and in the process generate many billions of dollars for Google.

Sure, that's great for Google, but is it great for practitioners like you? Yes, it is, and now we are going to show you how and why.

What are the Benefits of PPC Advertising?

- Instead of waiting months or years to get on top of Google's organic listings through SEO, you can get there immediately with an ad on top of the entire search results page.

- While it doesn't happen every time, sometimes you can get new patients right away. We've even seen practices get their first new patient the day their campaign launched.

- With PPC, you have the unique ability to target precisely the cases you want. For example, a dermatologist may have a bustling practice, and not want any more "bread and butter" cases. With PPC, she can target big money makers, i.e., skin cancer (including Mohs surgery) and aesthetics. Practices can also target precise geographies to build locations, or create campaigns to promote various providers.

- Pay-per-click is the leading "pull" medium, where prospects are actively searching for a solution. Most other advertising media (e.g., TV, radio, newspaper, billboards) are "push" marketing strategies, where you intrusively show your ad to the prospect and hope to catch them when they are ready to buy.

- While competition is already high in many markets, the online marketplace is wide open in others. If PPC competition is light in your city, you have a window of opportunity to build a dominant position in your market before your competitors even know what happened.

- Compared to traditional advertising, PPC and most digital advertising options are incredibly agile. With PPC, advertisers can make changes to campaigns almost instantly. With a billboard or television, changes in strategy are much more difficult to make.

- PPC and other online advertising options are also transparent. Through modern technology including online dashboards, you will be able to see exactly where your money is going, and how it is doing.

- As we mentioned earlier, when it works, PPC can become Predictable, Profitable, Passive, and Scalable.

- Looking at all of this another way, if your practice is not represented in the PPC listings, you are choosing to stay out of a marketplace where patients are going with the intent to buy. These patients will likely never have the opportunity to know your practice, and thus merely go somewhere else.

So, How Does PPC Work?

Google, Bing, and their respective search partners control virtually 100% of the search engine market. Every day, millions of people go to their websites to find the goods and services they need—including local healthcare.

Let's say a consumer searched Google for the phrase, "plastic surgeon near me." She'd find two to three ads at the top of Google, and click the one that seemed most relevant to her need. Google would instantaneously direct her to the advertiser's website, and the practice would pay for that click (as the name implies).

"But wait, I am smarter than that. I never click on the ads. Instead, I always stubbornly scroll down to the organic content." We certainly understand that you and a lot of other people skip the ads. But clearly, many millions of people *do* click on those PPC ads. Whenever the authors are personally looking to buy something, we both consider the PPC ads *first,* because we know those ads are from advertisers who want our business.

> Google did not build its fortune on Gmail, Android phones, Chromebooks, or Google Home. Last year, 71% of Google's $111 billion in revenue came from advertising on its proprietary sites, and another 16% came from Google network sites.[99]

Advertisers never pay when someone merely sees their PPC ad (that's called an impression). Instead, advertisers only pay for every click, knowing that a certain percentage of their website visitors will become new patients.

The price for each click is a function of the marketplace, and is determined by two factors:

1. The relative demand for each keyword, and
2. The quality and relevance of your PPC ad and website for each keyword. Google calls this metric a "Quality Score."

Since Google is all about creating a relevant search experience for consumers, the higher your Quality Score, the less you will pay per click.

The Magic of Control

Unlike SEO and organic social media, PPC is highly controllable. Most of the essential factors are under your control, including:

- Keywords: You can choose the keywords you want to advertise for, e.g., implant dentist near me, integrative medicine specialist Austin, vein doctor nearby, menopause specialist, hormone replacement therapy, etc.
- Geography: Choose the precise area for your ad.
- Time: You can choose when and when not to run your ads.
- Ad text: You control what your ads say, and can test many variations.
- Destination: You can send visitors to whichever website page you like.
- Unlimited testing potential: With PPC, it is easy to test new ideas, and results will come back relatively quickly and affordably.
- Budget: You have complete control over your daily spend. The bare minimum budget we recommend bothering with is $500 a month, or $17 a day, though impressive results usually require more, starting at $50 a day.

How to Get More People to Call You

As we mentioned previously, you pay for the number of clicks, not how many patients call you to set an appointment. To optimize the success of your campaign, you'll need to raise the percentage of people who call you after they click.

- The website or landing page must be "Conversion Rate Optimized," i.e., designed to compel visitors to inquire via phone calls and form submissions.
- The relevance of your ad copy and website to the searcher's intent.
- Phone skills - the ability of your staff to convert callers into first appointments.
- PPC Campaign optimization - Your campaign should be continually optimized by an expert to uncover the ideal combination of factors.

What Are Landing Pages?

Most websites are not optimized to convert visitors into inquiries. What's more, practice websites often provide prospective patients so many options unrelated to what they are looking for that they become lost, confused, and eventually leave the site without doing anything.

Take for example a patient with migraines who is looking for a doctor to help him. Upon landing upon a neurologist's website, he could quickly become so distracted with the competing information on diseases unrelated to his problem that he'd immediately "bounce" off the site, rather than dig through the information and eventually call.

Therefore, counter-intuitively, it is often better to send prospective patients to a "landing page," which is solely designed to satisfy the exact need the patients are searching for (e.g., migraines), and then convince them to inquire.

Tracking the Source of New Patients

In the old days, we taught practitioners to ask new patients on their first call into the office, "Whom may we thank for referring you?" That still works reasonably well, but it is a manual process, and staff compliance is usually a big problem. Today, tracking the source of new patients is much easier and far more scientific.

As consumers land on your website from PPC (or other digital) ads, technology can now track their behavior as they travel through your site, and very importantly, determine whether or not they filled out an inquiry form or if they called you.

Patient phone inquiries can be tracked via unique tracking numbers, which dynamically change for each visitor based upon the ad that got them there. Thus, your digital campaigns can be optimized based upon the combination of platforms, keywords, advertisements, landing pages, time of day, and geography that gets people to call you. What's more, phone calls can be recorded in a HIPAA-compliant manner. Best of all, the critical data is available to you and your digital team, 24 hours a day. Just as you can calculate the ROI from other types of advertising, you can conduct a similar calculation for your digital investment.

Digital Advertising Strategies That Reach Patients When They Aren't Actively Searching for You

While PPC is designed to target people who are actively seeking information via search engines, there are many options designed to capture prospective patients earlier in the buying cycle, *before* they actively search for solutions. Some of your leading options include the Google Display Network, YouTube advertising, Yahoo/Oath network, Pandora, Spotify, Facebook, and Instagram. We'll cover Facebook and Instagram advertising at length in Chapter 9: How to Make Social Media Work for You, so let's begin with Google Display Network.

Google Display Network

In addition to dominating the search engine advertising space, Google also owns the Google Display Network (GDN),[100] which is the most extensive online display advertising network.

- Boasting more than one million websites, apps, blogs and videos, GDN allows you to reach patients while they're browsing their favorite sites, watching YouTube, checking their Gmail account, or using their mobile devices.
- Practices can target prospective local consumers who are browsing content about topics such as healthcare, diet, and beauty, or keywords like integrative medicine or chiropractor.
- Display ads can be produced in various formats, including photos, videos or dynamic (interactive) HTML5.
- We usually recommend GDN as a secondary layer to a PPC campaign.

YouTube

Owned by Google, YouTube[101] has enjoyed spectacular growth in recent years and is fundamentally changing how people consume video content online. According to Google, "In the average month, 18+-year-olds in the United States spend more time watching YouTube than any television network." Some key points:

- You can advertise to prospective patients in your area as they browse YouTube videos,[102] either through GDN or by reserving specific, premium inventory through YouTube.

- YouTube allows you to target prospective patients by geography, demographics, and interests. Advertisers can also determine the maximum amount they are willing to pay.

- With YouTube, advertisers pay when people watch their ads.

- TrueView[103] in-stream ads play before or during another video from a YouTube partner. Viewers see five seconds of your video and then have a choice to keep watching or skip it. Advertisers pay when a viewer watches for at least 30 seconds or to the end of the video (whichever is first), or clicks on an interactive sliding card.

- TrueView video discovery ads appear alongside other YouTube search pages, or on GDN websites that match the advertiser's target audience. Advertisers only pay when a viewer chooses to watch its video by clicking on the ad.

Verizon's Oath Network (Including Yahoo!)

Verizon owns the Oath network, and it includes some of the Internet's most venerable content brands including Yahoo!, AOL, and Huffington Post. Some people underestimate the power of these brands, especially the various Yahoo! brands which still have over a billion monthly users. Yahoo.com remains one of the most trafficked websites in the United States, behind other leading sites including Google, YouTube, Facebook, and Amazon.[104]

Native display and video ads are designed to fit in with the content that surrounds them and are our favorite Yahoo! strategy. You can see examples of native display ads by going to yahoo.com, where they appear as "sponsored" content within the various news stories. Best practices include:

- Make sure your ad fits in and is relevant to the content that surrounds it.
- Choose high quality, impactful photos or videos.
- Write headlines that sound like news stories.
- Send click-through visitors to specially designed, relevant landing pages.

Search Ads. While the Google and Bing networks dominate the search engine landscape today, Yahoo Search offers a lesser, third option. According to Oath, Yahoo Search still reaches over 100 million unique searches per month, about 1/3 of which can't be found on other search engines.

Geofencing

Geofencing is an exciting new technology that allows advertisers to target people who enter particular geographic areas, for example, a senior center, a football stadium, or even competitors' locations.

1. The advertiser first defines the precise geographic area for the geofence.
2. When consumers enter the predetermined geofence, the system recognizes their location and tags their phones.
3. Consumers will then see push notifications or ads within various apps for up to 30 days.
4. Results can be tracked on a completely anonymous basis.

Other Digital Advertising Properties to Consider

Pandora's listeners are incredibly loyal to their platform. Audio ads periodically appear when free subscribers stream their favorite audio, and mobile ads appear when users interact with the Pandora app. Since the minimum price point to run a campaign is often high, more hospitals than practices advertise on their platform.

Spotify. Because it requires a much lower "buy-in" than Pandora, and also reaches a younger audience, Spotify is an option for some practices willing to work through its do-it-yourself platform.

Waze is a highly popular directions application that utilizes user interactions and cell phone data to help its users find the fastest possible routes. When users stop at traffic lights near your office, your ads can appear on their mobile phone.

How to Actually Implement These Ideas

As we come to the end of our marketing journey together, we need to consider the next steps. We hope that you are excited about the many ideas we have shared, but we worry you might also feel a bit overwhelmed, too. After all, "Who exactly is going to do all this stuff?"

Great question.

The answer is, someone on your team can and should handle much of the marketing implementation and administration, while some marketing strategies and tactics are better outsourced.

"Why not just hire a marketing person to handle everything?" Three reasons:

1. Like medicine, marketing today is a world of specialists. For example, some of the specialties outlined within this chapter include website and graphic design, website development (programming), copywriting, SEO, digital advertising, social media, videography, and editing. All those specialties require different skill sets, and no one does all of them well.

2. Digital marketing is complicated and requires expertise. In our seminars, I (Stewart) use the analogy, "Playing high stakes poker is easy. It's the winning that is hard." You can read a book and learn how to play poker in an hour, but that doesn't mean it is a good idea to sit down and join a high stakes game. (Though we are pretty sure the other players would welcome you if you did!) Likewise, SEO and digital adverting are highly competitive, zero-sum games. While we know it may sound self-serving, if you want to win, you really should hire experts.

3. Finally, outside firms typically have digital marketing systems and operations in place, so they can often handle the most important digital marketing functions for you, less expensively than you could do yourself. (And without the headaches and overhead of another salary.)

Keep in mind, though, you can't delegate everything to someone else. There are plenty of other things your internal team should do in-house:

- Organic social media
- Monitor and respond to reviews
- Patient recalls and emails
- Local events
- Doctor referral building
- Phone handling to convert inquiries to patients
- Case presentation (sales)
- Vendor coordination and administration

Examples of digital marketing strategies that are best outsourced

- Website development
- Local and national SEO
- Digital advertising
- Reputation management

Thank you for joining us on this journey. Good luck and good marketing!

> Get free articles, tips, resources, do-it-yourself tools and a
> free digital marketing audit at CashPayResources.com.

Chapter

How to Make Social Media Work for You

Organic Social Media

When social media first exploded onto the scene over a decade ago, both marketers and doctors were actually a little too excited about its potential for private practice marketing. Who could blame them? The fantasy was great. "All I have to do is figure out how to put up a free Facebook Page, and then the next day I'll get lots of new patients." (Everyone loves free patients.)

Sadly, the promise of social media fame and easy money far exceeded the reality, then as now. In our experience, while organic social media can bring in some new patients, it very rarely brings in lots of new patients. Also, while some people call organic social media "free" because you don't directly pay money directly to Facebook et al., organic social media entails a lot of work.

Granted, there are a few doctor social media celebrities out there, including the three who are arguably the most well-known.

- Dr. Kevin Pho, aka @kevinmd, who blogs about various healthcare stories and whose tweets became prominent during the early days of Twitter.

- Dr. Eric Topol, aka @EricTopol, who is a noted author and speaker on healthcare trends and technology.

- Dr. Sandra Lee, aka @SandraLeeMD or Dr. Pimple Popper,[105] who came up with a very unique, memorable concept.

What do these and other rising social media stars have in common? Well, most seem to be "naturals" who possess great social media instincts, enjoy the process of winning followers, have something unique to say, and work very hard at building a following.

Take for example Sheila Nazarian, MD, who has earned 37,000 Facebook followers and 182,000 Instagram followers. Nazarian is an attractive, charismatic, board-certified Beverly Hills plastic surgeon who, according to a recent MedEsthetics article, also employs two full-time social media staffers and recently hired a marketing company. Beyond Facebook and Instagram, she is also building her presence on YouTube, Pinterest, Snapchat, LinkedIn and Twitter.[106]

If you dream of becoming a social media celebrity, have the right stuff, and are willing to work very, very hard at it with no guarantee of success, the best practices recommendations in this section can help you get started. Be forewarned, however, that (1) likes and followers do not necessarily translate into direct revenue and new patients, and (2) worse, it is getting much harder to reach followers for free.

Alternatively, if you are like the vast majority of practitioners who don't have the time, budget, skills, or inclination to do what it takes to become famous online, the principles within this section can help you build a solid, prioritized social media presence that attracts some patients along the way. Assuming that sounds more like you, social media should be part of your marketing plan, but definitely not your only—or even primary—marketing strategy. Either way, let's get started.

"Facebook's Organic Reach is Dead."

Social media behemoth Facebook's evolution has been exciting to watch. In the very beginning, you had to have an email address from certain universities to even get onto the network. In 2007, "Fan Pages" became open to everyone, and major brands like Coca-Cola rushed in to set up their own free Facebook Pages. Those same corporations then spent millions of dollars online and offline to convince consumers to declare themselves fans on their respective Facebook Pages. (We have to wonder if Mark Zuckerberg ever sent the corporations thank you notes for promoting his site so well.)

Businesses and even healthcare practices loved Facebook because they could engage their best customers in an exciting new way, convert them into fans, and then build and maintain these relationships for free through Facebook's massive organic reach.

Starting in 2012, the music stopped and organic reach suddenly plummeted to 16%. By 2014, reach dropped again to between 2% and 6.5%. In early 2016, the remaining reach dropped again, possibly by as much as 42%.[107]

Think for a moment what this all means. It takes a near Herculean effort for the average practice to win 1,000 "likes" on its Facebook Page. Then, it takes creativity and time to come up with suitable Facebook posts. Now, each post will likely be exposed to less than 50 people, most of whom are already patients!

In January 2018, Facebook's Mark Zuckerberg confirmed another new round of algorithm changes, noting that the explosive growth in content had the potential to overwhelm Facebook users' limited amount of time to consume it. To keep Facebook relevant to what users want, Zuckerberg wrote:

> *"…you can expect to see more from your friends, family and groups.*
> *As we roll this out, you'll see less public content like posts*
> *from businesses, brands, and media."*[108]

So, while Facebook's organic reach had already reached historic lows, Zuckerberg confirmed it will go even lower. Several days after Zuckerberg's announcement, digital advertising news leader Digiday declared, "Organic reach on Facebook is dead. Advertisers expect price hikes after Facebook's feed purge."[109]

The bad news doesn't stop with Facebook. According to Hootsuite, Instagram and Twitter's organic reach is also declining. In retrospect, it sounds like a familiar story. As soon as the business users became hooked on social media, the free samples began to disappear.

Declining reach, combined with the labor and skill required to master social media, are the fundamental reasons most practices fail to attract many new patients from organic social media. However, it is still worth doing. There are some strategies to eek out a modicum of organic reach, and advertising offers additional opportunities. More on all of that later.

9 Ways Organic Social Media Can Benefit Your Practice

Even though organic social media's reach continues to drop, and is not likely to win you droves of new patients, you probably should still participate on at least Facebook. Here are some of the benefits of building your presence on Facebook and other social media:

1. **Brand advocacy and loyalty.** Chances are, a high percentage of your patients are already active on social media. Rather than miss out on this very important "party," you should at least create a solid Facebook Page so that your most loyal

patients can find and interact with your practice online. By joining the online conversation, you will make it easy for devoted patients to support and promote your practice for you.

2. **Generate patient referrals.** When your patients interact with your practice on social media, their friends will often take notice. Eventually, conversations will emerge, leading to online or offline referrals.

3. **Patient retention.** Your social media presence will allow you stay in front of patients and build loyalty with them. Thus, social media can help you keep your patients.

4. **Build community.** Some specialties are highly consumer-direct, and therefore lend themselves well to your building an online community that your patients can participate in. It is easier to get patients to engage with cash-based practices like orthodontics, LASIK, plastic surgery, weight loss, and integrative medicine than it is for insurance-based specialties like oncology and urology. Still, even practices in those specialties can do such a great job of building a community that their patients actually begin connecting and supporting each other.

5. **Thought leadership.** When you create and share lots of great content via social media, others (including traditional media) will begin to take notice.

6. **Search Engine Optimization.** Even though Google denies it, many SEO experts believe social signals such as likes and shares indirectly enhance your search engine optimization.

7. **Employee recruitment**. Prospective employees often check out your Facebook Page to evaluate your internal culture.

8. **Humanize your practice.** While patients want their healthcare providers to stay professional, they typically don't want to be treated by robots. Your social media presence can give them (a curated) behind-the-scenes look at the human beings who make up your practice.

9. **Share testimonials, case studies and before and afters.** Social media platforms are great for helping you to show off your great outcomes.

How to Avoid Social Media Disasters

Even though social media has been around for years, some providers are still afraid to participate. Frankly, it is true that things can go awry if you are not careful. However, remember that social media problems can arise whether or not you actively participate in the conversation. We asked our friend, Lee Aase, Communications Director, Social and Digital Innovation for Mayo Clinic, for his insights about this topic:

- Create your own social media accounts on the major networks to help manage your online reputation. We recommend that for search optimization, you claim and complete your Doximity profile and create accounts on Twitter and LinkedIn. You also may want to have a Facebook Page for engagement with potential patients. Having these platforms also gives you a vehicle to respond if an issue arises.

- Monitor social media activity for all these "owned" social media properties, and have an action plan ready for negative or problematic posts or comments. Also, periodically check leading social media and reputation sites where people may mention you or your practice. Google Alerts can help with this task.

- Be careful to ensure that any information you share is both accurate and from a reputable source, because everything you post online has the potential to stay in the public forum, forever.

- Never give medical advice online. Public forums are great for general education on health and medical issues, but not for practicing medicine.

- Create a social media policy or guidelines for anyone employed by your practice. It should cover the rules for both official messages from your practice and the online activities of employees that are related to your practice. Keep it as short and simple as possible. We recommend you review your policy or guidelines with an attorney and then train employees. To help you get started, we recommend you search online for Mayo Clinic's social media guidelines for employees.[110]

- We hope your practice never faces a public crisis, but if it does, be sure to seek the advice of both an attorney and a crisis management PR specialist before responding online. Be very careful so that you don't make the problem worse or create additional legal liability.

- Consider joining Mayo Clinic's Social Media Network (socialmedia.mayoclinic. org) to connect with others and learn from those who are applying social media in their practices.

Facebook (and Other Social Media) Best Practices

Boasting about 2.2 billion active users worldwide, Facebook remains by far the most important social media network for most healthcare practitioners to consider.[111] Since many Facebook best practices also apply to other social media platforms (including Instagram), let's start there.

- **Start by building out a great Facebook Page.** Your Facebook marketing should center on your practice's business Facebook Page, not your personal profile. (For privacy and ethical reasons, most providers should customize their own Facebook profile so that only Facebook friends can see their profiles, and then only accept "friend requests" from non-patients.)

    - If you haven't already, go to your Facebook account, click "create" on the top menu, and follow the prompts to create your Facebook Page.
    - Make sure you fully complete your Page profile. As you build out your Facebook Page, think about someone meeting your practice for the first time. What do you want to show them? What do you want them to know?
    - Be sure to select a great profile picture and cover photo.[112] Also feature target audience photos on your Page.

- **Facebook (and social media) basics**

    - Adhere to HIPAA. Patient privacy is of course paramount. Always get releases before posting patient names, stories, photos, or videos. Also, the AMA has published guidelines about Professionalism in the Use of Social Media.[113]
    - Consider adding a privacy notice to patients on your Facebook Page or elsewhere, such as: *Your healthcare is confidential, and our practice respects your right to privacy. Social media reaches far and wide, and records of your identity, posts, photos, videos or comments could theoretically last forever. Therefore, please use good judgment before sharing anything about your own health online. Also, never share confidential health information about any other individual. Thank you.*

- Be authentic. Patients expect your social media efforts to be a bit more transparent and less formal than your practice website.

- Have two-way conversations with people, not monologues. Be about them! Remember you are not the patient—they look at things completely different than you do. Keep your posts conversational.

- Use original photos and videos wherever and whenever possible. Try to avoid stock photos.

- Always consider how your posts can also build your authority.

- Create your own, consistent, social media "voice," so that you stand out from the crowd.

- People have the option to "like" or "follow" your Facebook Page. According to Facebook, people who want to show support for your Page and receive updates should like it, while people who merely want to receive updates should follow it.[114] Put another way, you want "likes," because you also automatically become followed. (Note: In 2010 Facebook phased out "fans" in favor of "likes.")[115]

- Since it is difficult for an outside firm to keep up on the day-to-day workings of a busy office, most practices should manage their organic social media internally. Find someone on staff who has the willingness and ability to do so.

- **Create shareable content.** Create and share excellent content on a regular basis—at least several times a month and ideally several times per week. Start a content calendar to ensure you don't fall behind. Examples of effective Facebook content include:

  - Create relevant educational healthcare posts.

  - Write informative SEO-friendly blog posts, and share summaries and links on Facebook.

  - Share relevant health information from additional, credible sources.

  - Cover your participation in community and charity events—before, during and after the occasion. Be sure to take lots of pictures.

  - Some providers like to include photos or videos of their travels to healthcare conferences. While "on the road" stories and photos are fun and show a commitment to continuing education, it is especially important to capture your thought leadership whenever you speak. Ask someone to take pictures of you standing at the podium during your speech, and when appropriate and possible, take a picture (or selfie) of the audience from your point of view.

- Share select "slice of life" stories about your doctor(s) or team when they are in the real world, outside of the office.
- Share appropriate in-office photos. For example, you could take pictures of an interesting gift from a patient or referring doctor, a puppy someone brought in, staff birthday parties, etc.
- Create compelling graphics and infographics. Tip: Canva.com is a great tool to help.
- Post video—patient or even doctor milestones (with permission, of course).
- Offer contests and quizzes to your Facebook visitors.
- If you are looking for real patient stories for video testimonials or your marketing efforts, announce a process to apply.
- Tell stories. People especially love emotional success stories.
- Post about trending health-related topics.
- Post selfies at interesting locations.
- Ask followers for input.
- Use humor. If you or someone on your team is funny, show it.
- Directly promote your services no more than 20% of the time. The other 80% should be valuable or entertaining content.
- Post before and after pictures
- Selectively post videos of procedures.

- **Very high-quality content.** *Highly compelling* content can sometimes break free of organic reach's downward death spiral and get some traction on Facebook.

  - Native videos (those posted directly on Facebook versus YouTube) get a nice boost compared to other posts. Pick a great topic like, "5 Tips to Improve Your Sleep." Whenever possible, show subtitles or words to match the script, so users can watch the videos (at work), without turning the sound on. Keep the video length to under 90 seconds. Tip: pond5.com is an excellent source of sound and video files. WeVideo.com and Apple's free iMovie are excellent tools for amateur video editing.
  - Since Facebook is currently pushing its video streaming service, Facebook Live, it does much better at reaching followers and their friends than ordinary content.

- Finally, content that is *remarkable* does best of all. A recent podcast interview Stewart conducted with Lee Aase featured a huge success story with emotional posts and videos about the hospital's first face transplant patient.[116]

- **How to get more Facebook followers**. In the early days of Facebook, marketers spent a lot of time and money to build Facebook likes and followers. Today, given the decline in organic social media reach, we rarely recommend practices that make special efforts to acquire more followers. Focus instead on creating great content that has the ability to catch on organically with your followers. (Note: there are some advertising options to boost likes; more about that soon.)

- **How to handle negative posts and comments.** If you want any Facebook presence at all, you'll need to enable comments and ratings. Make a plan as to how you will respond to both negative comments and reviews. Note: you generally can't take down reviews, but you have options with negative comments. For example, regarding your Facebook Page,[117] you (or your appointed social media manager) can:

  - Choose to ignore the negative post or comment (rarely the right move).
  - Respond to the post or comment appropriately (never angrily), and when appropriate ask them to take the conversation offline.
  - Hide the post or comment, so that only the poster and his Facebook friends can see it.
  - Delete the post or comment from the page entirely. This is the best option if someone posts egregious material or violates another patient's privacy.
  - Report the post or comment for spam, hate speech, personal attacks, sexually explicit comments, violence, or harmful behavior.
  - Ban the user from posting or commenting on your page in the future.

Instagram

With about 1 billion active users worldwide[118] (including 60% of US adults),[119] Instagram is the fastest growing, second most relevant network for practitioners. Owned by Facebook, Instagram is great for doctors who want to target a somewhat younger audience. Much of what we covered in the previous section also applies to Instagram, but here are some additional thoughts:

- Instagram, of course, is a mobile platform that is all about sharing photos with followers.

- Therefore, specialties that have a visual component naturally have a big advantage, e.g., plastic surgeons, medspas, OB/GYNs (cute babies), dermatologists, and veterinarians (cute pets).

- You can set up an account either through your Facebook Page, or through your business email (you do not want to link to your personal account).

- Your username will begin with the @ sign, and it will be your user name going forward. A lot of people choose cute but confusing and obscure abbreviations; however, we recommend you choose your practice name, a keyword-based name, or a memorable variation of your own name.

- As with Facebook, choose a great profile picture and complete your profile and settings. Be sure to switch your new profile to a business profile, and link it with your Facebook account so you can manage any advertising from one place.

- Hashtags are fundamental to both Instagram and Twitter. Hashtags start with the pound sign (#) and include a word, string of words, or abbreviation that users can easily search for. Some examples include cities (#PalmSprings), professional conferences (#asps2018), professional associations (#a4m), schools (#ocsa), and topics of interest (#integrativemedicine). You can create your practice's own hashtag over time, but it is also important to explore which hashtags people routinely use by trying keywords in the magnifying glass icon at the bottom of the app. In that way, a plastic surgeon could include the keyword #beauty in her post in order to reach some of the highly-involved people who browse that hashtag's 266,000 posts.

- Lots of people admire great photography on Instagram, so try to take great photos in the different size formats Instagram offers, and be sure to experiment with the various filters that come with the app. Amateurs often stumble into some stunning results. Tip: if you have an iPhone (and what doctor doesn't), sign up for one of the free iPhone photography classes at the Apple store. You'll learn how to get the most from your phone, attachments, and additional apps.

- Behind-the-scenes photos or videos can work well.

- Images can include a lot more than just photos, including all kinds of instructional graphics, infographics, quotes, etc. Be sure no one inadvertently uploads copyrighted material.

- Like Facebook, videos stand out and work particularly well on Instagram. Impromptu videos are authentic and can work well, as can professionally-produced videos. Be sure to try out the Boomerang setting, which is a 3 second video that loops back and forth, often comically.

- Like Snapchat, Instagram stories are videos that are posted for only for 24 hours. They are often more impromptu and less polished than other videos. Engaged followers tend to love these.

- Instagram Live broadcasts live video, just like Facebook Live.

- Perfect captions. While Instagram captions can be up to 2200 words long, users will only see the first three or four lines of text until they click "More." So, make sure you take the extra time to write engaging captions. Remember to ask users to follow you, view another post, or visit a blog post.

- Try to create a consistent brand "look" on Instagram, rather than include hundreds of disparate looking photos.

- When you create great content, more and more people will follow you and come back to your posts over time.

Twitter

While Twitter boasts 330 million worldwide users, it is of much more limited use to doctors than Facebook or Instagram.[120] Still, here are some useful highlights:

- As with all social media platforms, create a great profile with great descriptions and great profile and background photos. You can include keywords and links in your profile description.

- Like Instagram, Twitter user names begin with an @ symbol. Choose your Twitter handle carefully.

- Because Twitter endlessly streams updates in real time, and because many people follow thousands of others, hashtags are even more critical on Twitter. Without hashtags, next to no one will find your posts.

- Also because of the endless streams, the time of day that you post is even more important on Twitter than other social networks. Advanced social media users choose third party tools like HootSuite or Sprout Social to organize all their social media posts and time them to when their audiences will most likely be watching.

- We simplistically categorize Twitter content into news, celebrity watching, special interests, local interests (like the local high school), and thought leadership. For most doctors, the primary Twitter benefit is to build thought leadership.

- A lot of people have a profile for both their business and themselves personally. I (Stewart) for example, have a personal profile (@stewartgandolf) that I update myself whenever it occurs to me. My interests vary, but tend to include our content, digital marketing articles, smart articles on varied topics, personal things I don't mind strangers seeing (versus Facebook which I save for people I know), music, travel adventures, and occasionally political stuff. Meanwhile, our editor updates our company Twitter account, @HCSuccess, almost exclusively with our own blog posts. Mark, on the other hand, finds Twitter of little interest for business, and therefore rarely posts.

- A lot of people still use "bots" on Twitter to automatically post articles and follow people, in the hopes they will follow them back. Please don't!

- As you build momentum on Twitter, be sure to follow the notifications tab to see how your posts are performing. Expert Twitter users (who have the time) will often reach out to people who engage with their content.

- You can "Direct Message" people who follow you on Twitter.

- You can tweet to a user and all his/her followers by starting your tweet with their Twitter handle (with the @ sign).

YouTube

Owned by Google, YouTube boasts 1.9 billion users.[121] It is the second most trafficked search engine, behind Google. Some highlights:

- Content types can include how-to instructions (e.g., exercises, makeup, etc.), doctor or patient testimonials, thought leader interviews, case studies, regular video blogs, live video, and events.

- Some of the most popular categories on YouTube include health and wellness, beauty and fashion, how-to videos, music, and silly entertainment (e.g., cat videos).

- Start by creating a YouTube channel with the usual complete profile and photos. Be sure to include keywords in your profile description.

- Because YouTube is owned by Google, your channel and videos have the opportunity to show up well in search results. Since Google has a hard time deciphering videos, make sure you include keywords in the descriptions and tags for each video you upload. Also take care to name your video files appropriately.

- Pick interesting video topics, such as, "What to do if you kid has a persistent cough."

- To show up well in Google and YouTube search results, you should also attempt to engage visitors on your YouTube channel, and engage with other YouTube channels. Advanced YouTube users have a sense of community.

- Usually you'll want to keep videos as short as possible, often a couple of minutes or less. However, if the user really wants your content, they will watch a surprisingly long video. Make your video as long as it needs to be, but not a second more.

- If you are going to do a lot of videos, it makes sense to use some of the tools we mentioned above to create simple opening and closing title cards; include some pleasing music.

- While YouTube suggests up to three thumbnail pictures for your video, sometimes none of them work. However, if you have a verified profile, you can choose whatever frame or image you want.

- To shoot videos by yourself, pick a great background, make sure you have proper lighting, be ready to pick up all kinds of unexpected background sounds, shoot more than you need to (including "B-Roll"), and remember the real magic is in editing.

- In terms of equipment, if you are shooting videos yourself, you can obtain good results using your smartphone, a simple lighting kit, a mini or full-size tripod, and a microphone (lavalier, iRig, or Zoom iQ6).

- YouTube comes with surprisingly detailed analytics. Metrics you can review include watch time, audience retention, traffic sources, and demographics.

- Leverage your videos by sharing them on Twitter, by email, and on your blog.

- YouTube is really more for exposure than results.

LinkedIn

With 562 million worldwide users, LinkedIn is a "special case" opportunity for doctors.[122] Here are some tips:

- While statistics vary, more than half of US doctors and lots of other healthcare professionals are on LinkedIn.[123] Thus, LinkedIn can be an adjunct strategy to your professional referring efforts.

- Most serious US businesspeople have a LinkedIn profile, which creates opportunities for you if you want to contract with area businesses (e.g., occupational medicine).

- LinkedIn allows you to "follow" anyone, but when it comes to "connecting" with someone, you are supposed to actually know them. However, in today's dynamic social media world, many people ignore the higher standard for connecting. Because we are both highly visible due to our speaking and writing, the authors receive multiple LinkedIn requests to connect each day. If the person inviting us looks credible and relevant to our professional interests, we'll usually go ahead and say, "yes." (If *you* reach out to us via LinkedIn and mention this book, we will almost certainly say yes.) When someone turns out to simply want to sell us something, we simply un-connect with them.

- There are some important benefits to having a large network on LinkedIn:

  - Your expanded network will give you more 1st, 2nd and 3rd degree of separation contacts, which means your searches will uncover far more LinkedIn member profiles.
  - You can message and network with people who share connections with you.
  - You can obtain contact data (including phone numbers and sometimes emails) from your connected profiles.
  - If you are looking to grow your professional reputation as a thought leader, it helps to connect with other thought leaders.

- Whenever you connect with someone new, be sure to send them a personalized, engaging note through the platform. If you really want to build a relationship, compliment them on something specific in their profile and ask them a question. While everyone is busy and time is limited, you will do well if you try to help your new connections to the extent that you reasonably can.

- If you are just getting started on LinkedIn, you can build a core network of people by uploading your contact list into LinkedIn's tool, which will then invite people you know to connect on the platform. This is method can get a lot of connections quickly. From there you have the option to invite others to connect, including people you know or at least have a lot in common with professionally. Warning: do not start an abusive, spammy connection outreach campaign. If you do, LinkedIn's algorithm will eventually catch you and freeze your account.

- You can write your own articles, or share posts on LinkedIn.

- In recent years, LinkedIn acquired both online learning platform *Lynda.com*, and deck sharing platform *SlideShare.com*.
- Some LinkedIn Groups are great, but most are not worth the effort or time.

- As with all the social media platforms we've discussed, be sure to complete a great LinkedIn profile for both yourself and your business.

- LinkedIn has some premium features available, including premium user accounts, InMails (where you can solicit people you don't know through the platform), recruitment options at varying levels, and advertising.

259

More Information About Social Media Platforms

We only have room in this book for the most important highlights about Facebook, Instagram, Twitter, YouTube, and LinkedIn. Also, while we often get questions about podcasts, Snapchat, and Pinterest, in our experience they just aren't that relevant for the vast majority of healthcare practices.

FACEBOOK AND INSTAGRAM ADVERTISING

Chances are, you were pretty disappointed to discover that organically Facebook and Instagram rarely generate many new patients. We hope you will be excited to discover how Facebook and Instagram advertising can help you:

1. Recruit new patients.
2. Generate more followers.
3. Reach the 95% of followers who otherwise would not see your organic posts.

Facebook and Instagram are the only social media platforms we generally recommend advertising in. Because Facebook owns Instagram, you can purchase both networks via your Facebook Page. Since the advertising principles are similar for both properties, we will cover them together here. Let's start with the most familiar ad type you may have considered:

Boosted Posts

No matter who you are, the truth is some Facebook and Instagram posts will always be better than others. You may want to consider boosting your best posts, i.e., the non-promotional, educational, and entertaining posts that people seem to care about.

You can boost a post quite inexpensively (as low as $1 a day). You can target your followers who did not see your post organically, or you can reach thousands of prospective patients in your area beyond your current followers. You can define your audiences within your Facebook Page; targeting options are improving. Boosted posts can show up on Facebook desktop and mobile newsfeeds, Instagram, and Facebook Audience Network. Boosted posts usually send traffic back to Facebook or Instagram, though they now can include links. Generally, boosted posts are more effective at building followers than generating patients.

Better Facebook and Instagram Advertising Options

Facebook and Instagram offer additional advertising options that allow you to affordably reach tens of thousands of prospects in your community, outside of your follower base. Most of these options allow you to send traffic to your website or landing page instead of Facebook or Instagram. That means you'll have a better chance of converting a prospect into a patient.

What's more, while you will pay for "impressions" with a nominal cost per thousand charge (CPM), you mostly pay when people click on the ads. So, the exposure to the tens of thousands of people who do not click is almost free. When prospects click, you win. When they don't click, you win. Some additional points:

- Facebook may deny your ads if they do not fit within their advertising guidelines.[124] They are especially sensitive to ads that are too promotional, e.g., more than 20% text.

- We believe Facebook advertising rates are currently below market and will likely increase over time.

- Your ads can often draw likes to your Facebook Page.

Facebook offers advertisers a very robust choice of advertising options. We will cover those most applicable to private practices here.[125]

Types of Ads

- **Image Ads** can be photos or any jpg or png image. These are the ads you see most often on Facebook and Instagram, and importantly, they can link to your website. Image ads are available on Facebook desktop and mobile newsfeeds, Facebook right column, Facebook Audience Network, and Instagram.

- **Video Ads** are worth the extra effort because they work well. We sometimes see 10x the response with video compared to static image ads. Like image ads, they can link to your website or landing page. Video ads are available for Facebook desktop and mobile newsfeeds, Facebook Audience Network, and Instagram. Note: Instagram videos need to be 60 seconds or less.

- **Carousel Ads** allow you to feature up to ten images or videos within a single ad, each with its own link. You will get better results if you allow Facebook to adjust the order of the images based on user interaction. Carousel ads are available for Facebook desktop and mobile newsfeeds, Facebook Audience Network, and Instagram.

- **Other Advertising Options** include Marketplace ads, Messenger ads, Canvas ads, and Instagram stories.

Campaign Objectives

Most of the time we recommend sending traffic from your ads to a website or landing page, letting them handle the heavy lifting of inciting visitors to make an inquiry via a phone call or form request. These are called conversions. However, Facebook and Instagram offer some additional compelling options. These include:

- **Lead Generation Ads** allow you to generate inquiries from prospective patients in classic direct marketing form. For example, you could offer a free eBook, "7 Things to Consider When Choosing an Integrative Medicine Doctor." Targeted users in your community see the ad in their news feed, click a button, and most of the info is pre-populated for them. These ads can be delivered with Image ads, Video, or Carousels. Best of all, the entire lead generation sign-up process is handled within Facebook.

- **Offer Ads** can be used for time-sensitive sales, including percent off; dollar amount off; buy one, get one free; or free offers. These could apply to very retail-oriented business like medspas. You can design your offer to show up as an image, video, or carousel.

- **Event Responses** are used to promote your events and can appear as an image or video.

- **Page Like** campaigns deliver ads designed to get users to "like" your Facebook Page. We usually prefer spending money to drive prospective new patients to your website, but there are special cases where doctors feel the need to engage with a local niche audience, such as alternative medicine. Page Like campaign ads can be an image or a video and can be delivered through Facebook desktop, Facebook mobile, Facebook right column, or Instagram.

Special Targeting Options

On Facebook and Instagram,[126] you can (1) Target your own followers, (2) Target by demographics and interests, or (3) Target with the following specialized options:

- **Contact Lists.** Facebook and Instagram allow you to reach the contacts you already have, using data such as phone numbers or emails. This option could work for lists of names from community events or perhaps referring doctors. If you are interested in using this tool for patient lists, check with your attorney first to confirm that the idea is HIPAA-compliant.

- **Retarget Website Visitors.** Retargeting is one of Facebook's most powerful features. You have seen retargeting before when, for example you look at a pair of shoes online, and suddenly ads for those exact shoes follow you around the Internet for 30 days. Whether you personally like retargeting or not, it is extremely powerful. While Google does not permit retargeting due to HIPAA concerns—because users have to log into Facebook or Instagram—you CAN retarget through their platforms. To take advantage of this feature, your web developer will need to properly install a snippet of code on your website called a Facebook pixel.[127] Then, when people visit your site, their browser will get a cookie that alerts Facebook and Instagram so the user can be retargeted.

- **Lookalike Audiences.** You can create custom audiences on Facebook and Instagram who are similar to your customer and prospect lists, people who have visited your website, or people who have interacted with your Facebook Page and ads, or your Instagram profile or ads.

Organic and paid social media offer practitioners numerous practice-building opportunities. In the next and final chapter, Mark will provide specific advice on how to build your professional presence.

CHAPTER

HOW TO GET NOTICED, KNOWN & REMEMBERED

Since I (Mark) no longer practice medicine, many people ask me what I now do. I keep it short and sweet replying, "I help healthcare practitioners go from good to great." The wonderful thing about this retort is, it inevitably invites the second question, "How do you do that?" To which I reply, "I help practitioners enhance their presence in person, on camera, and online." The conversation, if there is interest at this point, then turns into a discussion on the person's needs and whether the work that I do helps meet those needs.

Over the last three years, I've worked with my colleague, Robert John Hughes, at ChangeWell Training Academy conducting Enhance Your Presence™ programs for small to mid-sized groups of healthcare practitioners. Some sessions draw participants from all over the country, and others are in-house courses for companies who want to improve the effectiveness of their key opinion leaders, sales, or marketing professionals.. The programs vary from a half-day to two-days in length, and every participant improves their presentation, persuasion, and promotion skills. We take the anxious and shy and help them get over their trepidation; we take the good and make them great; and the great, even better as we fine tune their abilities. Robert and I have written a book, *Enhance Your Presence: The Path to Personal Power, Professional Influence & Business Results*, and created an accompanying online training and coaching program. We have also curated a free series of 3-minute videos on the Presentation Secrets of America's Leading Motivational Healthcare Speakers. You can learn more about these resources at changewell.com.

We've learned a great deal about presence from spending countless hours with hundreds of practitioners. In this chapter, we'll go over how to enhance your presence to get your practice noticed, known and remembered.

What Is Presence and Why Do I Need It?

One of the questions I'm often asked is whether mindfulness is the same as presence. While mindfulness is a component of presence, it really only deals with one aspect, namely, attending and being in the moment. This is a good start. The ability to calm one's mind, to focus on the breath, and to observe without judgement is a great ability, and one that can be learned. But in the healthcare setting, there's more to presence than just attending. This is shown in the model below.

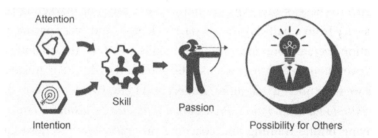

Healthcare presence begins by attending to the patient, and it includes a synergy with your intention. It is our hope that this intention is noble, focused on the patient's needs, and reflects a sincere desire to help them get what they need or want. We have seen practitioners—motivated by money—enter into a therapeutic relationship with the intent of selling something to a patient. Increasingly, patients know when they are being sold. If not in the moment, then days or weeks later when they surface their resentment online.

There is a great deal of energy that can be channeled from the marriage of attention and intention, and it can be deployed by a practitioner who has mastered skills and is passionate about his or her work. Patients can detect passion. It is highly contagious.

The energy, skills, and passion may well culminate in a prescription, a lifestyle program, advanced testing, nutrition education, coaching, counseling, or needed supplements. However, the real power of presence in the context of a patient-practitioner relationship comes from the ultimate outcome, which, in fact goes back to intention. You will always be most powerful and most effective when you tie your intention to providing a possibility for the patient. The possibility may be a life without pain, improved confidence and self-esteem, energy to play with one's kids, additional quality years, or another positive outcome.

To put it all together:

Presence is the intentional act of attending to another, and using your skills to passionately create a possibility in the minds and hearts of those who receive your message.

This model of presence holds true no matter when and where you engage with an audience, be it one-on-one, one-to-many, or through media such as video, audio, or print.

Presence Is Diluted

THE POWER OF PRESENCE

| ONE-ON-ONE | ONE-TO-MANY | VIDEO | AUDIO | PRINT |

If you were to think of presence as fine, dark red wine, your "drink" is most potent when you are one-on-one. Individuals can actually feel your attention and caring from your words, voice, and body language. Presence becomes diluted when you are reaching larger audiences. In a keynote presentation, those beyond the first dozen rows may be watching you on a big screen and listening to you over speakers. However, with the right skill training, you can learn to engage with a large percentage of the audience. Increasingly, practitioners are using video to get their presence across, and for those who master this medium, the power of their presence can rival that of a large talk. With audio, you are dependent upon creating resonance as your audience hears, imagines, and emotes based upon your skills as an orator. Finally, there is print. In many ways, your presence is most diluted by this medium. Why? Because, with just visual clues, you are depending upon the reader to interpret your words without the benefit of facial expressions, tone of voice, and body gestures. Let's look more closely at the skills that underpin these media.

THE ART OF THE LIVE HEALTHCARE PRESENTATION

There is no shortage of venues for practitioners to deliver their health-related message in the flesh. Basically, two types of opportunities exist: professional meetings where you present research, teach techniques, or impart clinical wisdom; and direct-to-consumer talks in which you engage individuals in groups both small and large. We will not be discussing the professional seven-minute research or literature-review PowerPoint presentation replete with its graphs, charts, and references that often fly past the viewer at speeds beyond comprehension. Instead, we will focus on the tools of engaging consumers and to some extent colleagues (who are consumers as well) that gather to hear your words.

With more digital tools at our command than ever before, we have entered what some call the "Presentation Generation." Impactful visuals can help you get your message across more easily, but they can only augment, not supplant your ability to speak passionately, clearly, and concisely about a given health topic. Nor can great visuals alone captivate and motivate your audience.

As noted, a quality presentation starts with the presence of the presenter. It is reinforced with appropriate visuals, peppered with engaging stories, augmented with interactive exercises, and delivered in a manner that takes into account the unique interests and needs of the audience.

Here are a dozen tips to create a meaningful presentation:

1. Recognize What Sets Healthcare Presentations Apart

You've probably heard a great sales presentation at one point in your life. Chances are it moved you to take action: either sign up for something, commit to a purchase, or enroll in a club or membership scheme. Stated or unstated, every presentation involves selling. You want to get your point across, to champion an idea or position, to convey important information, and to inspire others to take action. However, unlike the car salesman, you are dealing with the deeply personal realm of health. Your presentation is imbued with meaning. Some attendees come to hear you based upon interest in a specific topic, while others are drawn to you from positions of need, either for themselves or for a loved one or friend. Your message may be just the trigger that dispels misconceptions, ignites health behavior change, informs about resources, or enables action for an acute or chronic condition.

Few things can be more rewarding than delivering a meaningful health presentation in which you share something that you believe is very important with others. Always approach your presentation with the gravitas it deserves. You are embarking on a noble adventure. You may never again have the opportunity to be with the people in the audience; this may be your only chance to reach out to them.

2. Understand the Presentation Is for Them, Not for You

A presentation that goes well can be extremely fulfilling for both you and the audience. The presentation may draw new patients to your practice, engender positive social media notice, or elicit word-of-mouth referrals. A good presentation might even help your career. But remember: the major benefit should accrue to the participants. Your presentation should be "other centered." Sure, you can—and should, to an extent—roll out your credentials and expertise, and mention your products and services; but it is better to regard these more self-promotional elements as a tasty appetizer, with the main course devoted to understanding the audience, meeting their needs, and providing an emotional experience.

All presenters want to please their audiences. We want to address attendees' needs and answer their questions. However, in the healthcare presentation, if you are a licensed clinician, you must be careful not to cross the line by delivering medical advice. It is all too common for a consumer to ask you a question that relates to their (or their family member's) unique condition. Never hesitate to begin your remarks by noting that, you cannot give out specific medical advice, and then shift to a more general statement about the condition being raised. You can always qualify remarks further by prefacing them with, "In my experience…" Clinicians must also be cognizant that they are not going overboard in promoting products or services. When discussing treatment options, watch out for two troublesome words: "always" and "never." Instead of "always," be sure to say "often." The word "never" should be replaced by the word "rarely." And remember, no treatment is ever 100% safe; there are only safer or relatively safe treatments.

3. Clarify the Context

Each and every health-related presentation should be centered around meeting and exceeding the audience's expectations. In order to meet and exceed these expectations, you will want to gather as much background information as possible to fine tune your presentation. If you are planning on conducting a talk or workshop in your clinic or healthcare institution, you already have sufficient background to be well-prepared.

However, if you are asked by a third party, or conference organizer to present to consumers or colleagues, you'll want to make certain to get the answers to these questions:

- Why was I asked to speak?
- Who will be attending and what do I need to know about them?
- What would you like the audience to come away with from my session?
- What other speakers has this group been exposed to and how were they received?
- How scientifically/medically literate is this group?
- How much time will I have to present my talk?
- How will participants be seated? Theater style, rounds, lecture tables?
- What time of day will the session occur?
- What AV equipment is available? Will I have access to a lavaliere or an untethered handheld mike?
- Will we be using my laptop or a conference laptop? Do I have the necessary connectors and the presentation in the correct software version?
- Is audio available if I choose to show a video, or do I need to bring small speakers?

Getting answers to these basic questions can help set the context for a focused presentation and help you avoid making an easily preventable mistake.

4. Know Thy Audience

Spending time getting to know your audience has two functions. First, it helps to alleviate anxiety. Whenever possible, arrive at a presentation early and speak with some of the participants. Learn their names. Ask them why they are attending your talk. The beauty of this approach is one of focus. When you do your presentation, you are no longer looking out at a sea of unrecognized faces. You are initially directing your remarks to those attendees whom you have briefly gotten to know. This helps put you at ease. Depending upon the nature and formality of your presentation, it is always helpful to be able to relate personally to one or more participants and, if appropriate, to acknowledge them in the course of your talk.

If you are entering unfamiliar territory, for example, a consumer health group or association with whom you have little familiarity, or you are called on to give a health presentation to a corporate audience, try to arrange some time in advance to talk with one or more representative participants. Ask them to brief you on the audience and their expectations.

You can always begin a small to mid-sized talk by directly asking the audience why are they attending. I (Mark) will often do this in a manner that thanks participants for being at the venue. "I'm honored that you folks have decided to give up part of your Saturday to be with me…So, tell me, what would you like to learn or accomplish during our time together?" This opening provides the second advantage of getting to know your audience. You can modify your presentation to directly address some of the items brought up by the attendees.

One word of caution: I have seen too many presenters, in response to audience inquiries, promise, "We'll cover that…" They then disregard the input and fail to reference the concern, and instead just go ahead with their prepared remarks. This type of behavior often results in negative feedback from the participant whose request was disregarded.

5. Make Emotion Your Ally

"What, I have to provide attendees with 'an emotional experience?' Isn't that what tear-jerker movies are for?" Wrong sentiment! Noted author/teacher Seth Godin, writing in his blog, put it quite nicely when he discussed appealing to attendees' minds and hearts:[128]

> "Communication is about getting others to adopt your point of view, to help them understand why you're excited (or sad, or optimistic, or whatever else you are). If all you want to do is create a file of facts and figures, then cancel the (presentation) and send in a report. Our brains have two sides. The right side is emotional, musical, and moody. The left side is focused on dexterity, facts, and hard data. When you show up to give a presentation, people want to use both parts of their brains. So, they use the right side to judge the way you talk, the way you dress, and your body language. Often, people come to a conclusion about your presentation by the time you're on the second slide. After that, it's often too late for your bullet points to do you much good. You can wreck a communication process with lousy logic or unsupported facts, but you can't complete it without emotion. Logic is not enough. Communication is the transfer of emotion."

Tell Stories

Every clinician has stories that touch the heartstrings of listeners. You have helped individuals allay fears, overcome barriers, gain confidence in their care, make health behavior changes, and build support for treatment plans. You can work these stories into your presentation while maintaining confidentiality.

In the appropriate setting, you can always tell the story of how and why you went into healthcare (assuming of course that you can tap into your passion for helping others). This will humanize you. What motivated you to go into healthcare? Why did you choose your specialty? You might address what you learned at different points during your training. If you had other careers along the way, what did you find out about yourself from these endeavors that could help others? Have you overcome a personal health challenge or issue and feel comfortable bringing this into your talk?

Reflect upon the characteristics you enjoy in other human beings and ask yourself, "How does your story reflect some of these characteristics?" When you consider telling a story, work backwards from the point you want to make. Your story must have a reason to exist, beyond just entertainment. Keep it tight.

6. Err on the Side of Simplicity, Especially with Your Slides

One axiom remains true for all presentations: less is more. While each situation is different, in general you will always be best served by reducing the number of slides, the amount of text on the slides, and the number of syllables in the words. We've all had the experience of suffering through "death by PowerPoint." If you want to communicate with greater clarity, integrity, appeal, and wisdom, you must naturally be more restrained, and yes, simpler. Resist the temptation to put two hours of slides into a 30-minute talk.

For those of us who present at conferences, it has increasingly become the norm for conference organizers to include a set of your slides in the handout material. This has led to presenters creating text heavy slides that reference the scientific literature—ostensibly for attendees to go back and refer to the articles. Presenters feel that they must cram the slides full of the key points from the literature.

This type of presentation does not extend well to consumers or patients. In reality, it doesn't even extend well to our peers. For starters, people have difficulty processing information if it comes at them simultaneously in verbal and written forms. When you overload people with text on a slide, they can either listen to you or read the slides, but they can't do both simultaneously. And if the purpose of the presentation is solely to convey the content on the slides, why do participants even need you to deliver the talk? They can just read the slides. You have to provide more than bullet points; for example, contextualizing the message, inspiring others to adopt your point of view, formulating disparate ideas into a new paradigm, or sharing your clinical experience. You can always put your research-based, statistically-laden, referenced material into a separate handout.

For consumer presentations, you want to emphasize images, and whenever necessary include visualizations of quantitative information in their simplest formats.

7. Prepare Well

It takes time to "own" a specific presentation. It takes time to get the pacing, the story telling, the humor, and the emotion dialed in. The major advantage of slides is their ability to help you organize and pace your presentation. Try to organize your message around no more than five, but preferably three key points. These are your anchors for your presentation, and you can build your preparation around them.

Many people find it helpful to practice in front of a full-length mirror; this can also serve to help coordinate one's movements and hand gestures. Others will find great value in doing a first time talk in front of a friendly audience of friends and staff.

The real payoff lies in mastering a presentation. The presentation can stay—in whole or in part—the same. You "perform" to a new audience each time you give it.

I rarely rehearse an entire presentation; instead I rely on the anchor slides to keep me organized and on time. However, I always rehearse, and commit to memory the first two-three minutes of a talk, and the two to three-minute conclusion. I rehearse what I'm going to say as an audience warms up, perhaps some gentle self-deprecating humor. Or, if I am giving a presentation to a group that speaks another language, I will often memorize a paragraph in that language, telling the audience how honored I am to be there and apologizing for my poor speaking skills in their native tongue. I mentally rehearse where I intend to pause in my opening remarks so the audience can become comfortable with my slight New York accent, or my cadence. I rehearse placing the pauses strategically either before or after the key messages I intend to deliver in my opening. I mentally review the key points I want to drive home. Two to three minutes into a presentation, I am usually relaxed enough to trust that the body of my session will flow smoothly.

8. Overcome Your Anxiety

Having anticipatory energy is a good thing. You need it to keep your spirits up and to project strength. Too much energy—in the form of anxiety, however, can be detrimental to your session. Here are a few tips to help overcome the jitters:

- Start sipping water 20 minutes before you begin talking. While we are on the subject of water, go to the bathroom right before your presentation, even if you don't think you have a lot to contribute in that department.

- Ground yourself. This can be done by using your toes to grab the ground, almost as if you were developing roots.

- Remember to breathe. Some deep, slow breaths (breathe deeply in for a count of 5 and out for a count of five) will help strengthen the workings of your parasympathetic nervous system, slow the heart rate, lower blood pressure, warm your extremities, and allow the brain waves to generate a more fluid flow state.

- Psych yourself up. Use affirmations like, "Go crush it." "Wow them." "Unleash your power." Find a word or picture on your laptop to gaze upon prior to going on stage. Silently hum the theme to Rocky before you go on stage. Imagine you are accepting an Oscar or Golden Globe for the great work you have already done.

I have always used a four-part "mantra" to harness my pre-presentation energy. The repetition of these phrases also helps to establish the tone for my presentation:

I am glad I'm here.
I am glad you are here.
I know what I know.
I care about you.

The first two sentences are self-explanatory. You want to project happiness, and also honor your attendees for their contribution of time and energy to hear you speak. The third sentence is designed to address "the imposter syndrome" that resides in all of us to some extent. This belief looms even larger when we present to other healthcare professionals who are critical by nature, or who know as much or more about your subject as you do. It is all too easy in this circumstance for you to fill your head with negative thoughts, particularly as you compare your current knowledge and experience with those in the audience. I always remind myself that while others may know more than I do about a given topic, my synthesis, my approach, my message is unique and worthy of being heard.

In longer presentations and those that most notably take place after lunch, I vigorously guard against a potentially lethal condition: ischemia of the posterior ischial tuberosities accompanied by postprandial hyperglycemia. Simple translation: when you sit too long after a big lunch, your butt hurts and you get sleepy. The treatment is simple as well; get the audience up for an interactive exercise.

274

9. Attend to Your Non-Verbals

There's a lot more being transferred in a presentation than just content. In the first two minutes of your talk, your audience is picking up dozens of subconscious clues that determine whether they will understand and be inspired by your remarks. Whether words are coming out of your mouth or not, your body is speaking the entire time that others observe you.

Find Your Position of Power

Bodies radiate energy. We can observe this phenomenon as we observe the collapsed posture of individuals who are depressed, the shaky movements of anxious individuals, or the quiet confidence and alignment of a yoga or mediation teacher.

You can find your position of power by standing up straight and aligning your spine. Bring your shoulders back and down. Uplift your sternum by imagining a wire lifting it to the ceiling. Straighten your head and tilt your chin slightly down. Arrange your pelvis in a neutral position.

Spend a bit of time in front of a full-length mirror to identify how and what you can do to find this starting point. Then while maintaining this position, allow your body to relax. Soften your grip, remove tension from your forehead, eyes and jaw. You can always work with a posture or yoga coach to provide some necessary feedback.

Use Movement Wisely

It can be helpful to set three or four spots on a stage and practice moving to each area. This is particularly important if you want to address your remarks to the entire audience. Always get a handheld microphone or lavalier and try to never get trapped behind the podium.

Your hand gestures should be purposeful and precise. Use them to reinforce a point. For example, if you want to illustrate something increasing you could move hands outward from a centered position near your chest. To emphasize an emotional point or something you deeply believe, touching you heart with one or two hands amplifies the message. You can also use your fingers as counting points, especially when you tell the audience that you'd like to leave them with "three key take-homes." You can count these off on your fingers.

Whenever you are on video you'll want to keep your gestures to a minimum, and keep your hands closer to your chest. When you reach out with your hands directly to the camera, this has the effect of distorting perspective, so your hands become disproportionately large and potentially distracting.

Roll with the Punches

Breathe deeply. No matter how well you prepare, there will always be some unexpected challenges. The microphone screeches, the projector fails to work, there's a loud noise or periodic laughter emanating from the adjacent room. Go with the flow. Say something lighthearted. A squeaking noise coming from the ceiling? "Well, that must be the NSA grabbing our metadata." A thumping noise from the speakers? A great time to practice tap dancing. A broken projector and no slides? An opportunity to roll up your sleeves and ask the audience to share their experiences. You always go from being a presenter to acting more as a facilitator and commentator.

One of my most impactful presentations took place during a daytime session in which, right before I was to begin, we lost electric power. No slides. The subject of my talk was on stress management. I had the group rearrange their chairs to sit in a circle, and I then posed this question: "Each of you has a technique you use to deal with stress and change. Tell us, what works for you." I then used each person's answers as the jumping off point to further discuss and elaborate upon their contributions.

10. Use Humor, but Appropriately

Humor in a healthcare presentation is not about joking or clown-like remarks. Rather it comprises generally acceptable and timely statements that result in genuine laughter. Humor should be used early in a presentation to put the audience at ease and to relax you. This can often be achieved easily through some gentle self-deprecating remarks, an observation on a current event, reference to a funny remark, or a comment made by an earlier presenter.

You can borrow liberally from pictures and jokes on the Internet to lighten the tone in the room. (Be aware of copyright issues.) Clever remarks and visuals also allow you to drive home your points. To be successful, humor must be well timed. Comedians follow a tested format. They employ a set up that engages the audience's attention and then follow this up with the punch line. Set up, punch line. Set up, punch line.

11. Check for Understanding

Healthcare professionals spend a great deal of their time communicating in the jargon of medicine. This jargon is split between multi-syllabic medical terms like laparoscopic cholecystectomy, and their abbreviations, in this case "lap chole". We have COPD, PVD, CHF, DVTs...and the list goes on.

It's always a good idea to define any medical terms when you first use them. Let people know what the acronym stands for and that you'll be using it throughout the talk. The same goes for herbal names, nutraceuticals, dermatological conditions—in short, terms we take for granted, but require definition.

You also want to check for another type of understanding: whether or not you have gotten your point across. Keep your eyes peeled for quizzical looks, and even more so for yawns or frequent mobile device checking.

If you ever sense that you are losing your audience's attention, you can stop and summarize what you have discussed up to this point in your presentation. Ask if there are any questions before you go further in your remarks. You can even throw out some rhetorical questions such as, "Does this seem to make sense? How are we doing? Are you all with me on this?"

12. Attend to the Pacing of Your Presentation

First of all, it is not a race. It is also not a quest to see how many words you can deliver in the shortest period of time. Classically when people are under pressure or get anxious (perhaps after seeing a yawn from the audience), they increase the speed of their presentation.

You want to vary the pacing of your delivery: speed up some sections, draw out others. Perhaps most important, learn to pause. Pause intentionally and comfortably. Stop talking. Make eye contact with the audience. Why? The pause allows a key message to sink in. It also prepares the audience for a key message that is about to come.

There is power in the pause. In musical terms, this is called a rest. Rests are built into all musical scores where their length varies from a whole rest (one beat) to fractions. Composers and conductors will often also write in breath marks (apostrophes) that instruct the wind instruments to take a breath and the non-wind instruments to take a slight pause. An even longer silent period is known as a caesura, indicated by two slash marks. This is a silent break in the music, the duration of which is dictated by the conductor.

Variety is the spice of life. So too is variety of pacing when championing your point of view.

THE POWER OF YOUR VOICE

If you think of your presentation as a symphony, you'll want to first tune up your instrument—your voice. You can dramatically improve your presentation skills with voice coaching and training. It need not be a drawn-out affair. Speech therapists and acting coaches can help you get over your bad habits and provide you with personal feedback. Robert John Hughes, Mark's partner in ChangeWell Training Academy, has been involved in radio for the better part of three decades and conducts online coaching sessions that help practitioners make immediate improvements in their voices. Here are a few of his tips:

Eliminate your auditory "hiccups." These are the all too common verbal distractions in your delivery. They range from too many "Umms and Ahs" to the ubiquitous "You know" or even the overworked "I think…" construction. After all, if you didn't think, you wouldn't have anything to say.

Speak in your natural register. Avoid the tendency to tighten your vocal chords and raise your pitch in an attempt to "sound energetic." Find and use the middle part of your natural register. This is the voice you use in relaxed group conversation.

Come from your chest. Your most pleasing and powerful voice will usually originate in your chest, not your head or your throat, and it will be powered by abdominal breathing. However, when you have a bad case of nerves, abdominal breathing will not seem like a good idea.

Vocal warm up. Before you go on stage, find a private space (your car!!). Limber up your lips, teeth, tongue with a simple vocal warm-up exercise. Do this several times in sequence:

Say: lah, lah, lah, lah, lah, lah
Say: bop, bop, bop, bob, bop, bop
Say: yum, yum, yum, yum, yum, yum
Say: lee, lee, lee, lee, lee, lee
Say: nay no, nee no, nigh no, neh no
Say, tip top, toe tip tee tie, tok
Say: hah hah, hee hee, hoh, hoh, hi, hi

Imitate the sound of a motorboat by making a motor noise with your voice while blowing out and letting your lips flap.

Imitate the sound of a siren starting at your lowest pitch, rising to your highest. Do it backwards.

Repeat several times.

Adjust volume accordingly. How loud should you be? If you are using a microphone, remember that "micro" means "small" and "phone" means "sound." Don't yell into a microphone. If there is a sound engineer, he will just turn your volume down. If you'll be speaking to a convention, find a voice that you would use to address a group in a small- to medium-sized room. Let the microphone make it big enough to be heard.

Vary your volume. This adds interest. But keep in mind that if you soften your vocal texture to a whisper, you must boost your volume. This is paradoxical. You will need to experiment with the idea of softening the sound of your voice to create a whisper, while simultaneously powering that sound with all the energy of a very loud yell. That's a "stage whisper," a soft sound that carries to the back of the theater.

Don't shout. A loud voice is not necessarily a friendly or persuasive voice. Some of the ugliest voices are those of politicians trying to address a large crowd. They raise their pitch, increase their volume, and tighten down their vocal chords to mistakenly add force and power. This makes them sound tense, combative, and angry rather than excited, as if they are on the losing side of a bitter argument. The result is that the crowd feels like they are being yelled at—because they are. And after a while, these speakers end up with hoarse, permanently damaged vocal chords.

Practice talking with the intention of finding a comfortable, persuasive, relaxed but energized way of speaking. Video-record your practice sessions and get feedback. Once you've found your sound, practice it until it becomes second nature.

MASTERING VIDEO

Most people hate seeing themselves on video. All they see are their flaws. There are those who quake in fear with the very idea of being on camera. They compare themselves to professionals who come across as confident, competent, and occasionally eloquent. We're here to disabuse you of this mindset, as well as to provide you with the tools to become comfortable on camera and produce some professional-quality recordings. A few introductory thoughts:

- Getting good or better on video is a learned skill. It does take some practice, but it is not that difficult to master.
- Your audience doesn't expect you to be a movie star; they expect you to come across as a kind, caring, compassionate, knowledgeable professional who is eager to help them get what they want.

- If you are comfortable communicating one-on-one with patients, you can easily transfer this context, comfort, and communication to video. Chances are your video will only be watched by one person at a time.
- There are four components to utilizing video in your practice:
    1. Hardware
    2. Delivery
    3. Editing
    4. Deployment

Hardware

The easiest path, but also the most expensive, is to hire a professional who will show up with camera, audio, and lights. The videographer will usually need 45 minutes to get the "set" ready, clearing away clutter, and getting the lighting done. When deciding on a location, see if you can use a good-sized room so that the objects in the background can be blurred out (a shallow depth of field). This can give the video a nice professional feeling. The same professional can also edit the production. The costs for a half-day (usually minimum time requirement, due to travel set-up and break-down) range from $350-$600; editing runs anywhere from $35-$75 an hour. Videographers can easily be found online and you can preview their work. The major advantage is that you are engaging a professional and the quality of the video will be good. The videographer can also direct your performance. You may want to consider this route for crafting a "welcome to our practice" video. Another advantage is that since you have booked a half day, you may be able to shoot a number of pieces, the easiest of which are responses to frequently asked questions. You can use these as video blogs or send them out in a newsletter.

Do It Yourself

The second option is to do it yourself. Technology has gotten so much better that you can use your smartphone with or without an external microphone (depending on how quiet the room is), and augment the lighting with some low-cost, readily available LED lights. If you want to avoid the tech and have a modest budget, look for a high school or college student who owns video equipment and can help you produce your video series.

The latest generation of "smart phones" like the Samsung Galaxy and the Apple iPhone contain cameras that are capable of near professional quality. They have two major weaknesses:

- **It is not easy to "zoom" in or out.** If you want the camera closer to—or farther away from the action—you have to move the camera to the right spot.

- **Audio quality depends on the position of the built-in microphone.** This means you must move the camera to the right spot, depending on the sound you want. Remember that the microphone on a smartphone is located at the bottom of the camera, the part that is closest to your mouth when you are on the phone.

- **Buy a microphone.** There are several inexpensive lavalier (clip-on) type microphones that will work with your cell phone or tablet. While you can use the built-in microphone in your device, the plug-in option will almost always deliver better sound quality. If you are recording on your computer, a plug-in USB microphone like the Blue Yeti, is a great investment. The iRig microphone and the Zoom iQ6 are additional options. Always be aware of the background noise. If the background noise level is high, it will be difficult to hear you. So, find a quieter location or time.

- **Positioning your phone.** You always want to shoot your video horizontally, and while it is tempting to center your image, professionals usually use what is known as the rule of thirds. The presenter's face is centered 1/3 of the way in from left or right, and 1/3 of the way down from the top. In addition to being more visually interesting, this also allows your editor to put words or graphics in the blank space.

- **Lighting the scene.** In general, you want to have two light sources at 45 degree angles from your face. This can be natural light, lamps, or LED lights. Dracast makes some reasonably good, moderately priced LED lights that allow you to control the intensity and the color (more yellow or blue).

- **Make certain the camera is stable.** You can use a tripod or a clamp to position your smartphone. For most smartphones, the rear facing camera is usually higher quality, so you will want to position it accordingly. The camera should be at eye level. If you are going to record directly into the computer, the camera on many of the newer laptops is adequate, but we prefer using a dedicated camera. Our preferences are those made by Logitech.

Delivery

There are three ways to deliver your content.

1. **Direct to camera.** This is where you look at and speak right into the lens. You have two choices. First you can ad lib. There are many practitioners who really know their stuff and can succinctly, and with proper grammar and emphasis, deliver short, educational clips direct to camera. They have the ability to come across as both personable and knowledgeable. If that's you, go for it.

The second way is to script your talk and use a teleprompter. Assuming you can master reading scrolling text (We teach this in our coaching and it usually takes around 45 minutes to learn how to appear naturally), we've found that you are more likely to deliver a tighter, more impactful performance with this method. You can use a tablet and a downloadable app called PromptSmart Pro which scrolls the words. You need to position the tablet just beneath the camera lens. There are also some mirror-based hardware systems that will project the words so they go right over the lens. Because you are looking at the script, you make great eye contact with the viewer.

When you write, rewrite, edit, and practice your script, always remember that you want to use the spoken, and not the written word. Keep sentences short. Avoid using big words. Imagine you are talking to a 9th grader.

2. **Via interview.** Trying to perform a script so that it sounds spontaneous can be difficult. Trying to talk to a camera lens instead of a human being is hard. Instead, you can talk to someone you like who just happens to be seated either next to or behind the camera outside the shot. Have them ask you the questions and you answer them in your best impromptu style. The camera will capture you being present with and serving them, and that may end up being the best possible result of all. If you need a "cheat sheet" to help you, write out the key points for every question. Get them all on one page, outline style and print the cheat sheet out using big print. Have your interviewer hold this where you can see it as you speak.

3. **Voice-over slides.** If direct to camera is the hardest, this is the easiest. You simply transfer your script to slides, you plug a microphone into your computer, you activate a screen recording tool, and you deliver the script while you change the slides. If you are not comfortable with how you look performing in front of a camera, this is the option for you.

If you choose the voice-over slide method, you will need a way to record what happens on your computer screen together with your audio narration. Both Powerpoint and Keynote have recording options built in. Once you have recorded your presentation, export the video.

A Professional Tip: Cameras and lighting reveal imperfections, and a shiny face can lead to a major glare. We recommend men and women alike use at least a tinted or transparent powder makeup to even out skin tone and cut down on facial shine.

Editing

You can do this yourself or encourage a staff member to learn how to do it. We prefer a Mac program called Screenflow which is a reasonably easy-to-learn tool. The PC version is Camtasia which is equally capable, but a bit more expensive. For those who have Macs, if you want to do the editing yourself and live close to an Apple store, they have free classes that you can investigate. The big drawback is that unless you really are excited to edit, there's a fairly steep learning curve, and it is usually a big waste of your time. It is amazing how many young people—from 10-30 years old—are adept at video editing. You can usually grab one for $15-$20 an hour. They are usually delighted with the challenge and the cash. Ask your patients or friends if they know of someone. Inquire at the local high school or even junior high school. You will be pleasantly surprised at what might be a daunting task for you is kids-play for them.

Deployment

Once you've got your videos in hand, it's time to get them working for you. Here are a few recommendations.

- **Create a YouTube channel.** YouTube will host your videos for you and allow you to embed them in your website, as well as permit you to link to them on your Facebook Page and in your email blasts. You can also use Vimeo to host your video but it doesn't attract as many people.
- **Embed the link to your YouTube videos on your website.** Ask your webmaster to create a page on your site that presents your videos. This is a quick way to get videos where your current and future patients can see them and consume the content you created.
- **Use the videos in your email campaigns.** There is genuine magic in a thoughtful, useful email. It's even better when your email contains a link to a video that provides helpful information.
- **Use your videos in your Facebook posts.** Facebook loves it when you create useful content. When you feature a video in your weekly email, link that email to your Facebook and Twitter feeds so you maximize exposure. Once you get comfortable on camera, you can also record and stream in real time using Facebook Live.
- **Be sure that you pay attention to the call to action and the traffic destination.** In most cases, you want to direct traffic to your website where your viewer can take a single specific action such as calling for an appointment, emailing with

a question, signing up for your newsletter, or placing a supplement order. Only provide one option at a time.

Strive for Continuous Improvement

No matter whether you are using your communication skills in person or on camera, you'll want to continually hone your message. This means constantly evaluating how you did—celebrating what you did well, and identifying what you could improve. Try using the following checklist:

On a scale from 1 to 10, with ten being best, how would you rate your:

- Pacing and timing
- Voice quality
- Understandability of message
- Audiovisuals
- Emphasis of key points
- Ability to clarify your remarks when necessary
- Effectiveness in providing an emotional experience
- Introduction
- Conclusion
- Answering audience members' questions
- Your ability to hold the audience's attention
- Voice quality
- Level of interactivity

Many of us take great pride—no matter what our field—in our ability to diagnose and treat effectively. We can take equal pride in our ability to present material to audiences in a way that challenges their thinking, touches their emotions, answers their questions, and provides them with knowledge, skills, and support to lead healthier lives. Do this with integrity, a focus on being "other centered," and a genuine sense of caring for your attendees. You will come away as enriched as those who engage with you.

The Power of Print

So far, we've examined those media elements that create the strongest presence. For those who want to memorialize their thoughts in print, we've already provided some how-to suggestions in Chapter 5: Where Do I Start? You will note that print is on the lower end of the presence spectrum. So why do so many professionals write books? We have a few biases, the first of which relates to engaging the sense of touch. If you purchased the print version of *Cash-Pay Healthcare*, we thank you for holding our baby in your hands and encourage you to mark her up, highlight, fold, scribble, and underline. In an era of ever-increasing technology, many of us still take comfort in that which is physical and tangible. If you've acquired the book at one of our talks or workshops, we are honored that you are taking a little bit of us home with you. If you are reading the Kindle edition, we hope you find value in the interactivity.

While you may very well have been attracted to this book because it held promise to make you more money, we'd like to think that you are leaving with a lot more. Reflecting on the art of healthcare, we will often remark that, "What you have to give is who you are." If you find joy in life, meaning in your work, and comfort in helping others, then you will deliver a great, "wow" experience for your patients, and they will look to you as their guide and teacher. We hope you have found some value in our guidance.

ABOUT THE AUTHORS

Mark J. Tager, MD

Dr. Mark Tager is Chief Enhancement Officer (CEO) of ChangeWell, Inc., (changewell.com) a San Diego organization that trains and coaches healthcare practitioners to enhance their presence in person, on camera and online. A veteran of more than 1,000 presentations, Mark shares his skills and passion to empower those who attend his trainings. He brings a wealth of experience to his professional development work. As a consultant and change agent he has worked with a broad spectrum of organizations, from Fortune 100 companies to small non-profits. As a physician, he is well grounded in aesthetic, lifestyle, regenerative and integrative medicine. A highly sought-after speaker he has lectured and trained extensively in the United States, Europe and Asia.

Mark's career was founded on a passion for health promotion and disease prevention. As a medical student at Duke University Medical School, he created one of the first training programs for medical students in nutrition. He also spent time training *promotores de salud* (barefoot doctors) in the mountains of Guatemala.

During his tenure in Portland, Oregon, Mark founded one of the first integrative medicine centers in the US, the Institute of Preventive Medicine. He also served as corporate Medical Director for Electroscientific Industries (NASDAQ: ESIO) and as Director of Health Promotion for Kaiser Permanente, Northwest Region. Early in his career he wrote a syndicated newspaper column on wellness, produced videos and films, and authored books on health promotion.

In the mid 1980s, Mark founded a consumer health and medical publishing company that he ran for ten years before it was acquired by Mosby Yearbook, a Times Mirror Company. As VP of Business Development for Mosby Consumer Health, he oversaw the acquisition of five companies as well as the design and deployment of wellness and disease management programs for major corporations, pharmaceutical companies, hospitals, insurers and non-profits.

Mark has served as the founding Vice President of Marketing for Reliant Technologies (NASDAQ: SLTM), where he launched the Fraxel® laser and introduced the science of fractional photothermolysis to physicians around the world. He then served as Chief Marketing Officer for Syneron (NASDAQ: ELOS) where he was responsible for corporate positioning, public and luminary relations, and new product launches.

As a medical messenger, he specializes in working with aesthetic, nutrition, medical device, and laboratory testing companies to help them translate their science so it is readily understandable by practitioners and consumers. Over the last four years, he has helped shape the messaging and training of practitioners for more than 40 companies. He is active with many of the integrative and functional medicine associations, most notably The American Academy of Anti-Aging Medicine (A4M) where he conducts programs in practice enhancement.

In addition to *Cash-Pay Healthcare*, he has written nine other books including *Enhance Your Presence: The Path to Personal Power, Professional Influence, and Business Results* (with Robert John Hughes); *Total Engagement: The Healthcare Practitioner's Guide to Heal Yourself, Your Patients and Your Practice* (With Mimi Guarneri, MD), *The Art of Aesthetic Practice* (with Stephen Mulholland, MD) and *Transforming Stress into Power*. Mark attended Duke University Medical School and trained in family practice at The Oregon Health & Science University.

Mark lives outside of San Diego with his wife Carolyn and two of the cutest poodle-mix dogs in the world. He is visited often by his two adult-aged children who continue to make him proud.

He can be reached at @marktager and www.linkedin.com/in/marktager.

Stewart Gandolf, MBA

Stewart Gandolf, MBA, is CEO of Healthcare Success, one of the United States' leading healthcare marketing agencies. Additionally, Stewart has personally consulted with over 1,500 practices and hospitals over the past twenty years. Stewart's company Healthcare Success brings a depth of expertise far beyond what is typical within the world of private practice marketing. His team of 25 marketing "subspecialists" represents about 80 practices and hospitals throughout the USA, and abroad. Healthcare Success' capabilities include digital marketing, doctor referral building, patient experience training, branding, advertising, and public relations.

Stewart has spoken at over 200 venues, including dozens of medical association Annual Meetings, corporate events, and his company's 2-day Advanced Medical Marketing Strategies seminars. Stewart is an inspirational speaker and dynamic storyteller, who uses anecdotes from his work to inspire his audiences and demonstrate the difference between effective marketing campaigns and those that flop.

As a passionate educator and writer, Stewart has authored countless articles on results-driven marketing for leading healthcare publications. He also frequently offers his insights during interviews as an expert resource. Stewart is also Publisher of the Healthcare Success Insight blog, which today boasts over 19,000 doctor and hospital executive subscribers worldwide.

People who know Stewart often comment on his rare mix of creativity and analytical thinking, innovative ideas, and high energy. Digital marketing is Stewart's favorite professional passion, and it literally keeps him up at night. Stewart's company's tagline, "Scientific Marketing That Delivers Patients," sums up his business philosophy well. Before co-founding Healthcare Success, Stewart's career included marketing for a variety of America's leading companies, including J. Walter Thompson, Bally Total Fitness, Citicorp, Wells Fargo, and Chase Manhattan.

Stewart completed his undergraduate education at Ohio State, received his MBA at San Diego State, and since then has completed studies at UCLA, UCI, UCSD, along with dozens of seminars and continuing education classes. Stewart's business and personal accomplishments are supported by his loving wife Clara, and two beautiful daughters Natalie and Cristina, and Cosmo, the dog. When he isn't working (almost never), Stewart plays electric guitar. Loudly.

He can be reached at @stewartgandolf and https://www.linkedin.com/in/stewartgandolf/.

INDEX

A

Aarts 6, 124
Aase 249, 253
Academy of Integrative Health and Medicine
  35, 50
Access Healthcare Direct 73
Aethern 127
Ajinomoto 127
Allscripts 43
AMA Doctor Finder 223
Ambra Bioscience 128
Amen Clinics 107
Amen, Daniel 107
American Academy of Anti-Aging Medicine
  51, 129, 290
American College of Lifestyle Medicine 53
American College of Preventive Medicine 54
American College of Private Physicians 73
American College of Sports Medicine 56
American Medical Association 27
American Med Spa Association 55, 101
American Well 89
Amnio Aesthetics 103
Amwell 39
Anatara Medicine 35
AngiesList 224
AOL 240
Apple Maps 221
AstaMed 128
AthenaHealth 43
Axe, Josh 84

B

Babylon Health 39
Bale, Brad 84
BBB.org 226
Beeson, Stephen 28
Belk, David 30
Bellus 123
Best of the Web Local 224
Better Business Bureau 224
Binder, Silvia 113
Bing Local 226
Biohm 122
BioReference Laboratories 121
Bitter, Patrick 67
Bland, Jeffrey 51
Bliss, Garrison 73
BlueStar 44

BodyLogicMD 57, 117
BodySite 50
Brainmaster Technologies 108
Business.com 224

C

Canva.com 252
Canyon Ranch Medicine 67
Capsiate Gold 127
CareCredit 65, 201
Carnahan, Jill 84
Carpenter, Lorin 142
Carter, Jarod 83
Cash Practice Systems 44
Castellano, Richard 144
Castle Connolly Top Doctors 223
Center for Health and Well Being 35
Center for Medical Weight Loss 55, 134
Cerescan 108
Cerner 43
Christakis, Paul 80
CityMD 204
Citysearch 224
Claritas 167
Cleveland Clinic 87, 156
Cleveland HeartLab 119
CleveMed 132
CMS Physician Compare 223
CNS Vital Signs 107
Coachcare 133, 198
Cognitive Clarity Inc 108
Cohen, Jillian 95
Color.com 37
Colorscience 111
Comite Center for Precision Medicine 68
Comite, Florence 68
Connected Health Policy 90
ConstantContact 194
CoolSculpting 105
Crowe, Doug 151
CVS 162
Cypress 77
Cyrex Laboratories 119

D

Dall, Tara 48
DaVinci Laboratories 125
Dayan, Stephen 6
Desert Clinic Pain Institute 35, 56

294

REFERENCES

1 Mundell, E.J. "More Americans Pushed Into High-Deductible Health Plans." U.S. News & World Report, 22 Feb. 2018, health.usnews.com/health-care/articles/2018-02-22/more-americans-pushed-into-high-deductible-health-plans.

2 Fry, Richard. "Millennials Expected to Outnumber Boomers in 2019." Pew Research Center, Pew Research Center, 1 Mar. 2018, www.pewresearch.org/fact-tank/2018/03/01/millennials-overtake-baby-boomers.

3 Kumar, Sanjaya, and Nash, David. "Health Care Myth Busters: Is There a High Degree of Scientific Certainty in Modern Medicine?" Scientific American, 25 Mar. 2011, www.scientificamerican.com/article/demand-better-health-care-book.

4 Belk, David, http://www.truecostofhealthcare.com.

5 Kumar, Sanjaya, and David B. Nash. Demand Better!: Revive Our Broken Healthcare System. Second River Healthcare Press, 2011.

6 "Overweight & Obesity Statistics." National Institute of Diabetes and Digestive and Kidney Diseases, U.S. Department of Health and Human Services, 1 Aug. 2017, www.niddk.nih.gov/health-information/health-statistics/overweight-obesity.

7 Collins, Sarah. "Primary Care Shortages: Strengthening This Sector Is Urgently Needed, Now and in Preparation for Healthcare Reform." American Health & Drug Benefits, vol. 5, no. 1, Jan. 2012, pp. 40–47.

8 Peckham, Carol. "Medscape National Physician Burnout & Depression Report 2018." Medscape Family Medicine, Medscape, 17 Jan. 2018, www.medscape.com/slideshow/2018-lifestyle-burnout-depression-6009235#1.

9 Sinsky, Christine, et al. "Allocation of Physician Time in Ambulatory Practice: A Time and Motion Study in 4 Specialties." Annals of Internal Medicine, vol. 165, no. 11, June 2016, pp. 753–760., doi:10.7326/m16-0961.

10 Blechter, Batel, et al. "Correlates of Burnout in Small Independent Primary Care Practices in an Urban Setting." The Journal of the American Board of Family Medicine, vol. 31, no. 4, 2018, pp. 529–536., doi:10.3122/jabfm.2018.04.170360.

11 Bliss, Garrison. Interview. 20 Aug. 2018.

12 Belk, David. "True Cost of Health Care." True Cost of Healthcare, truecostofhealthcare.org.

13 "Opting Out of Medicare: A Guide for Physicians." AAPS | Association of American Physicians and Surgeons, 22 July 2017, aapsonline.org/opting-out-of-medicare-a-guide-for-physicians.

14 "HSA-Eligible High-Deductible Health Plans." University of Michigan V-BID Center, vbidcenter.org/initiatives/hsa-high-deductible-health-plans-2.

15 Ross, Casey, et al. "Medicine with a side of mysticism: Top US hospitals promote unproven therapies." STAT, 7 Mar. 2017, www.statnews.com/2017/03/07/alternative-medicine-hospitals-promote.

16 Nahin Richard, et al. "Expenditures on complementary health approaches: United States, 2012, National Health Statistics Reports; No 95." National Center for Health Statistics. 2016, www.cdc.gov/nchs/data/nhsr/nhsr095.pdf.

17 Aston, Geri. "Consumers Drive Complementary and Alternative Medicine Movement." Hospitals & Health Networks, 14 Dec.2016, www.hhnmag.com/articles/7699-consumers-clamor-for-complementary-and-alternative-medicine.

18 Picchi, Aimee. "Drug Ads: $5.2 Billion Annually -- and Rising." CBS News, CBS Interactive, 11 Mar. 2016, www.cbsnews.com/news/drug-ads-5-2-billion-annually-and-rising.

19 Allyse, Meghan, et al. "Direct-to-Consumer Testing 2.0: Emerging Models of Direct-to-Consumer Genetic Testing." Mayo Clinic Proceedings, Jan. 2018, www.mayoclinicproceedings.org/article/S0025-6196(17)30772-3/fulltext.

20 "Home-Use Beauty Devices Market by Type (Hair Removal, Anti-Aging, Cleansing, Hair Growth, Cellulite Reduction and Body Toning, Acne Elimination), by Geography (U.S., Canada, Germany, France, Italy, Spain, U.K., China, Japan, India, Brazil) – Global Market Size, Share, Development, Growth, and Demand Forecast, 2013–2023." Home-Use Beauty Devices Market | Industry Share Report 2023, June 2018, www.psmarketresearch.com/market-analysis/home-use-beauty-devices-market.

21 "The Market for Direct-to-Consumer Genetic Testing and Routine Laboratory Testing." The Market for Direct-to-Consumer Genetic Testing and Routine Laboratory Testing: Market Research Report, 1 Jan. 2016, www.kaloramainformation.com/Direct-Consumer-DTC-9588755.

22 Keshavan, Meghana. "20 Key Players in the Direct-to-Consumer Lab Testing Market." MedCity News, 20 Jan. 2016, medcitynews.com/2016/01/20-key-players-in-the-direct-to-consumer-lab-testing-market.

23 Woollett, Gillian, and Jackson, Jay. "FDA Has Received $7.67 Billion from Manufactures to Fund Drug Review." Avalere Health, 15 Aug. 2016, avalere.com/expertise/life-sciences/insights/fda-has-received-7.67-billion-from-manufactures-to-fund-drug-review.

24 Goldman, Erik. "With FDA's Approval of Epidiolex, CBD Supplements Face Uncertain Fate." Holistic Primary Care, 28 June 2018, holisticprimarycare.net/topics/topics-h-n/herbal-medicine/1964-with-fda-s-approval-of-epidiolex-cbd-supplements-face-uncertain-fate.html.

25 Center for Devices and Radiological Health. "Safety Communications - FDA Warns Against Use of Energy-Based Devices to Perform Vaginal 'Rejuvenation' or Vaginal Cosmetic Procedures: FDA Safety Communication." U S Food and Drug Administration, 30 July 2018, www.fda.gov/MedicalDevices/Safety/AlertsandNotices/ucm615013.htm.

26 Center for Drug Evaluation and Research. "Compounding - Bulk Drug Substances Used in Compounding Under Section 503A of the FD&C Act." U S Food and Drug Administration, 23 July 2018, www.fda.gov/Drugs/GuidanceComplianceRegulatoryInformation/PharmacyCompounding/ucm614204.htm.

27 Sweeney, Evan. "CMS Physician Payment Proposal Nudges Open the Door for Telehealth." The Direct Primary Care Journal (DPC Journal), 16 July 2018, directprimarycare.com/2018/07/26/cms-physician-payment-proposal-nudges-open-the-door-for-telehealth.

28 Pear, Robert. "Bruises? Cancer? Under Medicare Plan, Payments for Office Visits Would Be Same for Both." The New York Times, 22 July 2018, www.nytimes.com/2018/07/22/us/politics/medicare-payments-trump.html.

29 Monegain, Bernie. "Cerner Still Leads in EHR Marketshare, Though Smaller Vendors Are Making Moves." Healthcare IT News, 28 Apr. 2017, www.healthcareitnews.com/news/cerner-still-leads-ehr-marketshare-though-smaller-vendors-are-making-moves.

30 "4 Digital Health App Trends to Consider for 2018." Liquid State, 29 Jan. 2018, liquid-state.com/digital-health-app-trends-2018.

31 "Drug-Nutrient Interactions." Integrative Therapeutics, LLC, www.integrativepro.com/Resources/Drug-Nutrient-Interaction-Checker.

32 Tai-Seale, Ming, et al. "Time Allocation in Primary Care Office Visits." Health Services Research, vol. 42, no. 5, Oct. 2007, pp. 1871–1894., doi:10.1111/j.1475-6773.2006.00689.x.

33 Cross, Ryan. "This $25,000 Physical Has Found Some 'Serious' Health Problems. Others Say It Has Serious Problems." Science | AAAS, 12 May 2017, www.sciencemag.org/news/2017/05/25000-physical-has-found-some-serious-health-problems-others-say-it-has-serious.

34 "2017 Medical Spa State of the Industry Report." American Med Spa Association, www.americanmedspa.org/page/med-spa-statistics.

35 Thiersch, Alex R. "The Rise of Non-Core Doctors, and What It Means." Modern Aesthetics, Aug. 2018, modernaesthetics.com/2018/08/the-rise-of-non-core-doctors-and-what-it-means.

36 Cohen, Michael H. "Are Physician Online Dietary Supplement Sales Kickbacks?" Cohen Healthcare Law Group | Healthcare Lawyers | Life Sciences | FDA & FTC Law, 1 Apr. 2016, cohenhealthcarelaw.com/2016/04/are-physician-online-dietary-supplement-sales-kickbacks-or-fee-splitting.

37 Bowman, Patrick. "How Physician Office Lab Testing Enhances Chronic Care Management." McKesson, 20 Nov. 2017, www.mckesson.com/blog/how-physician-office-lab-testing-enhances-chronic-care-management.

38 Harrison, Jazz. "Palmetto GBA Video Script for Part B Established patient Office Visits (CPT Codes 99211-99215)." American Medical Association, www.palmettogba.com/Palmetto/Providers.Nsf/files/Video_Part_B_CPT-Codes-for-Evaluation-and-Management-Office-Visits-Established.pdf/$File/Video_Part_B_CPT-Codes-for-Evaluation-and-Management-Office-Visits-Established.pdf.

39 Ramsey, Lydia. "There's a Growing Movement of Surgery Centers and Specialists That List Their Prices and Don't Take Insurance." Business Insider, 8 Apr. 2017, www.businessinsider.com/surgery-centers-and-specialists-that-take-cash-not-insurance-2017-3.

40 Klemes, Andrea, et al. "Personalized Preventive Care Leads to Significant Reductions in Hospital Utilization." The American Journal of Managed Care, vol. 18, no. 12, 1 Dec. 2012, pp. e453–e460.

41 Saxena, Shilpa Patel. "Leveraging Time With Lifestyle-Based Group Visits." American Journal of Lifestyle Medicine, vol. 10, no. 5, 2016, pp. 330–337., doi:10.1177/1559827616638018.

42 Kessels, Roy PC. "Patients Memory for Medical Information." Journal of the Royal Society of Medicine, vol. 96, no. 5, Jan. 2003, pp. 219–222., doi:10.1258/jrsm.96.5.219.

43 Schroeder, Michael. "Group Visit: Why Shared Medical Appointments Are Gaining in Popularity." U.S. News & World Report, 12 July 2016, health.usnews.com/health-news/patient-advice/articles/2016-07-12/group-visit-why-shared-medical-appointments-are-gaining-in-popularity.

44 "Global Telehealth Market to Reach US$ 19.5 Bn by 2025; Improving Services and Increase in Applications of Telehealth to Boost the Market: Transparency Market Research." Transparency Market Research, 27 Mar. 2018, www.transparencymarketresearch.com/pressrelease/telehealth-market.htm.

45 "VA Telehealth Services Served Over 690,000 Veterans In Fiscal Year 2014." Office of Public and Intergovernmental Affairs, U.S. Department of Veterans Affairs, 1 Sept. 2016, www.va.gov/opa/pressrel/pressrelease.cfm?id=2646.

46 "Physician Practice Benchmark Survey: Policy Research Perspectives Based on the 2016 Benchmark Survey." American Medical Association, www.ama-assn.org/about/physician-practice-benchmark-survey.

47 Shergill, Ajainder. "Six Lessons I Learned from My Failed Direct Primary Care Practice." LinkedIn, 10 June 2018, www.linkedin.com/pulse/six-lessons-i-learned-from-my-failed-direct-primary-shergill-do-mba.

10 "2017 Medical Spa State of the Industry Report." American Med Spa Association, www.americanmedspa.org/page/med-spa-statistics.

49 Wang, Christine. "Apparently the Average Person Takes 25,000 Selfies in a Lifetime. Seems about Right." Mashable, 29 Mar. 2017, mashable.com/2017/03/29/samsung-selfie/#z7R93gjSCiqH).

50 "Body Contouring Market: Global Industry Trends, Share, Size, Growth, Opportunity and Forecast 2018-2023." IMARC, www.imarcgroup.com/body-contouring-market.

51 Houston, Mark. "The Role of Noninvasive Cardiovascular Testing, Applied Clinical Nutrition and Nutritional Supplements in the Prevention and Treatment of Coronary Heart Disease." Therapeutic Advances in Cardiovascular Disease, vol. 12, no. 3, Mar. 2018, pp. 85–108., doi:10.1177/1753944717743920.

52 Bale, Bradley Field, et al. "High-Risk Periodontal Pathogens Contribute to the Pathogenesis of Atherosclerosis." Postgraduate Medical Journal, vol. 93, no. 1098, 2016, pp. 215–220., doi:10.1136/postgradmedj-2016-134279.

53 Strouse, Thomas B. "Cannabinoids in Medical Practice." Cannabis and Cannabinoid Research, vol. 1, no. 1, Jan. 2016, pp. 38–43., doi:10.1089/can.2015.0010.

54 "Market Studies." Medical Insight, miinews.com/market-studies.

55 HeartMath Institute. "The Heart's Intuitive Intelligence: A Path to Personal, Social and Global Coherence." YouTube, YouTube, 22 Apr. 2013, www.youtube.com/watch?v=QdneZ4fIIHE.

56 Hałasa, Maciej, et al. "Oral Supplementation with Bovine Colostrum Decreases Intestinal Permeability and Stool Concentrations of Zonulin in Athletes." Nutrients, vol. 9, no. 4, Aug. 2017, p. 370., doi:10.3390/nu9040370.

57 Keech, Andrew M. Peptide Immunotherapy: Colostrum – A Physician's Reference Guide. AKS Publishing, 2009.

58 Ablon, Glynis and Kogan, Sophia. "A Six-Month, Randomized, Double-Blind, Placebo-Controlled Study Evaluating the Safety and Efficacy of a Nutraceutical Supplement for Promoting Hair Growth in Women With Self-Perceived Thinning Hair." Journal of Drugs in Dermatology, vol. 17, no.5, May 2018, pp. 558–565.

59 Puig, Carlos J., et al. "Double-Blind, Placebo-Controlled Pilot Study on the Use of Platelet-Rich Plasma in Women With Female Androgenetic Alopecia." Dermatologic Surgery, vol. 42, no. 11, 2016, pp. 1243–1247., doi:10.1097/dss.0000000000000883.

60 Giordano, Salvatore, et al. "A Meta-Analysis on Evidence of Platelet-Rich Plasma for Androgenetic Alopecia." International Journal of Trichology, vol. 10, no. 1, 2018, pp. 1–10., doi:10.4103/ijt.ijt_74_16.

61 Huber, Colleen. "Best Practices Guidelines for IV Preparation." INCRI / ANRI / NORI, 20 Feb. 2015, naturopathicstandards.org/best-practices-guidelines-for-iv-preparation.

62 Hinz, Marty, et al. "Neurotransmitter Testing of the Urine: a Comprehensive Analysis." Open Access Journal of Urology, Dove Medical Press, 7 Oct. 2010, www.ncbi.nlm.nih.gov/pmc/articles/PMC3818889/.

63 McDonald, Daniel, et al. "American Gut: an Open Platform for Citizen Science Microbiome Research." American Society for Microbiology Journals, 26 June 2018, msystems.asm.org/content/3/3/e00031-18.

64 Adebowale, Abimbola, et al. "Analysis of glucosamine and chondroitin sulfate content in marketed products and the Caco-2 permeability of chondroitin sulfate raw materials." Journal of the American Nutraceutical Association, vol. 3, no. 1, Jan. 2000, pp.37–44.

65 O'Connor, Anahad. "Knowing What's in Your Supplements." The New York Times, 12 Feb. 2015, well.blogs.nytimes.com/2015/02/12/107141/.

66 "2015 CRN Consumer Survey on Dietary Supplements." Council for Responsible Nutrition, 2015, www.crnusa.org/CRN-consumersurvey-archives/2015/.

67 Ansari, Shahidh, et al. "Current Concepts and Prospects of Herbal Nutraceutical: A Review." Journal of Advanced Pharmaceutical Technology & Research, vol. 4, no. 1, Jan. 2013, pp. 4–8., doi:10.4103/2231–4040.107494.

68 Aarts, Tom. Personal Communication, 16 Oct. 2018.

69 Liu, Sophia Z., et al. "Building Strength, Endurance, and Mobility Using an Astaxanthin Formulation with Functional Training in Elderly." Journal of Cachexia, Sarcopenia and Muscle, 26 Sept. 2018, doi:10.1002/jcsm.12318.

70 Rossman, Matthew J., et al. "Chronic Supplementation With a Mitochondrial Antioxidant (MitoQ) Improves Vascular Function in Healthy Older Adults." Hypertension, vol. 71, no. 6, June 2018, pp. 1056–1063., doi:10.1101/hypertensionaha.117.10787.

71 Salvador, Laura, et al. "A Natural Product Telomerase Activator Lengthens Telomeres in Humans: A Randomized, Double Blind, and Placebo Controlled Study." Rejuvenation Research, vol. 19, no. 6, Dec. 2016, pp. 478–484., doi:10.1089/rej.2015.1793.

72 Lubkowska, A., et al. "Growth factor content in PRP and their applicability in medicine." Journal of Biological Regulators and Homeostatic Agents, vol. 26, no. 2 (Suppl 1), Apr. 2012, pp. 3s–22s.

73 Kim, Dae Hun, et al. "Can Platelet-Rich Plasma Be Used for Skin Rejuvenation? Evaluation of Effects of Platelet-Rich Plasma on Human Dermal Fibroblast." Annals of Dermatology, vol. 23, no. 4, Nov. 2011, p. 424–431., doi:10.5021/ad.2011.23.4.424.

74 "Platelet-Rich Plasma for Cosmetic Facial Procedures – Promising Results, but Evidence Has Limitations." American Society of Plastic Surgeons, 27 Apr. 2018, www.plasticsurgery.org/news/press-releases/platelet-rich-plasma-for-cosmetic-facial-procedures-promising-results-but-evidence-has-limitations.

75 Nishimoto, Soh, et al. "Growth Factor Measurement and Histological Analysis in Platelet Rich Fibrin: A Pilot Study." Journal of Maxillofacial and Oral Surgery, vol. 14, no. 4, Dec. 2015, pp. 907–913., doi:10.1007/s12663-015-0768-3.

76 "PRIZM® PREMIER." Claritas, claritas360.claritas.com/mybestsegments/.

77 "Nike Ad Spend Worldwide 2014-2018 | Statistic" Statista, 2018, www.statista.com/statistics/685734/nike-ad-spend/.

78 Mulholland, Stephen, and Tager, Mark. The Art of Aesthetic Practice: How to Profit from the Cosmetic Boom. ChangeWell, Inc., 2008.

79 Rakel, David P. "Number 406, 'Standard'". Family Medicine, vol. 41, no. 4, Apr. 2009, pp. 289-290.

80 Kaptchuk, Ted J, et al. "Components of Placebo Effect: Randomised Controlled Trial in Patients with Irritable Bowel Syndrome." BMJ, vol. 336, no. 7651, 3 May 2008, pp. 999–1003., doi:10.1136/bmj.39524.439618.25.

81 Brenan, Megan. "Nurses Keep Healthy Lead as Most Honest, Ethical Profession." Gallup.com, 26 Dec. 2017, news.gallup.com/poll/224639/nurses-keep-healthy-lead-honest-ethical-profession.aspx?g_source=CATEGORY_SOCIAL_POLICY_ISSUES&g_medium=topic&g_campaign=tiles.

82 Krug, Steve. Don't Make Me Think!: a Common Sense Approach to Web Usability. New Riders, 2004.

83 "Bounce Rate vs. Page Load Time." Think With Google, Google SOASTA, 2017, www.thinkwithgoogle.com/data/page-load-time-bounce-rate-increase/.

84 "Street View – Hire a Trusted Pro to Boost Your Visibility." Google, Google, www.google.com/streetview/hire/.

85 "Bounce Rate vs. Page Load Time." Think With Google, Google SOASTA, 2017, www.thinkwithgoogle.com/data/page-load-time-bounce-rate-increase/.

86 "How near Me Shopping Searches Have Changed - Think with Google." Google, Google, 2017, www.thinkwithgoogle.com/consumer-insights/near-me-searches/.

87 "Using Page Speed in Mobile Search Ranking." Official Google Webmaster Central Blog, 17 Jan. 2018, webmasters.googleblog.com/2018/01/using-page-speed-in-mobile-search.html.

88 "Make Your Business Listing Awesome." Google My Business Help, Google, support.google.com/business/answer/6335804?hl=en.

89 "Improve Your Local Ranking on Google." Google My Business Help, Google, support.google.com/business/answer/7091?hl=en.

90 "Local Consumer Review Survey | Online Reviews Statistics & Trends." BrightLocal, www.brightlocal.com/learn/local-consumer-review-survey/#Q4.

91 "Will Yelp Remove a False or Defamatory Review?" Will Yelp Remove a False or Defamatory Review? | Support Center | Yelp, www.yelp-support.com/article/Will-Yelp-remove-a-false-or-defamatory-review?l=en_US.

92 "Consumer Review Fairness Act: What Businesses Need to Know." Federal Trade Commission, 31 May 2017, www.ftc.gov/tips-advice/business-center/guidance/consumer-review-fairness-act-what-businesses-need-know.

93 "Don't Ask for Reviews." Don't Ask for Reviews | Support Center | Yelp, www.yelp-support.com/article/Don-t-Ask-for-Reviews?l=en_US.

94 Carroll, John. "Want a Find Us On Yelp Sticker? Request One Here!" Yelp, 14 Nov. 2017, www.yelpblog.com/2015/04/want-a-find-us-on-yelp-sticker-request-one-here

95 "How Do I Get a 'People Love Us on Yelp' Window Cling for My Business?" How Do I Get a "People Love Us on Yelp" Window Cling for My Business? | Support Center | Yelp, www.yelp-support.com/article/How-do-I-get-a-People-Love-Us-on-Yelp-window-cling-for-my-business?l=en_US.

96 "Yelp Does Not Extort Local Businesses or Manipulate Ratings." Yelp, www.yelp.com/extortion.

97 Reichheld, Frederick F. "The One Number You Need to Grow." Harvard Business Review, 16 July 2015, hbr.org/2003/12/the-one-number-you-need-to-grow.

98 How Does Yelp's Review Solicitation Penalty Work?" Search Engine Land, 19 June 2018, searchengineland.com/how-does-yelps-review-solicitation-penalty-work-299893.

99 Rosenberg, Eric. "How Google Makes Money." Investopedia, Investopedia, 10 Oct. 2018, www.investopedia.com/articles/investing/020515/business-google.asp.

100 About the Google Display Network." Google Ads Help, Google, support.google.com/google-ads/answer/2404190?hl=en.

101 "Online Video Advertising Campaigns – YouTube Advertising." YouTube, YouTube, www.youtube.com/yt/advertise/?subid=us-en-ha-yt-bkexa-a%21o3~1405946861-294530899679-kwd-5020163344~https%3A%2F%2Fwww.youtube.com%2Fyt%2Fadvertise&gclid=Cj0KCQjwxvbdBRC0ARIsAKmec9a03_yX8Fn88D2sA_q3W-_ExSQDhE8NcU3dPHxnGI4YNJ3O73AMJ5caAleLEALw_wcB&gclsrc=aw.ds.

102 "Companion Banner." Google Partners Help, Google, support.google.com/partners/answer/6293542?hl=en.

103 YouTube Advertising with TrueView - Think with Google." Google, Google, www.thinkwithgoogle.com/products/youtube-trueview/.

104 "Top Sites in United States. The Sites in the Top Sites Lists Are Ordered by Their 1 Month Alexa Traffic Rank. The 1 Month Rank Is Calculated Using a Combination of Average Daily Visitors and Pageviews over the Past Month. The Site with the Highest Combination of Visitors and Pageviews Is Ranked #1." Top Sites in United States - Alexa, www.alexa.com/topsites/countries/US.

105 Dr. Sandra Lee. "Dr. Sandra Lee (Aka Dr. Pimple Popper)." YouTube, YouTube, www.youtube.com/channel/UCgrsF4TYwmrV0QsXb8AoeHQ?reload=9.

106 Loria, Keith. "The Social Practice." Medesthetics, Apr. 2018, medesthetics.epubxp.com/i/958248-apr-2018/52.

107 Bernazzani, Sophia. "The Decline of Organic Facebook Reach & How to Adjust to the Algorithm." HubSpot Blog, 2018, blog.hubspot.com/marketing/facebook-organic-reach-declining.

108 Mosseri, Adam. "Bringing People Closer Together." Facebook Newsroom, 11 Jan. 2018, newsroom.fb.com/news/2018/01/news-feed-fyi-bringing-people-closer-together/.

109 Joseph, Seb. "'Organic Reach on Facebook Is Dead': Advertisers Expect Price Hikes after Facebook's Feed Purge." Digiday, 15 Jan. 2018, digiday.com/marketing/organic-reach-facebook-dead-advertisers-will-spend-reach-facebooks-feed-purge/.

110 "Social Media Guidelines for Mayo Clinic Staff." Mayo Clinic, Mayo Foundation for Medical Education and Research, socialmedia.mayoclinic.org/mayo-clinic-employee-social-media-guidelines/.

111 "Company Info." Facebook Newsroom, newsroom.fb.com/company-info/.

112 "Take Great Photos for Your Facebook Page." Facebook Business, www.facebook.com/business/learn/facebook-page-post-photos-videos.

113 "Professionalism in the Use of Social Media." Professionalism in the Use of Social Media | American Medical Association, www.ama-assn.org/delivering-care/professionalism-use-social-media.

114 How Do I like or Follow a Business Page on Facebook? | Facebook Help Center | Facebook, www.facebook.com/help/216630288356463.

115 "Facebook 'Like Button' Replaces 'Become A Fan.'" The Huffington Post, TheHuffingtonPost.com, 19 June 2010, www.huffingtonpost.com/2010/04/19/facebook-like-button-repl_n_543439.html.

116 Gandolf, Stewart. "Mayo Clinic Social Media Network: Shared Content and the Warm Arizona Sun [Podcast]." Healthcare Success, 9 Oct. 2017, www.healthcaresuccess.com/blog/podcast-interview/mayo-clinic-social-media-network-podcast.html.

117 Andrus, Aubre. "7 Ways to Deal With A-Hole Facebook Fans." Mashable, Mashable, 4 Jan. 2014, mashable.com/2014/01/04/facebook-customer-service/.

118 Constine, Josh. "Instagram Hits 1 Billion Monthly Users, up from 800M in September." TechCrunch, TechCrunch, 20 June 2018, techcrunch.com/2018/06/20/instagram-1-billion-users/.

119 Smith, Aaron, and Monica Anderson. "Social Media Use 2018: Demographics and Statistics | Pew Research Center." Pew Research Center: Internet, Science & Tech, Pew Research Center: Internet, Science & Tech, 1 Mar. 2018, www.pewinternet.org/2018/03/01/social-media-use-in-2018/.

120 Fiegerman, Seth. "Twitter Is Profitable Again and Adding Users." CNNMoney, Cable News Network, 25 Apr. 2018, money.cnn.com/2018/04/25/technology/twitter-earnings/index.html.

121 "Global Social Media Ranking 2018 | Statistic." Statista, www.statista.com/statistics/272014/global-social-networks-ranked-by-number-of-users/.

122 "About LinkedIn." About LinkedIn, about.linkedin.com/.

123 Humphrey, Rob. "Over 2 Million North American Doctors and Nurses Are on LinkedIn [INFOGRAPHIC]." LinkedIn Talent Blog, 31 July 2014, business.linkedin.com/talent-solutions/blog/2014/07/over-2-million-north-american-doctors-and-nurses-are-on-linkedin-infographic.

124 "Facebook." Advertising Policies, www.facebook.com/policies/ads/#

125 "Ad Formats." Facebook Business, https://www.facebook.com/business/learn/facebook-create-ad-basics?ref=ads_guide.

126 "Choose Your Audience." Facebook Business, www.facebook.com/business/products/ads/ad-targeting.

127 "Facebook Pixel." Facebook Business, www.facebook.com/business/learn/facebook-ads-pixel.

128 Godin, Seth. "Really Bad Powerpoint." Seth's Blog, 29 Jan. 2007, seths.blog/2007/01/really_bad_powe/.

Made in the USA
Middletown, DE
03 December 2018